William Wordsworth Selected Poems

Edited, with an introduction
and notes, by
WALFORD DAVIES
St. Anne's College, Oxford

J. M. Dent & Sons Limited   London
Rowman & Littlefield, Totowa, N.J.

© Introduction, notes and selection
J. M. Dent & Sons Ltd, 1975

Dent|edition
Hardback ISBN 0 460 10203 6
Paperback ISBN 0 460 11203 1

Rowman & Littlefield edition
Hardback ISBN 0-87471-594-6
Paperback ISBN 0-87471-595-4

CONTENTS

Introduction   ix

From LYRICAL BALLADS, 1798 and 1800

The Reverie of Poor Susan   1
The Old Cumberland Beggar   1
Animal Tranquillity and Decay   6
Goody Blake and Harry Gill   6
To My Sister   9
Lines Written in Early Spring   10
Anecdote for Fathers   11
Simon Lee   13
We Are Seven   15
The Idiot Boy   17
The Thorn   29
The Complaint of a Forsaken Indian Woman   35
Expostulation and Reply   37
The Tables Turned   38
Lines Composed a Few Miles Above Tintern Abbey   39
Nutting   43
'There was a boy'   44
'Strange fits of passion have I known'   45
'She dwelt among the untrodden ways'   46
'A slumber did my spirit seal'   46
'Three years she grew in sun and shower'   46
'I travelled among unknown men' (from *Poems*, 1807)   47
Lucy Gray   48
Matthew   50
A Poet's Epitaph   55

Hart-Leap Well 57

Michael 62

''Tis said, that some have died for love' 72

Peter Bell 74

From POEMS, 1807

To a Butterfly 103

To the Cuckoo 104

'My heart leaps up' 105

Ode: Intimations of Immortality 105

Resolution and Independence 110

'I grieved for Buonaparté' 114

Composed Upon Westminster Bridge 115

'It is a beauteous evening, calm and free' 115

On the Extinction of the Venetian Republic 116

To Toussaint L'Ouverture 116

Near Dover, September 1802 116

London, 1802 117

To H.C. Six Years Old 117

'There is a bondage worse, far worse, to bear' 118

'Nuns fret not at their convent's narrow room' 118

'Methought I saw the footsteps of a throne' 119

'The world is too much with us' 119

Ode to Duty 120

'I wandered lonely as a cloud' 121

Stepping Westward 122

The Solitary Reaper 123

Character of the Happy Warrior 124

Elegiac Stanzas suggested by a Picture of Peele Castle, in a Storm 126

Lines Composed at Grasmere 128

Thought of a Briton on the Subjugation of Switzerland 129

From THE RECLUSE 130

From THE PRELUDE
Prelude (1850 text):
Bk. I, lines 301–475 133
Bk. III, lines 46–169 137
Bk. IV, lines 256–460 140
Bk. VI, lines 541–640 144
Bk. XII, lines 208–286 146
Bk. XIV, lines 1–111 148

From THE EXCURSION (The Ruined Cottage) 151

The White Doe of Rylstone 164

LATER POEMS
Characteristics of a Child Three Years Old 206
'Surprised by joy—impatient as the wind' 207
Laodamia 207
Inside of King's College Chapel, Cambridge 212
Mutability 212
Extempore Effusion Upon the Death of James Hogg 213

INTRODUCTION

The poem Wordsworth projected as his masterpiece was never finished. This was not *The Prelude*, which of course is complete and stands, with a weight of personal relevance, as the corner-stone of his career. The major work, planned from as early as 1797–8, and encouraged by Coleridge, was *The Recluse*. It was to incorporate the autobiographical *Prelude* and the narrative *Excursion*, but was to over-reach both of those works in a more purely philosophical examination of Wordsworth's 'views of Man, Nature, and Society'. This plan was not abandoned until very late in the poet's career. In 1814, Wordsworth still saw *The Prelude*'s relationship to *The Recluse* as that of an 'Ante-chapel' to the body of a large 'gothic Church'. Indeed, the aim of the autobiographical poem was to see what experiences had fitted the poet to undertake a major work. When we note this, and when we nowadays tend to isolate the fine story of 'The Ruined Cottage' (p. 151) from the rest of *The Excursion*, we realize that Wordsworth wrote his real masterpieces as if by default, conceiving them or adapting them as subsidiaries to something more philosophically adventurous. In the event, the abortion of *The Recluse* does nothing to lower our estimate of Wordsworth's achievement in poetry. That achievement came from the examination of direct experience, and not from the 'opinions of a Poet living in retirement', his principles settled, and his mind made up.

Only the first book of *The Recluse* was finished, in 1800. Its final argument, outlining 'the design and scope of the whole Poem', is included in this selection (p. 130). The reader would do well to start with that passage, as a useful corrective to any notion of Wordsworth as a tidy celebrator of rainbows, cuckoos, daffodils and timid hares, or as a counterweight to the implications of Byron's phrase, 'the simple Wordsworth'. Nor is it a self-contradiction, after the above comments on *The Recluse*, to recommend the reader to start there. The significance of the passage is documentary. Its best touches *as poetry*—'A simple produce of the common day', 'words/ Which speak of nothing more than what we are', 'hang/ Brooding above the fierce confederate storm/ Of sorrow'—will be found more richly bedded elsewhere, in the body of achieved work to which we shall let this abstract programme direct us.

⌣ The magisterial discursiveness of the lines nevertheless makes us understand that the Romantic poet, and Wordsworth pre-eminently, is not only absorbed in the writing of individual poems, but conscious at the same time that his work is something he can oversee, direct, and dedicate. The eighteenth century idea of a poem as a professionally finished object, with fixed consumer values, already seems ages away. Wordsworth is here measuring himself against Milton, through covert references, stylistic echoes, and direct quotation. His aim 'to weigh the good and evil of our mortal state' parallels Milton's aim in *Paradise Lost* of justifying the ways of God to men. We remember that *The Prelude* on its first page quotes the end of *Paradise Lost*: 'the world is all before me'. Wordsworth's poetry brings Milton's aim into the real world of Time, into this world which (as Wordsworth put it) is the world of all of us, and the one in which we find our happiness, or not at all. Wordsworth also described his shorter poems as reflections of the same high aim. What is epic in Wordsworth is not simply the scope and size of *The Prelude*, *The Excursion*, or the planned *Recluse*, but the pattern in the whole body of poems, major and minor, of a man's imaginative growth and moral survival.

Therefore, just as he measures himself against Milton, Wordsworth also marks himself off from Milton in kind. Like Milton, he conceives of himself as a poet-prophet, but he is not above straightforward autobiography. He will, he says, describe 'who, and what he was,/ The transitory Being that beheld/ That vision, —when and where, and how he lived'. He will therefore de-mythologize and secularize Milton's Classical-Christian terms of reference (just as he wrote his own naturalistic version of Coleridge's magical 'The Ancient Mariner' in 'Peter Bell'— whose Prologue is another important document of Wordsworth's desire to level downwards towards realism). Wordsworth's 'awe' and 'fear' will not be bred from received literary frameworks:

>   Not Chaos, not
> The darkest pit of lowest Erebus,
> Nor aught of blinder vacancy—scooped out
> By help of dreams, can breed such fear and awe
> As fall upon us often when we look

> Into our Minds, into the Mind of Man,
> My haunt, and the main region of my Song.

This awed self-respect shocked William Blake, who wittily claimed that these specific lines caused him a bowel complaint which nearly killed him! 'Does Mr Wordsworth think his mind can surpass Jehovah?', Blake retorted. But let us also emphasize the 'fear'—that glimpse into the heart of darkness which makes Wordsworth in some ways peculiarly modern. In our own time, Robert Frost made the same self-affrighting power of the individual mind the theme of his poem 'Desert Places':

> They cannot scare me with their empty spaces
> Between stars—on stars where no human race is.
> I have it in me so much nearer home
> To scare myself with my own desert places.

That inner threat of 'blind vacancy', driving the poet to seek for pattern and re-assurance in the outer world, is always felt in Wordsworth. We think of the theme of death which counterpoints and prompts the necessary intimations of *im*mortality in the famous 'Ode'; the 'blind thoughts' alleviated by the encounter with the leech-gatherer in 'Resolution and Independence'; the fear of obliteration externalized in the 'Lucy' poems; the total demoralization at the outcome of the French Revolution in *The Prelude*; or the fear, between the lines in 'Tintern Abbey' but writ large in *The Prelude*, that one's own life may not yield a meaningful answer to the questions, Who am I? and What am I still capable of becoming?

Yet it must be stressed that Wordsworth exercises a definite discipline in selecting from the darker side of his personal experience. The groundswell of doubt and hesitation is certainly felt, as indicated; but the crises brought into his published verse are those which can be managed and surmounted there—without damaging his aim of being, representatively, 'a man speaking to men'. Thus it is revealing, for example, what happens to the sad affair of Annette Vallon, the girl who gave birth to the poet's illegitimate daughter in France in 1792. The first full version of *The Prelude* (1805) disinfects the experience in the superficially parallel story of Vaudracour and Julia; and in the final version (1850) even this is pared to its barest outline. On the other hand, consider this:

> Away, away, it is the air
> That stirs among the withered leaves;

Away, away, it is not there,
Go, hunt among the harvest-sheaves.
There is a bed in shape as plain
As from a hare or lion's lair
It is the bed where we have lain
In anguish and despair

Away, and take the eagle's eye,
    The tiger's smell,
Ears that can hear the agonies
And murmurings of hell;
And when you there have stood
By that same bed of pain,
The groans are gone, the tears remain.
Then tell me if the thing be clear,
    The difference betwixt a tear
Of water and of blood.

This impressive lyric (from a MS. of early 1798) very likely reflects the guilt and sorrow of the Annette Vallon episode. But its confessional pain remained significantly unpublished. Wordsworth once remarked, 'Had I been a writer of love-poetry it would have been natural to me to write it with a degree of warmth which could hardly have been approved by my principles'. That the 'warmth' could also be a dark heat seems clear (and in this particular instance gives the lie to traditional assumptions of Wordsworth's sexlessness). But Wordsworth's career is a heroic building-up, a searching of the grounds for optimism. In comparison, Coleridge seems most memorable on the process of breaking down—a process given greater imaginative weight in 'The Ancient Mariner', 'Christabel', and the 'Dejection' Ode (but in 'The Pains of Sleep' also more self-pity) than in Wordsworth, who seems to have paced himself for a longer career. Characteristically, Wordsworth informs us that 'I gave [Coleridge] the subject of his *Three Graves*: but he made it too shocking and painful, and not sufficiently sweetened by any healing views'.

But equally characteristic is the dangerous ease with which later readers tended to let that notion of 'healing views' stand in for the much fuller emotional impact which Wordsworth's own poems have upon us in the actual act of reading. He does not simplify the underlying complexities of his own verse. Matthew Arnold's view of Wordsworth as a poet who 'laid us as we lay at

birth/ On the cool flowery lap of earth' or one whose 'eyes avert
their ken/ From half of human fate' is to be resisted. Wordsworth
solved the problem of how to relate the private to the public
world in poetry without Victorian hysterics, but 'the still sad
music of humanity' nevertheless shades the tone of his work
to something more steadily sombre than joy. The Victorians,
from John Stuart Mill onwards, tended to see Wordsworth's
'normality' in isolation from the hesitations against which it
struggled. We are today, just as much as the Victorians, likely to
misrepresent (if not actually misread) his tone, in the widest sense
of that word. It is as if callous materialism, loss of faith, and the
need to survive in modern cities were new problems of later
ages, to which Wordsworth's voice speaks comfort from simpler
times and cleaner places. But Wordsworth himself, in the lines
from *The Recluse*, speaks of his own desire to 'Express the image
of a better time,/ More wise desires, and simpler manners'.
His comparisons (*better, more wise, simpler*), however, are not
between different times, but between different *present* possi-
bilities. It is that sense of immediate possibilities which is so
deftly communicated in the sonnet 'Composed Upon West-
minster Bridge' (p. 115). It is easy to forget that the same social
conditions produced this sonnet as called forth Blake's 'London'.
Both poems stand at the beginning of a poetic tradition, cul-
minating in T. S. Eliot, which sees the modern city as the
central image of a Waste Land. If we want from Wordsworth
searing descriptions of the stultifying reality of London streets,
we must go to *The Prelude*. What is significant about 'Composed
Upon Westminster Bridge' is its communication of the city,
early in the morning, as a vision of *possible* majestic innocence.
It is the same possibility that flashes briefly across T. S. Eliot's
description of the city in his 'Preludes':

> I am moved by fancies that are curled
> Around these images, and cling:
> The notion of some infinitely gentle
> Infinitely suffering thing.

Blake, Wordsworth and Eliot are radical thinkers because they
understand that the equivalent innocence in man himself comes
not simply from social amelioration, but from a deeper level of
individual psychic health, and that this calls for radical explora-
tion. Society is man-made; it can be man-changed; but only
when each individual changes himself. Without minimizing the

crucial differences in sensibility between the two poets, we feel that Wordsworth would have agreed with the T. S. Eliot of *Ash-Wednesday*: 'Consequently I rejoice, having to construct something/ Upon which to rejoice'.

II

Remembering the Mississippi near his birthplace, T. S. Eliot wrote (in *Four Quartets*) that the river's 'rhythm was present in the nursery bedroom'. Remembering the Derwent running at the bottom of his father's garden at Cockermouth, Wordsworth fancied

> That one, the fairest of all rivers, loved
> To blend his murmurs with my nurse's song.

At the age of thirty-four, Eliot was writing *The Waste Land*, and Wordsworth was completing *The Prelude*. In Eliot's poem, and others which lead up to it, we witness an adult disaffection, with no lifelines backwards except an impersonal cultural memory. This was the same Eliot who had necessarily brought a Wordsworthian appeal to Nature to an end with one stroke in 'The Love Song of J. Alfred Prufrock':

> Let us go then, you and I,
> *When the evening is spread out against the sky*
> *Like a patient etherized upon a table*
> (my italics)

and the same Eliot who berated the pastoral celebration of childhood in the poetry of Henry Vaughan. Even in *Four Quartets* (a work fairly comparable with *The Prelude*), glimpses of a pastoral childhood have only a tenuous substance in the adult's attempt to validate Time; and we feel that, without the new support of Eliot's Christian orthodoxy, those early memories would be as nothing.

In contrast, his rural childhood in Cumberland, a rootedness in particular places and a fixed culture, stand substantially at Wordsworth's recall. In 1818, even Coleridge deplored Wordsworth's 'inferred dependency of the human soul on accidents of birthplace and abode'. But this was striking at everything that had made Wordsworth what he was—as the Coleridge of 'Frost at Midnight' (1798) had once known well and enviously enough. For Wordsworth, natural sensations had been inbred almost preconsciously, and more indelibly than any formal religion could have been at the same time. (In 1796 Coleridge could call Wordsworth 'at least a *Semi*-atheist'). In the educational principles which underlie it, Wordsworth's poetry is sound in two broad decisions: that in the making of character, what goes in first goes in deepest; and that an imaginatively activated childhood is not a presence to be put by, but the foundation on which we most securely build.

Wordsworth was also immensely fortunate in those individuals who marked the events and reciprocated the emotions of his development. His mother, for example, whom he constantly associated with natural as well as personal delights, with memories of her tying nosegays for the boy for local festivals, and standing as the 'dear Presence' who made possible 'the filial bond/ Of nature that connects him with the world'. She drew her sanity and strength, he says, from 'the times/ And spot in which she lived'. As his earliest *dea loci*, her presence was counterpointed by the remoteness of Wordsworth's father who was law-agent to Sir James Lowther, the largest land-owner and political figure of the district. The father brought to the boy's consciousness the different atmosphere of the world of affairs— the world of *doing* as opposed to the world of *being* surrounding the mother. Wordsworth's sister Dorothy early complemented the mother's role. By duplicating her brother's openness to the experience of Nature, Dorothy intensified it, and added to his male boisterousness her female attentiveness to detail ('she gave me eyes, she gave me ears').

The school-years at Hawkshead (1779–87) were chastened by the death of his mother and separation from Dorothy. And after the father's death in 1783, Sir James Lowther's immoral tardiness in paying a sum of £4,700 owed for business undertaken by his law-agent, seriously threatened the independence of the young orphaned family. But these factors must have heightened the compensations of Hawkshead. Life there was boisterously gregarious, but also afforded the chance to be for the first time measurably alone, in the neighbourhood of fells and high mountains. '*Fostered* alike by beauty and by fear': the verb shows the relay from human to natural dependence. Schoolboy pastimes like skating, boating, riding and climbing involved the natural world as organized games would never do, and when compounded by feelings of guilt, formed a threshold to visionary experience—a more than notional awareness of a living, significant universe. But this experience, initially dependent on the after-silence following strenuous action, slowly became the independent habit of his soul. 'I was often unable to think of external things as having external existence, and I communed with all I saw as something not apart from but inherent in my own immaterial nature'. At first worrying, this merging of 'self' and 'non-self' the later poet saw as a luminous contact with 'the life of things', which the adult (differently habituated by education, society, and responsibility) has either sadly to lose, or reclaim through memory, or replace with new compensations.

This solitary communion with Nature was complemented by an increasing awareness of those 'outsiders'—beggars, madmen, discharged soldiers, idiots—who marked the limits, and the limitations, of the ordinary 'social' world, as much at Hawkshead as previously at Cockermouth. This is important because what stood behind Wordsworth in later years was a *peopled* landscape, a culture, not simply a geography. And again a particular relationship consolidated what the boy was learning of his environment. At Hawkshead he formed an important friendship with a wandering 'Packman', who told him stories of his country youth, sang old ballads, and impressed him with an untutored, emotionally-based wisdom such as a sophisticated society could never fashion. This man prefigured both the world and the authorial attitude of *Lyrical Ballads*, where he is poignantly celebrated as the Matthew of 'The Two April Mornings' and 'The Fountain'. And as the main original of the Pedlar of 'The Ruined Cottage' (the Wanderer of *The Excursion*) the Packman's memory inspired Wordsworth's first attempt at tracing the growth of a man's mind from childhood to the point where 'He could *afford* to suffer/ With those whom he saw suffer'.

The worlds of Cambridge and London which followed could match these early satisfactions only where they confirmed a deeper education already started. Wordsworth found it gratifying at Cambridge, for example, that his responsiveness to Nature was not restricted to the dramatic Northern landscapes he had left. But he found no one at Cambridge as impressive as the Packman, or his schoolmaster William Taylor; and knowledge which did not issue as character was nothing. By letting organized studies (though not private reading) slide, he resisted what seemed an inevitable career in one of the professions or in the Church, as if afraid of sealing off what he called the hiding-places of his power. No doubt his growing commitment to the

French Revolution, seen at first hand between 1790 and 1793, marked a feeling that he could accommodate a public role, the world of man and human affairs, more readily in an event of large international scale than in intermediate 'society'. But the Revolution turned to factional Terror, England declared war on France, and he had to abandon Annette Vallon and his child. The traumatic shock to Wordsworth's moral nature is our real measure of the deep reserves of feeling which were seeking release and direction in the young man. (August 1793 found him wandering alone across Salisbury Plain, without food, and in a definitely neurotic state). One can see why the social theories of William Godwin's *Political Justice* (1793), urging as they did the rule of Reason and the strict control of the emotions, appealed initially to Wordsworth as a way out of this crisis of despair. But he gradually came to see that Godwinian theory, like the botched Revolution, could not rediscover 'the heart which had been turned aside/ From Nature's way by outward accidents'. What steadied him for the great creative decade of 1797–1808 were a permanent reunion with Dorothy (from 1794); a legacy (1795) which assured financial independence; settlement at Racedown and Alfoxden (from 1795) making possible the important collaboration with Coleridge; and settlement (from 1799) at Grasmere—'a spot that seemed/ Like the fixed centre of a troubled world'.

III

Wordsworth's poetry is a search for permanence. 'Permanent', its synonyms and opposites, are the key-words of the Preface to *Lyrical Ballads*, that document which shares the same year (1800) and the same democratizing emphasis as the lines from *The Recluse*. In the Preface Wordsworth says that rustic life is chosen for its more 'durable' manners, and its closeness to 'permanent forms of nature'. The treatment of characters like Michael, Simon Lee, or the Old Cumberland Beggar reveals in slow motion 'the primary laws of our nature', and Wordsworth shows a particular respect for the enduring composure of many such rustic figures—a quality of endurance which has only false doubles in the 'savage torpor' or the 'sleep of death' of sophisticated society, and which the poet probably found increasingly attractive in the light of his own demoralization of a few years earlier. 'We Are Seven' dramatizes a related composure, but this time a composure made possible by the young girl's blessed inablity to recognize that relationships, once established, can ever be broken. Wordsworth himself of course, at the age of twenty-eight or so, could partake completely of neither the static innocence of childhood nor the stoic resilience of old age. And we must also remember that it was his own relative social gentility which gave him such a usefully objective view of his rustic figures: his stance throughout is unmistakably *gentle*manly, as parodies of the poems have rather gleefully shown. But there is a profound understanding here that one gains an extended life in the observed lives of others.

Thus his search for the perennial human qualities which make possible a settled quietness of mind involves a dramatic understanding of human conditions separated from his own by differences of age, of social station, of intellectual capacity, and even of mental health. (This is the paradox in the very title, *Lyrical Ballads*—with 'lyrical' suggesting a *personal* interest in the emotions explored, and 'ballads' indicating a measure of *dramatic* distancing). The aim of *Lyrical Ballads* might be said to be the achievement of a 'comprehensiveness of thinking and feeling': the 'comprehensiveness' being the guarantee of the poems' permanent human relevance. The phrase comes from Wordsworth's own defence of 'The Idiot Boy' in a letter in which he urges that 'the loathing and disgust which many people have at the sight of an idiot, is a feeling which, though having some foundation in human nature, is not necessarily attached to it in any virtuous degree, but is owing in a great measure to a false delicacy'. That 'false delicacy' is what R. S. Thomas, a sub-Wordsworthian of our own time, describes as 'the refined,/ But affected, sense' which is shocked by the stark naturalness of Iago Prytherch in his poem 'A Peasant'. Like R. S. Thomas, though with a more persuasive sympathy, Wordsworth changes our concept of heroism. Thomas's poem ends on a note which makes us think of many of Wordsworth's characters:

> Remember him then, for he, too, is a winner of wars
> Enduring like a tree under the curious stars.

What such characters possess unconsciously as a kind of 'Animal Tranquillity' (p. 6) the educated poet has of course to gain through a different power. This is what in 'Expostulation and Reply' Wordsworth calls 'a wise passiveness'—an open receptiveness to the normalizing influence of Nature, which brings the mind into play, but the mind freed from cold logic or mere curiosity. It is the quality celebrated also in 'The Tables Turned', 'Lines Written in Early Spring', and 'To My Sister', and whose absence accounts for the moral callousness of Peter Bell, despite the fact that he and Nature 'had often been together'. What Peter Bell lacks is not a rationalized set of ethics, but an openness to a world of permanent relationships, which it takes almost a halt in time to see:

> On a fair prospect some have looked
> And felt, as I have heard them say,
> As if the moving time had been
> A thing as steadfast as the scene
> On which they gazed themselves away.

In accordance with such materials and concerns, Wordsworth chooses to evolve a language for poetry which will relate, as nearly as is possible or necessary, to the lower stations of society and to a spoken idiom. As celebrated in the Preface to *Lyrical Ballads*, this language is seen as being more 'permanent' than the 'arbitrary and capricious' poetic diction which Wordsworth saw as a pernicious legacy from the poetry of the eighteenth century. Though his theories of low diction (what the *Recluse* lines call 'words/ Which speak of nothing more than what we are') may seem, *as* theories, often question-begging, and though they were even contradicted in his own later poetry, Wordsworth did in practice bring to an end the eighteenth century poetic tradition, in a pastoral realism and a new language which was to be the main poetic influence for over a hundred years. The major poetry illustrates Wordsworth's deep understanding that language is no mere vehicle, to be decorated at will, but the very thing which dictates how and what we feel, and that it must resist the dictates of received fashions whenever a radically new order of feeling is to be explored. It always takes an anti-poetical impulse of this kind to break an inherited poetic idiom, whether the revolutionary poet be a John Donne, a Wordsworth, or a T. S. Eliot. 'Sensibility alters from generation to generation . . . but expression is only altered by a man of genius': the comment is significantly T. S. Eliot's, whose own poetry, as we saw, brought an end to Wordsworth's influential reign.

The clean spareness of his verse is evident when we consider Wordsworth as a descriptive writer. He is usually thought of as a detailed nature poet. This is true, if what is meant is a painter's

eye for items and arrangements in a landscape. But this was in
any case an eighteenth century virtue. That Wordsworth sprang
from that tradition is attested by the early poems, *Descriptive
Sketches* and *An Evening Walk* (both published 1793). The
latter is as good on detail as any loco-descriptive poem by Pope,
Thomson, Dyer or Cowper; and the same descriptive eye still
shaped the opening of 'Tintern Abbey'. Wordsworth had once
hoped to take that delight in the 'minuter properties' of things
much further. An oak tree outlined against an evening sky once
made him feel that poetry had slighted the individual uniqueness
of things. Again, an early notebook description of Dovedale is
decidedly Hopkinsian in its attention to peculiarities of shape,
colour, and size. And a detail like a pebble 'gingling downward
shrill and slow' from an early poem rivets the perception again
in an Hopkinsian way. The mention of Hopkins reminds us of
that particular kind of poetry in which language is used mimeti-
cally, where words are almost caused to *become* the things
described. The source of that stream for the nineteenth century
was Keats, not Wordsworth; and even Coleridge ('the nigh
thatch/ Smokes in the sun-thaw') is closer to that kind of in-
dividuation. The major Wordsworth stands by balder descrip-
tive strengths. The magnificent opening of 'Resolution and
Independence', for example, shows Wordsworth's different
readiness to ventilate and relax his language so that it reminds
the reader as much of his own as of the poet's sensations. Those
opening stanzas can contain a Keats-Hopkinsian detail like the
hare raising a mist from 'the plashy earth', but they wheel broadly
down to the detail, and then away from it. Speaking of the
spurious imagery of Macpherson's Ossian poems, Wordsworth
once commented that there 'everything . . . is defined, insulated,
dislocated, deadened—yet nothing distinct. It will always be so
when words are substituted for things', Hopkins, of course,
proved otherwise; but it is important to recognize Wordsworth's
different linguisitic disposition. Nature, he said elsewhere, 'does
not permit an inventory to be made of her charms', 'In every
scene many of the most brilliant details are but accidental'.

The need to separate the accidental from the permanent also
underlies his famous formula, 'emotion recollected in tran-
quillity'. His natural tendency to allow a gap of time between the
emotional experience (a scene, a human encounter, or even a
chance remark) and the resultant poem, enables that experience
to be not only recorded, but recreated, thereby outlasting its own

event as something more than anecdote. This tendency to grasp
the whole, rather than celebrate a part, has its most profound
exercise in those poems—'Tintern Abbey', *The Prelude*, the
'Immortality' Ode—which trace the poet's own growth. At the
end of D. H. Lawrence's *Women in Love*, we find Ursula looking
back: 'In one lifetime one travelled through aeons . . . The great
chasm of memory from her childhood . . . was so great, that it
seemed she had no identity, that the child she had been . . . was a
little creature of history, not really herself.' The same concern
prompted Wordsworth, against a background of great social
change, to question how one can separate the accidental ex-
periences of a 'transitory being' from the unified, sustaining
identity one hopes to have as man or poet. It says a great deal for
the adventurousness of Wordsworth's aim, especially in *The
Prelude*, that this is a subject we more readily associate with the
novel, whether fictive or autobiographical. What, Wordsworth
asks, is relayed from the past into the present for the future?
Where, and under what pressures, do responses become respon-
sibilities? In poetry, the use of memory is usually a lesser thing
than these questions imply. Consider a poem of our own time,
Philip Larkin's 'Reference Back':

> Truly, though our element is time,
> We are not suited to the long perspectives
> Open at each instant of our lives.
> They link us to our losses: worse,
> They show us what we have as it once was,
> Blindingly undiminished, just as though
> By acting differently we could have kept it so.

Larkin stems, magnificently, from Thomas Hardy. Wordsworth
is not an elegist in their sense. Memory becomes knowledge
when it links him, not to losses, but to what he calls 'spots of
time' (p. 146).—those chastening glimpses of an abiding, im-
personal life, which sustains rather than mocks man's enterprise.
It is no accident that his most frequent image in describing the
natural world is a conjoining of flux and stasis, 'the central peace
subsisting at the heart of endless agitation':

> The immeasurable height
> Of woods decaying, never to be decayed,
> The stationary blasts of waterfalls

or that his most audacious verbal effect, characteristically his
own, is a revivifying of the verb 'to be':

> Our destiny, our being's heart and home,
> Is with infinitude, and only there;
> With hope it is, hope that can never die,
> Effort, and expectation, and desire,
> And something evermore about to be.

Evermore about to be: the journey rather than the arrival.
George Eliot added exactness to insight when she described
Wordsworth's poems as 'symmetrical creations which have
within them *the conditions of* permanence' (my italics). None of
Wordsworth's poems have the shot-silk effect of, let us say,
Keats's 'Grecian Urn' or 'Autumn' Odes, where resistant
opposites (life-art, growth-decay) are fused in an apparently
permanent way in the actual texture of the self-contained poem,
and the poet's autobiographical presence falls away. Words-
worth's poems, unlike the irreducible song of his own Solitary
Reaper, who 'sang/ As if her song could have no ending',
remain consciously meditative. They weigh and judge, by
separating out, the evidences for man's sense of his own value,
and remain open-ended. They return us inevitably from the
words to the life. The feeling we get from them, therefore, is of
a constant process of *becoming*. Actual permanence, against
which man's development is measured, is the preserve of Nature.
Wordsworth had been closest to complete identity with that
permanence when as a boy, as we saw, he had doubted the
existence of any reality outside himself (he had had to grasp a
wall or tree to recall himself from this 'abyss of idealism'). By
the time the first major poems came to be written, that feeling
had given way to an acceptance of the fact that Man and Nature
were separate realities, though allied vehicles for the 'one life
within us and abroad'. But an increasingly stronger develop-
ment was towards the idea of a creative relationship between
Man and Nature. The two views had to co-exist even in 'Tintern
Abbey' (1798): 'For I have learned/ To look on nature . . .';
'And I have felt/ A presence that . . . rolls through all things'.
In the Preface to *Lyrical Ballads* and *The Recluse* lines (1800),
however, the concept of a productive *relationship* is explicit and
exclusive. The central metaphor of *The Recluse* passage, it will be
noticed, is the marriage of the Mind of Man with Nature. To see
this relationship at work at its most dramatic, the reader should

turn to Wordsworth's climactic description of the ascent of Snowdon in *The Prelude* (p. 148). The relationship as seen there confirms in man the powers, not of Mystical, but of Imaginative life: self-possession, amplitude of scope, the creative spirit.

Beyond that lies Divinity itself. Wordsworth's later career is as surely a climb-down from *that* presumption as it is a natural falling-away of sheer poetic virtuosity. Already in 'Ode to Duty' (1804) we see a reliance on the more sober public virtues which that title suggests. There, Wordsworth still yearns 'for a repose that ever is the same', but the prayer is realistically near to the verities which the later years did bring: orthodox Anglican belief, Toryism, patriotism, a place in the Establishment as civil servant and finally Poet Laureate. His completion of *The Prelude* in 1805 was sobered by the death of his best-loved brother John, which sapped an inner imaginative confidence in the poet. But what remained, if a lesser thing, was not nothing. His last great poem, *The White Doe of Rylstone* (1807–8), makes fortitude not a glum substitute, but a resilient acceptance of man's medial and reciprocating position half-way between the animal and the divine. Yet the poem needed the safe objectivity of its fictional narrative form—perhaps the same consideration which prompted Wordsworth to anchor Book I of *The Excursion* in the narrative concreteness of the story of Margaret and The Ruined Cottage. Beyond 1808, though with some striking exceptions, the poet's voice turns to a diffuse public rhetoric. Yet there is no room for mourning. The career has the logical shape of life itself. Genius that had done so much, relatively early, understandably did not know that it had done everything.

SELECT BIBLIOGRAPHY

A. TEXTS

The Poetical Works, ed. E. de Selincourt and H. Darbishire (5 vols. 1940–49). The standard edition, excluding *The Prelude*.

The Prelude: the 1805 text ed. E. de Selincourt (revised H. Darbishire 1960, and S. Gill 1970); parallel 1805 and 1850 texts ed. E. de Selincourt (revised H. Darbishire 1959), and ed. J. C. Maxwell (1971).

The Letters of William and Dorothy Wordsworth, 1787–1850, ed. E. de Selincourt (6 vols. 1935–39).

Dorothy Wordsworth's *Journals*, ed. E. de Selincourt (2 vols. 1941). *Journals of Dorothy Wordsworth*, ed. M. Moorman (1971) is a convenient edition of the Alfoxden and Grasmere journals.

B. BIOGRAPHY AND CRITICISM

S. T. Coleridge, *Biographia Literaria* (1817): ed. J. Shawcross (2 vols. revised 1954); cd. G. Watson (1956). Especially chapters 4, 14, 17–22.

E. Legouis, *The Early Life of William Wordsworth* (1897).

W. Raleigh, *Wordsworth* (1903).

H. W. Garrod, *Wordsworth* (revised 1927).

R. D. Havens, *The Mind of a Poet: A Study of Wordsworth's Thought with Particular Reference to 'The Prelude'* (1941).

H. Darbishire, *The Poet Wordsworth* (1950).

L. Abercrombie, *The Art of Wordsworth* (1952).

F. W. Bateson, *Wordsworth: A Re-Interpretation* (1954).

J. Jones, *The Egotistical Sublime: A History of Wordsworth's Imagination* (1954).

M. Moorman, *William Wordsworth: A Biography* (2 vols. 1957, 65). The standard biography.

F. M. Todd, *Politics and the Poet: A Study of Wordsworth* (1957).

J. Danby, *The Simple Wordsworth: Studies in the Poems 1797–1807* (1960).

G. Hartman, *Wordsworth's Poetry 1787–1814* (1964).

J. Wordsworth, *The Music of Humanity: A Critical Study of Wordsworth's 'Ruined Cottage'* (1969).

THE REVERIE OF POOR SUSAN

AT the corner of Wood Street, when daylight appears,
  Hangs a Thrush that sings loud, it has sung for three
  years:
Poor Susan has passed by the spot, and has heard
In the silence of morning the song of the Bird.

'Tis a note of enchantment; what ails her? She sees
A mountain ascending, a vision of trees;
Bright volumes of vapour through Lothbury glide,
And a river flows on through the vale of Cheapside.

Green pastures she views in the midst of the dale,
Down which she so often has tripped with her pail;   *10*
And a single small cottage, a nest like a dove's,
The one only dwelling on earth that she loves.

She looks, and her heart is in heaven: but they fade,
The mist and the river, the hill and the shade:
The stream will not flow, and the hill will not rise,
And the colours have all passed away from her eyes!

THE OLD CUMBERLAND BEGGAR

I SAW an aged Beggar in my walk;
  And he was seated, by the highway side,
On a low structure of rude masonry
Built at the foot of a huge hill, that they
Who lead their horses down the steep rough road
May thence remount at ease. The aged Man
Had placed his staff across the broad smooth stone
That overlays the pile; and, from a bag
All white with flour, the dole of village dames,

He drew his scraps and fragments, one by one;   *10*
And scanned them with a fixed and serious look
Of idle computation. In the sun,
Upon the second step of that small pile,
Surrounded by those wild unpeopled hills,
He sat, and ate his food in solitude:
And ever, scattered from his palsied hand,
That, still attempting to prevent the waste,
Was baffled still, the crumbs in little showers
Fell on the ground; and the small mountain birds,
Not venturing yet to peck their destined meal,   *20*
Approached within the length of half his staff.
    Him from my childhood have I known; and then
He was so old, he seems not older now;
He travels on, a solitary Man,
So helpless in appearance, that for him
The sauntering Horseman throws not with a slack
And careless hand his alms upon the ground,
But stops,—that he may safely lodge the coin
Within the old Man's hat; nor quits him so,
But still, when he has given his horse the rein,   *30*
Watches the aged Beggar with a look
Sidelong, and half-reverted. She who tends
The toll-gate, when in summer at her door
She turns her wheel, if on the road she sees
The aged beggar coming, quits her work,
And lifts the latch for him that he may pass.
The post-boy, when his rattling wheels o'ertake
The aged Beggar in the woody lane,
Shouts to him from behind; and if, thus warned,
The old man does not change his course, the boy   *40*
Turns with less noisy wheels to the roadside,
And passes gently by, without a curse
Upon his lips, or anger at his heart.
    He travels on, a solitary Man;
His age has no companion. On the ground
His eyes are turned, and, as he moves along
They move along the ground; and, evermore,
Instead of common and habitual sight
Of fields with rural works, of hill and dale,
And the blue sky, one little span of earth   *50*
Is all his prospect. Thus, from day to day,
Bow-bent, his eyes for ever on the ground,
He plies his weary journey; seeing still,
And seldom knowing that he sees, some straw,
Some scattered leaf, or marks which, in one track,
The nails of cart or chariot-wheel have left

Impressed on the white road,—in the same line,
At distance still the same.   Poor traveller!
His staff trails with him; scarcely do his feet
Disturb the summer dust; he is so still   60
In look and motion, that the cottage curs,
Ere he has passed the door, will turn away,
Weary of barking at him.   Boys and girls,
The vacant and the busy, maids and youths,
And urchins newly breeched—all pass him by:
Him even the slow-paced waggon leaves behind.
   But deem not this Man useless.—Statesmen! ye
Who are so restless in your wisdom, ye
Who have a broom still ready in your hands
To rid the world of nuisances; ye proud,   70
Heart-swoln, while in your pride ye contemplate
Your talents, power, or wisdom, deem him not
A burthen of the earth!   'Tis Nature's law
That none, the meanest of created things,
Or forms created the most vile and brute,
The dullest or most noxious, should exist
Divorced from good—a spirit and pulse of good,
A life and soul, to every mode of being
Inseparably linked.   Then be assured
That least of all can aught—that ever owned   80
The heaven-regarding eye and front sublime
Which man is born to—sink, howe'er depressed,
So low as to be scorned without a sin;
Without offence to God cast out of view;
Like the dry remnant of a garden-flower
Whose seeds are shed, or as an implement
Worn out and worthless.   While from door to door,
This old Man creeps, the villagers in him
Behold a record which together binds
Past deeds and offices of charity,   90
Else unremembered, and so keeps alive
The kindly mood in hearts which lapse of years,
And that half-wisdom half-experience gives,
Make slow to feel, and by sure steps resign
To selfishness and cold oblivious cares.
Among the farms and solitary huts,
Hamlets and thinly scattered villages,
Where'er the aged Beggar takes his rounds,
The mild necessity of use compels
To acts of love; and habit does the work   100
Of reason; yet prepares that after-joy
Which reason cherishes.   And thus the soul,
By that sweet taste of pleasure unpursued,

Doth find herself insensibly disposed
To virtue and true goodness.
                              Some there are,
By their good works exalted, lofty minds
And meditative, authors of delight
And happiness, which to the end of time
Will live, and spread, and kindle: even such minds
In childhood, from this solitary Being,   *110*
Or from like wanderer, haply have received
(A thing more precious far than all that books
Or the solicitudes of love can do!)
That first mild touch of sympathy and thought,
In which they found their kindred with a world
Where want and sorrow were.   The easy man
Who sits at his own door,—and, like the pear
That overhangs his head from the green wall,
Feeds in the sunshine; the robust and young,
The prosperous and unthinking, they who live   *120*
Sheltered, and flourish in a little grove
Of their own kindred;—all behold in him
A silent monitor, which on their minds
Must needs impress a transitory thought
Of self-congratulation, to the heart
Of each recalling his peculiar boons,
His charters and exemptions; and, perchance,
Though he to no one give the fortitude
And circumspection needful to preserve
His present blessings, and to husband up   *130*
The respite of the season, he, at least,
And 'tis no vulgar service, makes them felt.
      Yet further.——Many, I believe, there are
Who live a life of virtuous decency,
Men who can hear the Decalogue and feel
No self-reproach; who of the moral law
Established in the land where they abide
Are strict observers; and not negligent
In acts of love to those with whom they dwell,
Their kindred, and the children of their blood.   *140*
Praise be to such, and to their slumbers peace!
—But of the poor man ask, the abject poor;
Go, and demand of him, if there be here
In this cold abstinence from evil deeds,
And these inevitable charities,
Wherewith to satisfy the human soul?
No—man is dear to man; the poorest poor
Long for some moments in a weary life
When they can know and feel that they have been,

Themselves, the fathers and the dealers-out 150
Of some small blessings; have been kind to such
As needed kindness, for this single cause,
That we have all of us one human heart.
—Such pleasure is to one kind Being known,
My neighbour, when with punctual care, each week,
Duly as Friday comes, though pressed herself
By her own wants, she from her store of meal
Takes one unsparing handful for the scrip
Of this old Mendicant, and, from her door
Returning with exhilarated heart, 160
Sits by her fire, and builds her hope in heaven.
   Then let him pass, a blessing on his head!
And while in that vast solitude to which
The tide of things has borne him, he appears
To breathe and live but for himself alone,
Unblamed, uninjured, let him bear about
The good which the benignant law of Heaven
Has hung around him: and, while life is his,
Still let him prompt the unlettered villagers
To tender offices and pensive thoughts. 170
—Then let him pass, a blessing on his head!
And, long as he can wander, let him breathe
The freshness of the valleys; let his blood
Struggle with frosty air and winter snows;
And let the chartered wind that sweeps the heath
Beat his grey locks against his withered face.
Reverence the hope whose vital anxiousness
Gives the last human interest to his heart.
May never HOUSE, misnamed of INDUSTRY,
Make him a captive!—for that pent-up din, 180
Those life-consuming sounds that clog the air,
Be his the natural silence of old age!
Let him be free of mountain solitudes;
And have around him, whether heard or not,
The pleasant melody of woodland birds.
Few are his pleasures: if his eyes have now
Been doomed so long to settle upon earth
That not without some effort they behold
The countenance of the horizontal sun,
Rising or setting, let the light at least 190
Find a free entrance to their languid orbs.
And let him, *where* and *when* he will, sit down
Beneath the trees, or on a grassy bank
Of highway side, and with the little birds
Share his chance-gathered meal; and, finally,
As in the eye of Nature he has lived,
So in the eye of Nature let him die!

ANIMAL TRANQUILLITY AND DECAY

THE little hedgerow birds,
That peck along the roads, regard him not.
He travels on, and in his face, his step,
His gait, is one expression: every limb,
His look and bending figure, all bespeak
A man who does not move with pain, but moves
With thought—He is insensibly subdued
To settled quiet: he is one by whom
All effort seems forgotten; one to whom
Long patience hath such mild composure given,   *10*
That patience now doth seem a thing of which
He hath no need.   He is by nature led
To peace so perfect that the young behold
With envy, what the Old Man hardly feels.

GOODY BLAKE AND HARRY GILL

A TRUE STORY

OH! what's the matter? what's the matter?
    What is't that ails young Harry Gill?
That evermore his teeth they chatter,
Chatter, chatter, chatter still!
Of waistcoats Harry has no lack,
Good duffle grey, and flannel fine;
He has a blanket on his back,
And coats enough to smother nine.

In March, December, and in July,
'Tis all the same with Harry Gill;   *10*
The neighbours tell, and tell you truly,
His teeth they chatter, chatter still.
At night, at morning, and at noon,
'Tis all the same with Harry Gill;
Beneath the sun, beneath the moon,
His teeth they chatter, chatter still!

Young Harry was a lusty drover,
And who so stout of limb as he?
His cheeks were red as ruddy clover;
His voice was like the voice of three.   *20*
Old Goody Blake was old and poor;
Ill fed she was, and thinly clad;
And any man who passed her door
Might see how poor a hut she had.

All day she spun in her poor dwelling:
And then her three hours' work at night,
Alas! 'twas hardly worth the telling,
It would not pay for candle-light.
Remote from sheltered village-green,
On a hill's northern side she dwelt,   *30*
Where from sea-blasts the hawthorns lean,
And hoary dews are slow to melt.

By the same fire to boil their pottage,
Two poor old Dames, as I have known,
Will often live in one small cottage;
But she, poor Woman! housed alone.
'Twas well enough when summer came,
The long, warm, lightsome summer-day,
Then at her door the *canty* Dame
Would sit, as any linnet, gay.   *40*

But when the ice our streams did fetter,
Oh then how her old bones would shake!
You would have said, if you had met her,
'Twas a hard time for Goody Blake.
Her evenings then were dull and dead:
Sad case it was, as you may think,
For very cold to go to bed;
And then for cold not sleep a wink.

O joy for her! whene'er in winter
The winds at night had made a rout,   *50*
And scattered many a lusty splinter
And many a rotten bough about;
Yet never had she, well or sick,
As every man who knew her says,
A pile beforehand, turf or stick,
Enough to warm her for three days.

Now, when the frost was past enduring,
And made her poor old bones to ache,
Could any thing be more alluring
Than an old hedge to Goody Blake?   *60*
And, now and then, it must be said,
When her old bones were cold and chill,
She left her fire, or left her bed,
To seek the hedge of Harry Gill.

Now Harry he had long suspected
This trespass of old Goody Blake;
And vowed that she should be detected—
Then he on her would vengeance take.
And oft from his warm fire he'd go,
And to the fields his road would take; 70
And there, at night, in frost and snow,
He watched to seize old Goody Blake.

And once, behind a rick of barley,
Thus looking out did Harry stand:
The moon was full and shining clearly,
And crisp with frost the stubble land.
—He hears a noise—he's all awake—
Again?—on tip-toe down the hill
He softly creeps—'tis Goody Blake;
She's at the hedge of Harry Gill! 80

Right glad was he when he beheld her:
Stick after stick did Goody pull:
He stood behind a bush of elder,
Till she had filled her apron full.
When with her load she turned about,
The by-way back again to take;
He started forward, with a shout,
And sprang upon poor Goody Blake,

And fiercely by the arm he took her,
And by the arm he held her fast, 90
And fiercely by the arm he shook her,
And cried, 'I've caught you then at last!'
Then Goody, who had nothing said,
Her bundle from her lap let fall;
And, kneeling on the sticks, she prayed
To God that is the judge of all.

She prayed, her withered hand uprearing,
While Harry held her by the arm—
'God! who art never out of hearing,
O may he never more be warm!' 100
The cold, cold moon above her head,
Thus on her knees did Goody pray;
Young Harry heard what she had said:
And icy cold he turned away.

He went complaining all the morrow
That he was cold and very chill:
His face was gloom, his heart was sorrow,
Alas! that day for Harry Gill!
That day he wore a riding coat,
But not a whit the warmer he: *110*
Another was on Thursday bought,
And ere the Sabbath he had three.

'Twas all in vain, a useless matter,
And blankets were about him pinned;
Yet still his jaws and teeth they clatter;
Like a loose casement in the wind.
And Harry's flesh it fell away;
And all who see him say, 'tis plain,
That, live as long as live he may,
He never will be warm again.   *120*

No word to any man he utters,
A-bed or up, to young or old;
But ever to himself he mutters,
'Poor Harry Gill is very cold.'
A-bed or up, by night or day;
His teeth they chatter, chatter still.
Now think, ye farmers all, I pray,
Of Goody Blake and Harry Gill!

TO MY SISTER

IT is the first mild day of March:
Each minute sweeter than before
The redbreast sings from the tall larch
That stands beside our door.

There is a blessing in the air,
Which seems a sense of joy to yield
To the bare trees, and mountains bare,
And grass in the green field.

My sister! ('tis a wish of mine)
Now that our morning meal is done,   *10*
Make haste, your morning task resign;
Come forth and feel the sun.

Edward will come with you;—and, pray,
Put on with speed your woodland dress;
And bring no book: for this one day
We'll give to idleness.

No joyless forms shall regulate
Our living calendar: 20
We from to-day, my Friend, will date
The opening of the year.

Love, now a universal birth,
From heart to heart is stealing,
From earth to man, from man to earth:
—It is the hour of feeling.

One moment now may give us more
Than years of toiling reason:
Our minds shall drink at every pore
The spirit of the season.   30

Some silent laws our hearts will make,
Which they shall long obey:
We for the year to come may take
Our temper from to-day.

And from the blessed power that rolls
About, below, above,
We'll frame the measure of our souls:
They shall be tuned to love.

Then come, my Sister! come, I pray,
With speed put on your woodland dress;   40
And bring no book: for this one day
We'll give to idleness.

LINES WRITTEN IN EARLY SPRING

I HEARD a thousand blended notes,
  While in a grove I sate reclined,
In that sweet mood when pleasant thoughts
Bring sad thoughts to the mind.

To her fair works did Nature link
The human soul that through me ran;
And much it grieved my heart to think
What man has made of man.

Through primrose tufts, in that green bower,
The periwinkle trailed its wreaths;   *10*
And 'tis my faith that every flower
Enjoys the air it breathes.

The birds around me hopped and played,
Their thoughts I cannot measure:—
But the least motion which they made
It seemed a thrill of pleasure.

The budding twigs spread out their fan,
To catch the breezy air;
And I must think, do all I can,
That there was pleasure there.   *20*

If this belief from heaven be sent,
If such be Nature's holy plan,
Have I not reason to lament
What man has made of man?

ANECDOTE FOR FATHERS

'Retine vim istam, falsa enim dicam, si coges.' —EUSEBIUS.

I HAVE a boy of five years old;
  His face is fair and fresh to see;
His limbs are cast in beauty's mould,
And dearly he loves me.

One morn we strolled on our dry walk,
Our quiet home all full in view,
And held such intermitted talk
As we are wont to do.

My thoughts on former pleasures ran;
I thought of Kilve's delightful shore,   *10*
Our pleasant home when spring began,
A long, long year before.

A day it was when I could bear
Some fond regrets to entertain;
With so much happiness to spare,
I could not feel a pain.

The green earth echoed to the feet
Of lambs that bounded through the glade,
From shade to sunshine, and as fleet
From sunshine back to shade.   *20*

Birds warbled round me—and each trace
Of inward sadness had its charm;
Kilve, thought I, was a favoured place,
And so is Liswyn Farm.

My boy beside me tripped, so slim
And graceful in his rustic dress!
And, as we talked, I questioned him,
In very idleness.

'Now tell me, had you rather be,'
I said, and took him by the arm,   *30*
'On Kilve's smooth shore, by the green sea,
Or here at Liswyn Farm?'

In careless mood he looked at me,
While still I held him by the arm,
And said, 'At Kilve I'd rather be
Than here at Liswyn farm.'

'Now, little Edward, say why so:
My little Edward, tell me why.'—
'I cannot tell, I do not know.'—
'Why, this is strange,' said I;   *40*

'For here are woods, hills smooth and warm
There surely must some reason be
Why you should change sweet Liswyn farm
For Kilve by the green sea.'

At this, my boy hung down his head,
He blushed with shame, nor made reply;
And three times to the child I said,
'Why, Edward, tell me why?'

His head he raised—there was in sight,
It caught his eye, he saw it plain—   *50*
Upon the house-top, glittering bright,
A broad and gilded vane.

Then did the boy his tongue unlock,
And eased his mind with this reply:
'At Kilve there was no weather-cock;
And that's the reason why.'

O dearest, dearest boy! my heart
For better lore would seldom yearn,
Could I but teach the hundredth part
Of what from thee I learn.   *60*

SIMON LEE,

THE OLD HUNTSMAN;
WITH AN INCIDENT IN WHICH HE WAS CONCERNED

IN the sweet shire of Cardigan,
  Nor far from pleasant Ivor-hall,
An old Man dwells, a little man,—
'Tis said he once was tall.
Full five-and-thirty years he lived
A running huntsman merry;
And still the centre of his cheek
Is red as a ripe cherry.

No man like him the horn could sound,
And hill and valley rang with glee   *10*
When Echo bandied, round and round,
The halloo of Simon Lee.
In those proud days, he little cared
For husbandry or tillage;
To blither tasks did Simon rouse
The sleepers of the village.

He all the country could outrun,
Could leave both man and horse behind;
And often, ere the chase was done,
He reeled, and was stone-blind.   *20*
And still there's something in the world
At which his heart rejoices;
For when the chiming hounds are out,
He dearly loves their voices!

But, oh the heavy change!—bereft
Of health, strength, friends, and kindred, see!
Old Simon to the world is left
In liveried poverty.
His Master's dead,—and no one now
Dwells in the Hall of Ivor;   *30*
Men, dogs, and horses, all are dead;
He is the sole survivor.

And he is lean and he is sick;
His body, dwindled and awry,
Rests upon ankles swoln and thick;
His legs are thin and dry.

One prop he has, and only one,
His wife, an aged woman,
Lives with him, near the waterfall,
Upon the village Common.   *40*

Beside their moss-grown hut of clay,
Not twenty paces from the door,
A scrap of land they have, but they
Are poorest of the poor.
This scrap of land he from the heath
Enclosed when he was stronger;
But what to them avails the land
Which he can till no longer?

Oft, working by her Husband's side,
Ruth does what Simon cannot do;   *50*
For she, with scanty cause for pride,
Is stouter of the two.
And, though you with your utmost skill
From labour could not wean them,
'Tis little, very little—all
That they can do between them.

Few months of life has he in store
As he to you will tell,
For still, the more he works, the more
Do his weak ankles swell.   *60*
My gentle Reader, I perceive
How patiently you've waited,
And now I fear that you expect
Some tale will be related.

O Reader! had you in your mind
Such stores as silent thought can bring,
O gentle Reader! you would find
A tale in every thing.
What more I have to say is short,
And you must kindly take it: *70*
It is no tale; but, should you think,
Perhaps a tale you'll make it.

One summer-day I chanced to see
This old Man doing all he could
To unearth the root of an old tree,
A stump of rotten wood.

The mattock tottered in his hand;
So vain was his endeavour,
That at the root of the old tree
He might have worked for ever.   *80*

'You're overtasked, good Simon Lee,
Give me your tool,' to him I said;
And at the word right gladly he
Received my proffered aid.
I struck, and with a single blow
The tangled root I severed,
At which the poor old Man so long
And vainly had endeavoured.

The tears into his eyes were brought,
And thanks and praises seemed to run   *90*
So fast out of his heart, I thought
They never would have done.
—I've heard of hearts unkind, kind deeds
With coldness still returning;
Alas! the gratitude of men
Hath oftener left me mourning.

WE ARE SEVEN

—A simple Child,
     That lightly draws its breath,
And feels its life in every limb,
What should it know of death?

I met a little cottage Girl:
She was eight years old, she said;
Her hair was thick with many a curl
That clustered round her head.

She had a rustic, woodland air,
And she was wildly clad: *10*
Her eyes were fair, and very fair;
—Her beauty made me glad.

'Sisters and brothers, little Maid,
How many may you be?'
'How many? Seven in all,' she said,
And wondering looked at me.

'And where are they?   I pray you tell.'
She answered, 'Seven are we;
And two of us at Conway dwell,
And two are gone to sea.   *20*

'Two of us in the churchyard lie,
My sister and my brother;
And, in the churchyard cottage, I
Dwell near them with my mother.'

'You say that two at Conway dwell,
And two are gone to sea,
Yet ye are seven!—I pray you tell,
Sweet Maid, how this may be.'

Then did the little Maid reply,   *30*
'Seven boys and girls are we;
Two of us in the churchyard lie,
Beneath the churchyard tree.'

'You run about, my little Maid,
Your limbs they are alive;
If two are in the churchyard laid,
Then ye are only five.'

'Their graves are green, they may be seen,'
The little Maid replied,
'Twelve steps or more from my mother's door,
And they are side by side.   *40*

'My stockings there I often knit,
My kerchief there I hem;
And there upon the ground I sit,
And sing a song to them.

'And often after sunset, Sir,
When it is light and fair,
I take my little porringer,
And eat my supper there.

'The first that died was sister Jane;
In bed she moaning lay,   *50*
Till God released her of her pain;
And then she went away.

'So in the churchyard she was laid;
And, when the grass was dry,
Together round her grave we played,
My brother John and I.

'And when the ground was white with snow,
And I could run and slide,
My brother John was forced to go,
And he lies by her side.'   *60*

'How many are you then,' said I,
'If they two are in heaven?'
Quick was the little Maid's reply,
'O Master! we are seven.'

'But they are dead; those two are dead!
Their spirits are in heaven!'
'Twas throwing words away; for still
The little Maid would have her will,
And said, 'Nay, we are seven!'

THE IDIOT BOY

'TIS eight o'clock,—a clear March night,
  The moon is up,—the sky is blue,
The owlet, in the moonlight air,
Shouts from nobody knows where;
He lengthens out his lonely shout,
Halloo! halloo! a long halloo!

—Why bustle thus about your door,
What means this bustle, Betty Foy?
Why are you in this mighty fret?
And why on horseback have you set   *10*
Him whom you love, your Idiot Boy?

Scarcely a soul is out of bed;
Good Betty, put him down again;
His lips with joy they burr at you;
But, Betty! what has he to do
With stirrup, saddle, or with rein?

But Betty's bent on her intent;
For her good neighbour Susan Gale,
Old Susan, she who dwells alone,
Is sick, and makes a piteous moan,   *20*
As if her very life would fail.

There's not a house within a mile,
No hand to help them in distress;
Old Susan lies a-bed in pain,
And sorely puzzled are the twain,
For what she ails they cannot guess.

And Betty's husband's at the wood,
Where by the week he doth abide,
A woodman in the distant vale;
There's none to help poor Susan Gale;   *30*
What must be done? what will betide?

And Betty from the lane has fetched
Her Pony, that is mild and good;
Whether he be in joy or pain,
Feeding at will along the lane,
Or bringing faggots from the wood.

And he is all in travelling trim,—
And, by the moonlight, Betty Foy
Has on the well-girt saddle set
(The like was never heard of yet)   *40*
Him whom she loves, her Idiot Boy.

And he must post without delay
Across the bridge and through the dale,
And by the church, and o'er the down,
To bring a Doctor from the town,
Or she will die, old Susan Gale.

There is no need of boot or spur,
There is no need of whip or wand;
For Johnny has his holly-bough,
And with a *hurly-burly* now   *50*
He shakes the green bough in his hand.

And Betty o'er and o'er has told
The Boy, who is her best delight,
Both what to follow, what to shun,
What do, and what to leave undone,
How turn to left, and how to right.

And Betty's most especial charge,
Was 'Johnny! Johnny! mind that you
Come home again, nor stop at all,—
Come home again, whate'er befall,   *60*
My Johnny, do, I pray you do.'

To this did Johnny answer make,
Both with his head and with his hand,
And proudly shook the bridle too;
And then! his words were not a few,
Which Betty well could understand.

And now that Johnny is just going,
Though Betty's in a mighty flurry,
She gently pats the Pony's side, ,
On which her Idiot Boy must ride,   70
And seems no longer in a hurry.

But when the Pony moved his legs,
Oh! then for the poor Idiot Boy!
For joy he cannot hold the bridle,
For joy his head and heels are idle,
He's idle all for very joy.

And while the Pony moves his legs,
In Johnny's left hand you may see
The green bough motionless and dead:
The Moon that shines above his head   80
Is not more still and mute than he.

His heart it was so full of glee
That, till full fifty yards were gone,
He quite forgot his holly whip,
And all his skill in horsemanship:
Oh! happy, happy, happy John.

And while the Mother, at the door,
Stands fixed, her face with joy o'erflows,
Proud of herself, and proud of him,
She sees him in his travelling trim,   90
How quietly her Johnny goes.

The silence of her Idiot Boy,
What hopes it sends to Betty's heart!
He's at the guide-post—he turns right;
She watches till he's out of sight,
And Betty will not then depart.

Burr, burr—now Johnny's lips they burr,
As loud as any mill, or near it;
Meek as a lamb the Pony moves,
And Johnny makes the noise he loves,   100
And Betty listens, glad to hear it.

Away she hies to Susan Gale:
Her Messenger's in merry tune;
The owlets hoot, the owlets curr,
And Johnny's lips they burr, burr, burr,
As on he goes beneath the moon.

His steed and he right well agree;
For of this Pony there's a rumour,
That, should he lose his eyes and ears,
And should he live a thousand years,   *110*
He never will be out of humour.

But then he is a horse that thinks!
And when he thinks, his pace is slack;
Now, though he knows poor Johnny well,
Yet, for his life, he cannot tell
What he has got upon his back.

So through the moonlight lanes they go,
And far into the moonlight dale,
And by the church, and o'er the down,
To bring a Doctor from the town,   *120*
To comfort poor old Susan Gale.

And Betty, now at Susan's side,
Is in the middle of her story,
What speedy help her Boy will bring,
With many a most diverting thing,
Of Johnny's wit, and Johnny's glory.

And Betty, still at Susan's side,
By this time is not quite so flurried:
Demure with porringer and plate
She sits, as if in Susan's fate   *130*
Her life and soul were buried.

But Betty, poor good woman! she,
You plainly in her face may read it,
Could lend out of that moment's store
Five years of happiness or more
To any that might need it.

But yet I guess that now and then
With Betty all was not so well;
And to the road she turns her ears,
And thence full many a sound she hears,   *140*
Which she to Susan will not tell.

Poor Susan moans, poor Susan groans;
'As sure as there's a moon in heaven,'
Cries Betty, 'he'll be back again;
They'll both be here—'tis almost ten—
Both will be here before eleven.'

Poor Susan moans, poor Susan groans;
The clock gives warning for eleven;
'Tis on the stroke—'He must be near,'
Quoth Betty, 'and will soon be here,   *150*
As sure as there's a moon in heaven.'

The clock is on the stroke of twelve,
And Johnny is not yet in sight:
—The Moon's in heaven, as Betty sees,
But Betty is not quite at ease;
And Susan has a dreadful night.

And Betty, half an hour ago,
On Johnny vile reflections cast:
'A little idle sauntering Thing!'
With other names, an endless string;   *160*
But now that time is gone and past.

And Betty's drooping at the heart,
That happy time all past and gone,
'How can it be he is so late?
The Doctor, he has made him wait;
Susan! they'll both be here anon.'

And Susan's growing worse and worse,
And Betty's in a sad *quandary*;
And then there's nobody to say
If she must go, or she must stay!   *170*
—She's in a sad *quandary*.

The clock is on the stroke of one;
But neither Doctor nor his Guide
Appears along the moonlight road;
There's neither horse nor man abroad,
And Betty's still at Susan's side.

And Susan now begins to fear
Of sad mischances not a few,
That Johnny may perhaps be drowned;
Or lost, perhaps, and never found;   *180*
Which they must both for ever rue.

She prefaced half a hint of this
With, 'God forbid it should be true!'
At the first word that Susan said
Cried Betty, rising from the bed,
'Susan, I'd gladly stay with you.

'I must be gone, I must away:
Consider, Johnny's but half-wise;
Susan, we must take care of him,
If he is hurt in life or limb'—   *190*
'Oh God forbid!' poor Susan cries.

'What can I do?' says Betty, going,
'What can I do to ease your pain?
Good Susan, tell me, and I'll stay;
I fear you're in a dreadful way,
But I shall soon be back again.'

'Nay, Betty, go! good Betty, go!
There's nothing that can ease my pain.'
Then off she hies; but with a prayer
That God poor Susan's life would spare,   *200*
Till she comes back again.

So, through the moonlight lane she goes,
And far into the moonlight dale;
And how she ran, and how she walked,
And all that to herself she talked,
Would surely be a tedious tale.

In high and low, above, below,
In great and small, in round and square,
In tree and tower was Johnny seen,
In bush and brake, in black and green;   *210*
'Twas Johnny, Johnny, every where.

And while she crossed the bridge, there came
A thought with which her heart is sore—
Johnny perhaps his horse forsook,
To hunt the moon within the brook,
And never will be heard of more.

Now is she high upon the down,
Alone amid a prospect wide;
There's neither Johnny nor his Horse
Among the fern or in the gorse;   *220*
There's neither Doctor nor his Guide.

'O saints! what is become of him?
Perhaps he's climbed into an oak,
Where he will stay till he is dead;
Or, sadly he has been misled,
And joined the wandering gipsy-folk.

'Or him that wicked Pony's carried
To the dark cave, the goblin's hall;
Or in the castle he's pursuing
Among the ghosts his own undoing;   230
Or playing with the waterfall.'

At poor old Susan then she railed,
While to the town she posts away;
'If Susan had not been so ill,
Alas! I should have had him still,
My Johnny, till my dying day.'

Poor Betty, in this sad distemper,
The Doctor's self could hardly spare:
Unworthy things she talked, and wild;
Even he, of cattle the most mild,   240
The Pony had his share.

But now she's fairly in the town,
And to the Doctor's door she hies;
'Tis silence all on every side;
The town so long, the town so wide,
Is silent as the skies.

And now she's at the Doctor's door,
She lifts the knocker, rap, rap, rap;
The Doctor at the casement shows
His glimmering eyes that peep and doze!   250
And one hand rubs his old night-cap.

'O Doctor! Doctor! where's my Johnny?'
'I'm here, what is't you want with me?'
'O Sir! you know I'm Betty Foy,
And I have lost my poor dear Boy,
You know him—him you often see;

'He's not so wise as some folks be':
'The devil take his wisdom!' said
The Doctor, looking somewhat grim,
'What, Woman! should I know of him?'   260
And, grumbling, he went back to bed!

'O woe is me! O woe is me!
Here will I die; here will I die;
I thought to find my lost one here,
But he is neither far nor near,
Oh! what a wretched Mother I!'

She stops, she stands, she looks about;
Which way to turn she cannot tell.
Poor Betty! it would ease her pain
If she had heart to knock again;   270
—The clock strikes three—a dismal knell!

Then up along the town she hies,
No wonder if her senses fail;
This piteous news so much it shocked her,
She quite forgot to send the Doctor,
To comfort poor old Susan Gale.

And now she's high upon the down,
And she can see a mile of road:
'O cruel! I'm almost threescore;
Such night as this was ne'er before,   280
There's not a single soul abroad.'

She listens, but she cannot hear
The foot of horse, the voice of man;
The streams with softest sound are flowing,
The grass you almost hear it growing,
You hear it now, if e'er you can.

The owlets through the long blue night
Are shouting to each other still:
Fond lovers! yet not quite hob nob,
They lengthen out the tremulous sob,   290
That echoes far from hill to hill.

Poor Betty now has lost all hope,
Her thoughts are bent on deadly sin,
A green-grown pond she just has past,
And from the brink she hurries fast,
Lest she should drown herself therein.

And now she sits her down and weeps;
Such tears she never shed before;
'Oh dear, dear Pony! my sweet joy!
Oh carry back my Idiot Boy!   300
And we will ne'er o'erload thee more.'

A thought is come into her head:
The Pony he is mild and good,
And we have always used him well;
Perhaps he's gone along the dell,
And carried Johnny to the wood.

Then up she springs as if on wings;
She thinks no more of deadly sin;
If Betty fifty ponds should see,
The last of all her thoughts would be   310
To drown herself therein.

O Reader! now that I might tell
What Johnny and his Horse are doing,
What they've been doing all this time,
Oh could I put it into rhyme,
A most delightful tale pursuing!

Perhaps, and no unlikely thought!
He with his Pony now doth roam
The cliffs and peaks so high that are,
To lay his hands upon a star,   320
And in his pocket bring it home.

Perhaps he's turned himself about,
His face unto his horse's tail,
And, still and mute, in wonder lost,
All silent as a horseman-ghost,
He travels slowly down the vale.

And now, perhaps, is hunting sheep,
A fierce and dreadful hunter he;
Yon valley, now so trim and green,
In five months' time, should he be seen,   330
A desert wilderness will be!

Perhaps, with head and heels on fire,
And like the very soul of evil,
He's galloping away, away,
And so will gallop on for aye,
The bane of all that dread the devil!

I to the Muses have been bound
These fourteen years, by strong indentures:
O gentle Muses! let me tell
But half of what to him befell;   340
He surely met with strange adventures.

O gentle Muses! is this kind?
Why will ye thus my suit repel?
Why of your further aid bereave me?
And can ye thus unfriended leave me,
Ye Muses! whom I love so well?

Who's yon, that, near the waterfall,
Which thunders down with headlong force,
Beneath the moon, yet shining fair,
As careless as if nothing were,   *350*
Sits upright on a feeding horse?

Unto his horse—there feeding free,
He seems, I think, the rein to give:
Of moon or stars he takes no heed;
Of such we in romances read:
—'Tis Johnny! Johnny! as I live.

And that's the very Pony too!
Where is she, where is Betty Foy?
She hardly can sustain her fears;
The roaring waterfall she hears,   *360*
And cannot find her Idiot Boy.

Your Pony's worth his weight in gold:
Then calm your terrors, Betty Foy!
She's coming from among the trees,
And now all full in view she sees
Him whom she loves, her Idiot Boy.

And Betty sees the Pony too:
Why stand you thus, good Betty Foy?
It is no goblin, 'tis no ghost,
'Tis he whom you so long have lost,   *370*
He whom you love, your Idiot Boy.

She looks again—her arms are up—
She screams—she cannot move for joy;
She darts, as with a torrent's force
She almost has o'erturned the Horse,
And fast she holds her Idiot Boy.

And Johnny burrs, and laughs aloud;
Whether in cunning or in joy
I cannot tell; but while he laughs,
Betty a drunken pleasure quaffs
To hear again her Idiot Boy.   *380*

And now she's at the Pony's tail,
And now is at the Pony's head,—
On that side now, and now on this;
And, almost stifled with her bliss,
A few sad tears does Betty shed.

She kisses o'er and o'er again
Him whom she loves, her Idiot Boy;
She's happy here, is happy there,
She is uneasy every where;   *390*
Her limbs are all alive with joy.

She pats the Pony, where or when
She knows not, happy Betty Foy!
The little Pony glad may be,
But he is milder far than she,
You hardly can perceive his joy.

'Oh! Johnny, never mind the Doctor;
You've done your best, and that is all:'
She took the reins, when this was said,
And gently turned the Pony's head   *400*
From the loud waterfall.

By this the stars were almost gone,
The moon was setting on the hill,
So pale you scarcely looked at her:
The little birds began to stir,
Though yet their tongues were still.

The Pony, Betty, and her Boy,
Wind slowly through the woody dale;
And who is she, betimes abroad,
That hobbles up the steep rough road?   *410*
Who is it, but old Susan Gale?

Long time lay Susan lost in thought;
And many dreadful fears beset her,
Both for her Messenger and Nurse;
And, as her mind grew worse and worse,
Her body—it grew better.

She turned, she tossed herself in bed,
On all sides doubts and terrors met her;
Point after point did she discuss;
And, while her mind was fighting thus,   *420*
Her body still grew better.

'Alas! what is become of them?
These fears can never be endured;
I'll to the wood.'—The word scarce said,
Did Susan rise up from her bed,
As if by magic cured.

Away she goes up hill and down,
And to the wood at length is come;
She spies her Friends, she shouts a greeting;
Oh me! it is a merry meeting   *430*
As ever was in Christendom.

The owls have hardly sung their last,
While our four travellers homeward wend;
The owls have hooted all night long,
And with the owls began my song,
And with the owls must end.

For while they all were travelling home,
Cried Betty, 'Tell us, Johnny, do,
Where all this long night you have been,
What you have heard, what you have seen: *440*
And, Johnny, mind you tell us true.'

Now Johnny all night long had heard
The owls in tuneful concert strive;
No doubt too he the moon had seen;
For in the moonlight he had been
From eight o'clock till five.

And thus, to Betty's question, he
Made answer, like a traveller bold,
(His very words I give to you,)
'The cocks did crow to-whoo, to-whoo,   *450*
And the sun did shine so cold!'
—Thus answered Johnny in his glory,
And that was all his travel's story.

THE THORN

I

'THERE is a Thorn—it looks so old,
     In truth, you'd find it hard to say
How it could ever have been young,
It looks so old and grey.
Not higher than a two years' child
It stands erect, this aged Thorn;
No leaves it has, no prickly points;
It is a mass of knotted joints,
A wretched thing forlorn.
It stands erect, and like a stone   *10*
With lichens is it overgrown.

II

'Like rock or stone, it is o'ergrown,
With lichens to the very top,
And hung with heavy tufts of moss,
A melancholy crop:
Up from the earth these mosses creep,
And this poor Thorn they clasp it round
So close, you'd say that they are bent
With plain and manifest intent
To drag it to the ground;   *20*
And all have joined in one endeavour
To bury this poor Thorn for ever.

III

'High on a mountain's highest ridge,
Where oft the stormy winter gale
Cuts like a scythe, while through the clouds
It sweeps from vale to vale;
Not five yards from the mountain path,
This Thorn you on your left espy;
And to the left, three yards beyond,
You see a little muddy pond   *30*
Of water—never dry,
Though but of compass small, and bare
To thirsty suns and parching air.

IV

'And, close beside this aged Thorn,
There is a fresh and lovely sight,
A beauteous heap, a hill of moss,
Just half a foot in height.
All lovely colours there you see,
All colours that were ever seen;

And mossy network too is there,   40
As if by hand of lady fair
The work had woven been;
And cups, the darlings of the eye,
So deep is their vermilion dye.

V

'Ah me! what lovely tints are there
Of olive green and scarlet bright,
In spikes, in branches, and in stars,
Green, red, and pearly white!
This heap of earth o'ergrown with moss,
Which close beside the Thorn you see,   50
So fresh in all its beauteous dyes,
Is like an infant's grave in size,
As like as like can be:
But never, never any where,
An infant's grave was half so fair.

VI

'Now would you see this aged Thorn,
This pond, and beauteous hill of moss,
You must take care and choose your time
The mountain when to cross.
For oft there sits between the heap   60
So like an infant's grave in size,
And that same pond of which I spoke,
A Woman in a scarlet cloak,
And to herself she cries,
"Oh misery! oh misery!
Oh woe is me! oh misery!"

VII

'At all times of the day and night
This wretched Woman thither goes;
And she is known to every star,
And every wind that blows;   70
And there, beside the Thorn, she sits
When the blue daylight's in the skies,
And when the whirlwind's on the hill,
Or frosty air is keen and still,
And to herself she cries,
"Oh misery! oh misery!
Oh woe is me! oh misery!"

VIII

'Now wherefore, thus, by day and night
In rain, in tempest, and in snow,
Thus to the dreary mountain-top   *80*
Does this poor Woman go?
And why sits she beside the Thorn
When the blue daylight's in the sky
Or when the whirlwind's on the hill,
Or frosty air is keen and still,
And wherefore does she cry?—
O wherefore? wherefore? tell me why
Does she repeat that doleful cry?'

IX

'I cannot tell; I wish I could;
For the true reason no one knows: *90*
But would you gladly view the spot,
The spot to which she goes;
The hillock like an infant's grave,
The pond—and Thorn, so old and grey;
Pass by her door—'tis seldom shut—
And, if you see her in her hut—
Then to the spot away!
I never heard of such as dare
Approach the spot when she is there.'

X

'But wherefore to the mountain-top   *100*
Can this unhappy Woman go?
Whatever star is in the skies,
Whatever wind may blow?'
'Full twenty years are past and gone
Since she (her name is Martha Ray)
Gave with a maiden's true good-will
Her company to Stephen Hill;
And she was blithe and gay,
While friends and kindred all approved
Of him whom tenderly she loved.   *110*

XI

'And they had fixed the wedding day,
The morning that must wed them both;
But Stephen to another Maid
Had sworn another oath:
And, with this other Maid, to church
Unthinking Stephen went—

Poor Martha! on that woeful day
A pang of pitiless dismay
Into her soul was sent;
A fire was kindled in her breast,   *120*
Which might not burn itself to rest.

XII

'They say, full six months after this,
While yet the summer leaves were green,
She to the mountain-top would go,
And there was often seen.
What could she seek?—or wish to hide?
Her state to any eye was plain;
She was with child, and she was mad;
Yet often was she sober sad
From her exceeding pain.   *130*
O guilty Father—would that death
Had saved him from that breach of faith!

XIII

'Sad case for such a brain to hold
Communion with a stirring child!
Sad case, as you may think, for one
Who had a brain so wild!
Last Christmas-eve we talked of this,
And grey-haired Wilfred of the glen
Held that the unborn infant wrought
About its mother's heart, and brought   *140*
Her senses back again:
And, when at last her time drew near
Her looks were calm, her senses clear.

XIV

'More know I not, I wish I did,
And it should all be told to you;
For what became of this poor child
No mortal ever knew;
Nay—if a child to her was born
No earthly tongue could ever tell;
And if 'twas born alive or dead,   *150*
Far less could this with proof be said;
But some remember well,
That Martha Ray about this time
Would up the mountain often climb.

XV

'And all that winter, when at night
The wind blew from the mountain-peak,
'Twas worth your while, though in the dark,
The churchyard path to seek:
For many a time and oft were heard
Cries coming from the mountain head: *160*
Some plainly living voices were;
And others, I've heard many swear,
Were voices of the dead:
I cannot think, whate'er they say,
They had to do with Martha Ray.

XVI

'But that she goes to this old Thorn,
The Thorn which I described to you,
And there sits in a scarlet cloak
I will be sworn is true.
For one day with my telescope,   *170*
To view the ocean wide and bright,
When to this country first I came,
Ere I had heard of Martha's name,
I climbed the mountain's height:—
A storm came on, and I could see
No object higher than my knee.

XVII

''Twas mist and rain, and storm and rain:
No screen, no fence could I discover
And then the wind! in sooth, it was
A wind full ten times over.   *180*
I looked around, I thought I saw
A jutting crag,—and off I ran,
Head-foremost, through the driving rain,
The shelter of the crag to gain;
And, as I am a man,
Instead of jutting crag, I found
A Woman seated on the ground.

XVIII

'I did not speak—I saw her face;
Her face!—it was enough for me;
I turned about and heard her cry,   *190*
"Oh misery! oh misery!"
And there she sits, until the moon
Through half the clear blue sky will go;

And, when the little breezes make
The waters of the pond to shake,
As all the country know,
She shudders, and you hear her cry,
"Oh misery! oh misery!"'

XIX

'But what's the Thorn? and what the pond?
And what the hill of moss to her?   *200*
And what the creeping breeze that comes
The little pond to stir?'
'I cannot tell; but some will say
She hanged her baby on the tree;
Some say she drowned it in the pond,
Which is a little step beyond:
But all and each agree,
The little Babe was buried there,
Beneath that hill of moss so fair.

XX

'I've heard, the moss is spotted red   *210*
With drops of that poor infant's blood;
But kill a new-born infant thus,
I do not think she could!
Some say, if to the pond you go,
And fix on it a steady view,
The shadow of a babe you trace,
A baby and a baby's face,
And that it looks at you;
Whene'er you look on it, 'tis plain
The baby looks at you again.   *220*

XXI

'And some had sworn an oath that she
Should be to public justice brought;
And for the little infant's bones
With spades they would have sought.
But instantly the hill of moss
Before their eyes began to stir!
And, for full fifty yards around,
The grass—it shook upon the ground!
Yet all do still aver
The little Babe lies buried there,   *230*
Beneath that hill of moss so fair.

XXII

'I cannot tell how this may be,
But plain it is the Thorn is bound
With heavy tufts of moss that strive
To drag it to the ground;
And this I know, full many a time,
When she was on the mountain high,
By day, and in the silent night,
When all the stars shone clear and bright,
That I have heard her cry,   *240*
"Oh misery! oh misery!
Oh woe is me! oh misery!"'

THE COMPLAINT

OF A FORSAKEN INDIAN WOMAN

[When a Northern Indian, from sickness, is unable to continue his journey with his companions, he is left behind, covered over with deer-skins, and is supplied with water, food, and fuel, if the situation of the place will afford it.   He is informed of the track which his companions intend to pursue, and if he be unable to follow, or overtake them, he perishes alone in the desert; unless he should have the good fortune to fall in with some other tribes of Indians.   The females are equally, or still more, exposed to the same fate.   See that very interesting work HEARNE'S *Journey from Hudson's Bay to the Northern Ocean.*   In the high northern latitudes, as the same writer informs us, when the northern lights vary their position in the air, they make a rustling and a crackling noise, as alluded to in the following poem.]

I

BEFORE I see another day,
  Oh let my body die away!
In sleep I heard the northern gleams;
The stars, they were among my dreams;
In rustling conflict through the skies,
I heard, I saw the flashes drive,
And yet they are upon my eyes,
And yet I am alive;
Before I see another day,
Oh let my body die away!   *10*

II

My fire is dead: it knew no pain;
Yet is it dead, and I remain:
All stiff with ice the ashes lie;
And they are dead, and I will die.
When I was well, I wished to live,
For clothes, for warmth, for food, and fire;

But they to me no joy can give,
No pleasure now, and no desire
Then here contented will I lie!
Alone, I cannot fear to die.   20

III

Alas! ye might have dragged me on
Another day, a single one!
Too soon I yielded to despair;
Why did ye listen to my prayer?
When ye were gone my limbs were stronger;
And oh, how grievously I rue,
That, afterwards, a little longer,
My friends, I did not follow you!
For strong and without pain I lay,
Dear friends, when ye were gone away.   30

IV

My Child! they gave thee to another,
A woman who was not thy mother.
When from my arms my Babe they took,
On me how strangely did he look!
Through his whole body something ran,
A most strange working did I see;
—As if he strove to be a man,
That he might pull the sledge for me:
And then he stretched his arms, how wild!
Oh mercy! like a helpless child.   40

V

My little joy! my little pride!
In two days more I must have died.
Then do not weep and grieve for me;
I feel I must have died with thee.
O wind, that o'er my head art flying
The way my friends their course did bend,
I should not feel the pain of dying,
Could I with thee a message send;
Too soon, my friends, ye went away;
For I had many things to say.   50

VI

I'll follow you across the snow;
Ye travel heavily and slow;
In spite of all my weary pain
I'll look upon your tents again.
—My fire is dead, and snowy white
The water which beside it stood:

The wolf has come to me to-night,
And he has stolen away my food.
For ever left alone am I;
Then wherefore should I fear to die?　　60

VII

Young as I am, my course is run,
I shall not see another sun;
I cannot lift my limbs to know
If they have any life or no.
My poor forsaken Child, if I
For once could have thee close to me,
With happy heart I then would die
And my last thought would happy be;
But thou, dear Babe, art far away,
Nor shall I see another day.　　70

EXPOSTULATION AND REPLY

'WHY, William, on that old grey stone,
　　Thus, for the length of half a day,
Why, William, sit you thus alone,
And dream your time away?

'Where are your books?—that light bequeathed
To Beings else forlorn and blind!
Up! up! and drink the spirit breathed
From dead men to their kind.

'You look round on your Mother Earth,
As if she for no purpose bore you;　　10
As if you were her first-born birth,
And none had lived before you!'

One morning thus, by Esthwaite lake,
When life was sweet, I knew not why,
To me my good friend Matthew spake,
And thus I made reply:

'The eye—it cannot choose but see;
We cannot bid the ear be still;
Our bodies feel, where'er they be,
Against or with our will.　　20

'Nor less I deem that there are Powers
Which of themselves our minds impress;
That we can feed this mind of ours
In a wise passiveness.

'Think you, 'mid all this mighty sum
Of things for ever speaking,
That nothing of itself will come,
But we must still be seeking?

'—Then ask not wherefore, here, alone,   *30*
Conversing as I may,
I sit upon this old grey stone,
And dream my time away.'

THE TABLES TURNED

AN EVENING SCENE ON THE SAME SUBJECT

UP! up! my Friend, and quit your books;
Or surely you'll grow double:
Up! up! my Friend, and clear your looks;
Why all this toil and trouble?

The sun, above the mountain's head,
A freshening lustre mellow
Through all the long green fields has spread,
His first sweet evening yellow.

Books! 'tis a dull and endless strife:
Come, hear the woodland linnet,   *10*
How sweet his music! on my life,
There's more of wisdom in it.

And hark! how blithe the throstle sings!
He, too, is no mean preacher:
Come forth into the light of things,
Let Nature be your teacher.

She has a world of ready wealth,
Our minds and hearts to bless—
Spontaneous wisdom breathed by health,
Truth breathed by cheerfulness.   *20*

One impulse from a vernal wood
May teach you more of man,
Of moral evil and of good,
Than all the sages can.

Sweet is the lore which Nature brings;
Our meddling intellect
Mis-shapes the beauteous forms of things:
We murder to dissect.

Enough of Science and of Art;
Close up those barren leaves;   *30*
Come forth, and bring with you a heart
That watches and receives.

LINES

COMPOSED A FEW MILES ABOVE TINTERN ABBEY, ON
REVISITING THE BANKS OF THE WYE DURING A TOUR,
13TH JULY 1798

FIVE years have past; five summers, with the length
   Of five long winters! and again I hear
These waters, rolling from their mountain-springs
With a soft inland murmur.[2]—Once again
Do I behold these steep and lofty cliffs,
That on a wild secluded scene impress
Thoughts of more deep seclusion; and connect
The landscape with the quiet of the sky.
The day is come when I again repose
Here, under this dark sycamore, and view   *10*
These plots of cottage-ground, these orchard-tufts,
Which at this season, with their unripe fruits,
Are clad in one green hue, and lose themselves
'Mid groves and copses.   Once again I see
These hedge-rows, hardly hedge-rows, little lines
Of sportive wood run wild: these pastoral farms,
Green to the very door; and wreaths of smoke
Sent up, in silence, from among the trees!
With some uncertain notice, as might seem
Of vagrant dwellers in the houseless woods,   *20*
Or of some Hermit's cave, where by his fire
The Hermit sits alone.

These beauteous forms
Through a long absence, have not been to me
As is a landscape to a blind man's eye:
But oft, in lonely rooms, and 'mid the din
Of towns and cities, I have owed to them
In hours of weariness, sensations sweet,
Felt in the blood, and felt along the heart;
And passing even into my purer mind,
With tranquil restoration:—feelings too   30
Of unremembered pleasure: such, perhaps,
As have no slight or trivial influence
On that best portion of a good man's life,
His little, nameless, unremembered, acts
Of kindness and of love.   Nor less, I trust,
To them I may have owed another gift,
Of aspect more sublime; that blessed mood
In which the burthen of the mystery,
In which the heavy and the weary weight
Of all this unintelligible world,   40
Is lightened:—that serene and blessed mood,
In which the affections gently lead us on,—
Until, the breath of this corporeal frame
And even the motion of our human blood
Almost suspended, we are laid asleep
In body, and become a living soul:
While with an eye made quiet by the power
Of harmony, and the deep power of joy,
We see into the life of things.
                              If this
Be but a vain belief, yet, oh! how oft—   50
In darkness and amid the many shapes
Of joyless daylight; when the fretful stir
Unprofitable, and the fever of the world,
Have hung upon the beatings of my heart—
How oft, in spirit, have I turned to thee,
O sylvan Wye! thou wanderer thro' the woods,
How often has my spirit turned to thee!
    And now, with gleams of half-extinguished thought,
With many recognitions dim and faint,
And somewhat of a sad perplexity,   60
The picture of the mind revives again:
While here I stand, not only with the sense
Of present pleasure, but with pleasing thoughts
That in this moment there is life and food
For future years.   And so I dare to hope,
Though changed, no doubt, from what I was when **first**
I came among these hills; when like a roe

I bounded o'er the mountains, by the sides
Of the deep rivers, and the lonely streams,
Wherever nature led: more like a man   *70*
Flying from something that he dreads than one
Who sought the thing he loved.   For nature then
(The coarser pleasures of my boyish days,
And their glad animal movements all gone by)
To me was all in all.—I cannot paint
What then I was.   The sounding cataract
Haunted me like a passion: the tall rock,
The mountain, and the deep and gloomy wood,
Their colours and their forms, were then to me
An appetite; a feeling and a love,   *80*
That had no need of a remoter charm,
By thought supplied, nor any interest
Unborrowed from the eye.—That time is past,
And all its aching joys are now no more,
And all its dizzy raptures.   Not for this
Faint I, nor mourn nor murmur; other gifts
Have followed; for such loss, I would believe,
Abundant recompense.   For I have learned
To look on nature, not as in the hour
Of thoughtless youth; but hearing oftentimes   *90*
The still, sad music of humanity,
Nor harsh nor grating, though of ample power
To chasten and subdue.   And I have felt
A presence that disturbs me with the joy
Of elevated thoughts; a sense sublime
Of something far more deeply interfused,
Whose dwelling is the light of setting suns,
And the round ocean and the living air,
And the blue sky, and in the mind of man:
A motion and a spirit, that impels   *100*
All thinking things, all objects of all thought,
And rolls through all things.   Therefore am I still
A lover of the meadows and the woods,
And mountains; and of all that we behold
From this green earth; of all the mighty world
Of eye, and ear,—both what they half create,[1]
And what perceive; well pleased to recognize
In nature and the language of the sense
The anchor of my purest thoughts, the nurse,
The guide, the guardian of my heart, and soul   *110*
Of all my moral being.
                  Nor perchance,
If I were not thus taught, should I the more
Suffer my genial spirits to decay:

For thou art with me here upon the banks
Of this fair river; thou my dearest Friend,
My dear, dear Friend; and in thy voice I catch
The language of my former heart, and read
My former pleasures in the shooting lights
Of thy wild eyes.   Oh! yet a little while
May I behold in thee what I was once,   *120*
My dear, dear Sister! and this prayer I make,
Knowing that Nature never did betray
The heart that loved her; 'tis her privilege,
Through all the years of this our life, to lead
From joy to joy: for she can so inform
The mind that is within us, so impress
With quietness and beauty, and so feed
With lofty thoughts, that neither evil tongues,
Rash judgments, nor the sneers of selfish men,
Nor greetings where no kindness is, nor all
The dreary intercourse of daily life,   *130*
Shall e'er prevail against us, or disturb
Our cheerful faith, that all which we behold
Is full of blessings.   Therefore let the moon
Shine on thee in thy solitary walk;
And let the misty mountain-winds be free
To blow against thee: and, in after years,
When these wild ecstasies shall be matured
Into a sober pleasure; when thy mind
Shall be a mansion for all lovely forms,
Thy memory be as a dwelling-place   *140*
For all sweet sounds and harmonies; oh! then,
If solitude, or fear, or pain, or grief,
Should be thy portion, with what healing thoughts
Of tender joy wilt thou remember me,
And these my exhortations!   Nor, perchance—
If I should be where I no more can hear
Thy voice, nor catch from thy wild eyes these gleams
Of past existence—wilt thou then forget
That on the banks of this delightful stream
We stood together; and that I, so long   *150*
A worshipper of Nature, hither came
Unwearied in that service: rather say
With warmer love—oh! with far deeper zeal
Of holier love.   Nor wilt thou then forget,
That after many wanderings, many years
Of absence, these steep woods and lofty cliffs,
And this green pastoral landscape, were to me
More dear, both for themselves and for thy sake!

NUTTING

——————————————It seems a day
(I speak of one from many singled out)
One of those heavenly days that cannot die;
When, in the eagerness of boyish hope,
I left our cottage-threshold, sallying forth
With a huge wallet o'er my shoulders slung,
A nutting-crook in hand; and turned my steps
Tow'rd some far-distant wood, a Figure quaint,
Tricked out in proud disguise of cast-off weeds
Which for that service had been husbanded,   *10*
By exhortation of my frugal Dame—
Motley accoutrement, of power to smile
At thorns, and brakes, and brambles—and, in truth,
More raggèd than need was!   O'er pathless rocks,
Through beds of matted fern, and tangled thickets,
Forcing my way, I came to one dear nook
Unvisited, where not a broken bough
Drooped with its withered leaves, ungracious sign
Of devastation; but the hazels rose
Tall and erect, with tempting clusters hung,   *20*
A virgin scene!—A little while I stood,
Breathing with such suppression of the heart
As joy delights in; and, with wise restraint
Voluptuous, fearless of a rival, eyed
The banquet;—or beneath the trees I sate
Among the flowers, and with the flowers I played;
A temper known to those, who, after long
And weary expectation, have been blest
With sudden happiness beyond all hope.
Perhaps it was a bower beneath whose leaves   *30*
The violets of five seasons re-appear
And fade, unseen by any human eye;
Where fairy water-breaks do murmur on
For ever; and I saw the sparkling foam,
And—with my cheek on one of those green stones
That, fleeced with moss, under the shady trees,
Lay round me, scattered like a flock of sheep—
I heard the murmur and the murmuring sound,
In that sweet mood when pleasure loves to pay
Tribute to ease; and, if its joy secure,   *40*
The heart luxuriates with indifferent things,
Wasting its kindliness on stocks and stones,
And on the vacant air.   Then up I rose,
And dragged to earth both branch and bough, with crash
And merciless ravage: and the shady nook

Of hazels, and the green and mossy bower,
Deformed and sullied, patiently gave up
Their quiet being: and, unless I now
Confound my present feelings with the past,
Ere from the mutiliated bower I turned   *50*
Exulting, rich beyond the wealth of kings,
I felt a sense of pain when I beheld
The silent trees, and saw the intruding sky—
Then, dearest Maiden, move along these shades
In gentleness of heart; with gentle hand
Touch—for there is a spirit in the woods.

THERE WAS A BOY

There was a Boy: ye knew him well, ye cliffs
And islands of Winander!—many a time
At evening, when the earliest stars began
To move along the edges of the hills,
Rising or setting, would he stand alone
Beneath the trees or by the glimmering lake,
And there, with fingers interwoven, both hands
Pressed closely palm to palm, and to his mouth
Uplifted, he, as through an instrument,
Blew mimic hootings to the silent owls,   *10*
That they might answer him; and they would shout
Across the watery vale, and shout again,
Responsive to his call, with quivering peals,
And long halloos and screams, and echoes loud,
Redoubled and redoubled, concourse wild
Of jocund din; and, when a lengthened pause
Of silence came and baffled his best skill,
Then sometimes, in that silence while he hung
Listening, a gentle shock of mild surprise
Has carried far into his heart the voice   *20*
Of mountain torrents; or the visible scene
Would enter unawares into his mind,
With all its solemn imagery, its rocks,
Its woods, and that uncertain heaven, received
Into the bosom of the steady lake.

This Boy was taken from his mates, and died
In childhood, ere he was full twelve years old.
Fair is the spot, most beautiful the vale
Where he was born; the grassy churchyard hangs

Upon a slope above the village school,   *30*
And through that churchyard when my way has led
On summer evenings, I believe that there
A long half hour together I have stood
Mute, looking at the grave in which he lies!

STRANGE fits of passion have I known:
    And I will dare to tell,
But in the Lover's ear alone,
    What once to me befell.

When she I loved looked every day
    Fresh as a rose in June,
I to her cottage bent my way,
    Beneath an evening-moon.

Upon the moon I fixed my eye,
    All over the wide lea;   *10*
With quickening pace my horse drew nigh
    Those paths so dear to me.

And now we reached the orchard-plot;
    And, as we climbed the hill,
The sinking moon to Lucy's cot
    Came near, and nearer still.

In one of those sweet dreams I slept,
    Kind Nature's gentlest boon!
And all the while my eyes I kept
    On the descending moon.   *20*

My horse moved on; hoof after hoof
    He raised, and never stopped:
When down behind the cottage roof,
    At once, the bright moon dropped.

What fond and wayward thoughts will slide
    Into a Lover's head!
'O mercy!' to myself I cried,
    'If Lucy should be dead!'

SHE dwelt among the untrodden ways
   Beside the springs of Dove,
A Maid whom there were none to praise
   And very few to love:

A violet by a mossy stone
   Half hidden from the eye!
—Fair as a star, when only one
   Is shining in the sky.

She lived unknown, and few could know
   When Lucy ceased to be;
But she is in her grave, and, oh,
   The difference to me!   *10*

A SLUMBER did my spirit seal;
   I had no human fears:
She seemed a thing that could not feel
   The touch of earthly years.

No motion has she now, no force;
   She neither hears nor sees;
Rolled round in earth's diurnal course,
   With rocks, and stones, and trees.

THREE years she grew in sun and shower,
   Then Nature said, 'A lovelier flower
On earth was never sown;
This Child I to myself will take;
She shall be mine, and I will make
A Lady of my own.

'Myself will to my darling be
Both law and impulse: and with me
The Girl, in rock and plain,
In earth and heaven, in glade and bower,   *10*
Shall feel an overseeing power
To kindle or restrain.

'She shall be sportive as the fawn
That wild with glee across the lawn,
Or up the mountain springs;
And her's shall be the breathing balm,
And her's the silence and the calm
Of mute insensate things.

'The floating clouds their state shall lend
To her; for her the willow bend;   *20*
Nor shall she fail to see
Even in the motions of the Storm
Grace that shall mould the Maiden's form
By silent sympathy.

'The stars of midnight shall be dear
To her; and she shall lean her ear
In many a secret place
Where rivulets dance their wayward round,
And beauty born of murmuring sound
Shall pass into her face.   *30*

'And vital feelings of delight
Shall rear her form to stately height,
Her virgin bosom swell;
Such thoughts to Lucy I will give
While she and I together live
Here in this happy dell.'

Thus Nature spake—The work was done—
How soon my Lucy's race was run!
She died, and left to me
This heath, this calm, and quiet scene;   *40*
The memory of what has been,
And never more will be.

I TRAVELLED among unknown men,
    In lands beyond the sea;
Nor, England! did I know till then
    What love I bore to thee.

'Tis past, that melancholy dream!
  Nor will I quit thy shore
A second time; for still I seem
  To love thee more and more.

Among thy mountains did I feel
  The joy of my desire;   *10*
And she I cherished turned her wheel
  Beside an English fire.

Thy mornings showed, thy nights concealed
  The bowers where Lucy played;
And thine too is the last green field
  That Lucy's eyes surveyed.

LUCY GRAY;

OR, SOLITUDE

OFT I had heard of Lucy Gray:
  And, when I crossed the wild,
I chanced to see at break of day
  The solitary child.

No mate, no comrade Lucy knew;
  She dwelt on a wide moor,
—The sweetest thing that ever grew
  Beside a human door!

You yet may spy the fawn at play,
  The hare upon the green;   *10*
But the sweet face of Lucy Gray
  Will never more be seen.

'To-night will be a stormy night—
  You to the town must go;
And take a lantern, Child, to light
  Your mother through the snow.'

'That, Father! will I gladly do:
  'Tis scarcely afternoon—
The minster-clock has just struck two,
  And yonder is the moon!'   *20*

At this the Father raised his hook,
And snapped a faggot-band;
He plied his work;—and Lucy took
The lantern in her hand.

Not blither is the mountain roe:
With many a wanton stroke
Her feet disperse the powdery snow,
That rises up like smoke.

The storm came on before its time:
She wandered up and down;   *30*
And many a hill did Lucy climb:
But never reached the town.

The wretched parents all that night
Went shouting far and wide;
But there was neither sound nor sight
To serve them for a guide.

At day-break on a hill they stood
That overlooked the moor;
And thence they saw the bridge of wood,
A furlong from their door.   *40*

They wept—and, turning homeward, cried
'In heaven we all shall meet;'
—When in the snow the mother spied
The print of Lucy's feet.

Then downwards from the steep hill's edge
They tracked the footmarks small;
And through the broken hawthorn hedge,
And by the long stone-wall;

And then an open field they crossed:
The marks were still the same;   *50*
They tracked them on, nor ever lost;
And to the bridge they came.

They followed from the snowy bank
Those footmarks, one by one,
Into the middle of the plank;
And further there were none!

—Yet some maintain that to this day
She is a living child;
That you may see sweet Lucy Gray
Upon the lonesome wild.   *60*

O'er rough and smooth she trips along,
And never looks behind;
And sings a solitary song
That whistles in the wind.

MATTHEW

I

IF Nature, for a favourite child,
In thee hath tempered so her clay,
That every hour thy heart runs wild,
Yet never once doth go astray,

Read o'er these lines; and then review
This tablet, that thus humbly rears
In such diversity of hue
Its history of two hundred years.

—When through this little wreck of fame,
Cipher and syllable! thine eye   *10*
Has travelled down to Matthew's name,
Pause with no common sympathy.

And, if a sleeping tear should wake,
Then be it neither checked nor stayed:
For Matthew a request I make
Which for himself he had not made.

Poor Matthew, all his frolics o'er,
Is silent as a standing pool;
Far from the chimney's merry roar,
And murmur of the village school. ·   *20*

The sighs which Matthew heaved were sighs
Of one tired out with fun and madness;
The tears which came to Matthew's eyes
Were tears of light, the dew of gladness.

Yet, sometimes, when the secret cup
Of still and serious thought went round,
He seemed as if he drank it up—
He felt with spirit so profound.

—Thou soul of God's best earthly mould!
Thou happy Soul! and can it be   *30*
That these two words of glittering gold
Are all that must remain of thee?

II

THE TWO APRIL MORNINGS

WE walked along, while bright and red
   Uprose the morning sun;
And Matthew stopped, he looked, and said,
'The will of God be done!'

A village schoolmaster was he,
With hair of glittering grey;
As blithe a man as you could see
On a spring holiday.

And on that morning, through the grass,
And by the steaming rills,   *10*
We travelled merrily, to pass
A day among the hills.

'Our work,' said I, 'was well begun,
Then, from thy breast what thought,
Beneath so beautiful a sun,
So sad a sigh has brought?'

A second time did Matthew stop;
And fixing still his eye
Upon the eastern mountain-top,
To me he made reply: *20*

'Yon cloud with that long purple cleft
Brings fresh into my mind
A day like this which I have left
Full thirty years behind.

'And just above yon slope of corn
Such colours, and no other,
Were in the sky, that April morn,
Of this the very brother.

'With rod and line I sued the sport
Which that sweet season gave,   *30*
And, to the churchyard come, stopped short
Beside my daughter's grave.

'Nine summers had she scarcely seen,
The pride of all the vale;
And then she sang;—she would have been
A very nightingale.

'Six feet in earth my Emma lay;
And yet I loved her more,
For so it seemed, than till that day
I e'er had loved before.   *40*

'And, turning from her grave, I met,
Beside the churchyard yew,
A blooming Girl, whose hair was wet
With points of morning dew.

'A basket on her head she bare;
Her brow was smooth and white:
To see a child so very fair,
It was a pure delight!

'No fountain from its rocky cave
E'er tripped with foot so free;   *50*
She seemed as happy as a wave
That dances on the sea.

'There came from me a sigh of pain
Which I could ill confine;
I looked at her, and looked again:
And did not wish her mine!'

Matthew is in his grave, yet now,
Methinks, I see him stand,
As at that moment, with a bough
Of wilding in his hand.   *60*

III

THE FOUNTAIN
A CONVERSATION

WE talked with open heart, and tongue
      Affectionate and true,
A pair of friends, though I was young,
And Matthew seventy-two.

We lay beneath a spreading oak,
Beside a mossy seat;
And from the turf a fountain broke,
And gurgled at our feet.

'Now, Matthew!' said I, 'let us match
This water's pleasant tune   *10*
With some old border-song, or catch
That suits a summer's noon;

'Or of the church-clock and the chimes
Sing here beneath the shade,
That half-mad thing of witty rhymes
Which you last April made!'

In silence Matthew lay, and eyed
The spring beneath the tree;
And thus the dear old Man replied,
The grey-haired man of glee: *20*

'No check, no stay, this Streamlet fears;
How merrily it goes!
'Twill murmur on a thousand years,
And flow as now it flows.

'And here, on this delightful day,
I cannot choose but think
How oft, a vigorous man, I lay
Beside this fountain's brink.

'My eyes are dim with childish tears,
My heart is idly stirred,   *30*
For the same sound is in my ears
Which in those days I heard.

'Thus fares it still in our decay:
And yet the wiser mind
Mourns less for what age takes away
Than what it leaves behind.

'The blackbird amid leafy trees,
The lark above the hill,
Let loose their carols when they please,
Are quiet when they will.   *40*

'With Nature never do *they* wage
A foolish strife; they see
A happy youth, and their old age
Is beautiful and free:

'But we are pressed by heavy laws;
And often, glad no more,
We wear a face of joy, because
We have been glad of yore.

'If there be one who need bemoan
His kindred laid in earth,   *50*
The household hearts that were his own;
It is the man of mirth.

'My days, my Friend, are almost gone,
My life has been approved,
And many love me; but by none
Am I enough beloved.'

'Now both himself and me he wrongs,
The man who thus complains;
I live and sing my idle songs
Upon these happy plains;   *60*

'And, Matthew, for thy children dead
I'll be a son to thee!'
At this he grasped my hand, and said,
'Alas! that cannot be.'

We rose up from the fountain-side;
And down the smooth descent
Of the green sheep-track did we glide;
And through the wood we went;

And, ere we came to Leonard's rock,
He sang those witty rhymes   *70*
About the crazy old church-clock
And the bewildered chimes.

A POET'S EPITAPH

ART thou a Statist in the van
   Of public conflicts trained and bred?
—First learn to love one living man;
Then may'st thou think upon the dead.

A Lawyer art thou?—draw not nigh!
Go, carry to some fitter place
The keenness of that practised eye,
The hardness of that sallow face.

Art thou a Man of purple cheer?
A rosy Man, right plump to see?   *10*
Approach; yet, Doctor, not too near,
This grave no cushion is for thee.

Or art thou one of gallant pride,
A Soldier and no man of chaff?
Welcome! but lay thy sword aside,
And lean upon a peasant's staff.

Physician art thou?—one, all eyes,
Philosopher!—a fingering slave,
One that would peep and botanize
Upon his mother's grave?   *20*

Wrapt closely in thy sensual fleece,
O turn aside,—and take, I pray,
That he below may rest in peace,
Thy ever-dwindling soul, away!

A Moralist perchance appears;
Led, Heaven knows how! to this poor sod:
And he has neither eyes nor ears;
Himself his world, and his own God;

One to whose smooth-rubbed soul can cling
Nor form, nor feeling, great or small;   *30*
A reasoning, self-sufficing thing,
An intellectual All-in-all!

Shut close the door; press down the latch;
Sleep in thy intellectual crust;
Nor lose ten tickings of thy watch
Near this unprofitable dust.

But who is He, with modest looks,
And clad in homely russet brown?
He murmurs near the running brooks
A music sweeter than their own. *40*

He is retired as noontide dew,
Or fountain in a noon-day grove;
And you must love him, ere to you
He will seem worthy of your love.

The outward shows of sky and earth,
Of hill and valley, he has viewed;
And impulses of deeper birth
Have come to him in solitude.

In common things that round us lie
Some random truths he can impart,— *50*
The harvest of a quiet eye
That broods and sleeps on his own heart.

But he is weak; both Man and Boy,
Hath been an idler in the land;
Contented if he might enjoy
The things which others understand.

—Come hither in thy hour of strength;
Come, weak as is a breaking wave!
Here stretch thy body at full length;
Or build thy house upon this grave. *60*

HART-LEAP WELL

THE Knight had ridden down from Wensley Moor
  With the slow motion of a summer's cloud,
And now, as he approached a vassal's door
'Bring forth another horse!' he cried aloud.

'Another horse!'—That shout the vassal heard
And saddled his best Steed, a comely grey;
Sir Walter mounted him; he was the third
Which he had mounted on that glorious day.

Joy sparkled in the prancing courser's eyes;
The horse and horseman are a happy pair;   *10*
But, though Sir Walter like a falcon flies,
There is a doleful silence in the air.

A rout this morning left Sir Walter's Hall,
That as they galloped made the echoes roar;
But horse and man are vanished, one and all;
Such race, I think, was never seen before.

Sir Walter, restless as a veering wind,
Calls to the few tired dogs that yet remain:
Blanch, Swift, and Music, noblest of their kind,
Follow, and up the weary mountain strain.   *20*

The Knight hallooed, he cheered and chid them on
With suppliant gestures and upbraidings stern;
But breath and eyesight fail; and, one by one,
The dogs are stretched among the mountain fern.

Where is the throng, the tumult of the race?
The bugles that so joyfully were blown?
—This chase it looks not like an earthly chase;
Sir Walter and the Hart are left alone.

The poor Hart toils along the mountain-side;
I will not stop to tell how far he fled,   *30*
Nor will I mention by what death he died;
But now the Knight beholds him lying dead.

Dismounting, then, he leaned against a thorn:
He had no follower, dog, nor man, nor boy:
He neither cracked his whip, nor blew his horn,
But gazed upon the spoil with silent joy.

Close to the thorn on which Sir Walter leaned,
Stood his dumb partner in this glorious feat;
Weak as a lamb the hour that it is yeaned;
And white with foam as if with cleaving sleet.   *40*

Upon his side the Hart was lying stretched:
His nostril touched a spring beneath a hill,
And with the last deep groan his breath had fetched
The waters of the spring were trembling still.

And now, too happy for repose or rest,
(Never had living man such joyful lot!)
Sir Walter walked all round, north, south, and west,
And gazed and gazed upon that darling spot.

And climbing up the hill—(it was at least
Four roods of sheer ascent) Sir Walter found   *50*
Three several hoof-marks which the hunted Beast
Had left imprinted on the grassy ground.

Sir Walter wiped his face, and cried, 'Till now
Such sight was never seen by human eyes:
Three leaps have borne him from this lofty brow,
Down to the very fountain where he lies.

'I'll build a pleasure-house upon this spot,
And a small arbour, made for rural joy;
'Twill be the traveller's shed, the pilgrim's cot,
A place of love for damsels that are coy.   *60*

'A cunning artist will I have to frame
A basin for that fountain in the dell!
And they who do make mention of the same,
From this day forth, shall call it HART-LEAP WELL.

'And, gallant Stag! to make thy praises known,
Another monument shall here be raised;
Three several pillars, each a rough-hewn stone,
And planted where thy hoofs the turf have grazed.

'And, in the summer-time when days are long,
I will come hither with my Paramour;   *70*
And with the dancers and the minstrel's song
We will make merry in that pleasant bower.

'Till the foundations of the mountains fail
My mansion with its arbour shall endure;—
The joy of them who till the fields of Swale,
And them who dwell among the woods of Ure!'

Then home he went, and left the Hart, stone-dead,
With breathless nostrils stretched above the spring.
—Soon did the Knight perform what he had said;
And far and wide the fame thereof did ring.   *80*

Ere thrice the Moon into her port had steered,
A cup of stone received the living well;
Three pillars of rude stone Sir Walter reared,
And built a house of pleasure in the dell.

And, near the fountain, flowers of stature tall
With trailing plants and trees were intertwined,—
Which soon composed a little sylvan hall,
A leafy·shelter from the sun and wind.

And thither, when the summer days were long,
Sir Walter led his wondering Paramour;   *90*
And with the dancers and the minstrel's song
Made merriment within that pleasant bower.

The Knight, Sir Walter, died in course of time,
And his bones lie in his paternal vale.—
But there is matter for a second rhyme,
And I to this would add another tale.

PART SECOND

THE moving accident is not my trade;
    To freeze the blood I have no ready arts:
'Tis my delight, alone in summer shade,
To pipe a simple song for thinking hearts.

As I from Hawes to Richmond did repair,
It chanced that I saw standing in a dell
Three aspens at three corners of a square;
And one, not four yards distant, near a well.

What this imported I could ill divine:
And, pulling now the rein my horse to stop,   *10*
I saw three pillars standing in a line,—
The last stone-pillar on a dark hill-top.

The trees were grey, with neither arms nor head;
Half wasted the square mound of tawny green;
So that you just might say, as then I said,
'Here in old time the hand of man hath been.'

I looked upon the hill both far and near,
More doleful place did never eye survey;
It seemed as if the spring-time came not here,
And Nature here were willing to decay.   *20*

I stood in various thoughts and fancies lost,
When one, who was in shepherd's garb attired,
Came up the hollow:—him did I accost,
And what this place might be I then inquired.

The Shepherd stopped, and that same story told
Which in my former rhyme I have rehearsed.
'A jolly place,' said he, 'in times of old!
But something ails it now; the spot is curst.

'You see these lifeless stumps of aspen wood—
Some say that they are beeches, others elms—   *30*
These were the bower; and here a mansion stood,
The finest palace of a hundred realms!

'The arbour does its own condition tell;
You see the stones, the fountain, and the stream;
But as to the great Lodge! you might as well
Hunt half a day for a forgotten dream.

'There's neither dog nor heifer, horse nor sheep,
Will wet his lips within that cup of stone;
And oftentimes, when all are fast asleep,
This water doth send forth a dolorous groan.   *40*

'Some say that here a murder has been done,
And blood cries out for blood; but, for my part,
I've guessed, when I've been sitting in the sun,
That it was all for that unhappy Hart.

'What thoughts must through the creature's brain have past!
Even from the topmost stone, upon the steep,
Are but three bounds—and look, Sir, at this last—
O Master! it has been a cruel leap.

'For thirteen hours he ran a desperate race;
And in my simple mind we cannot tell   *50*
What cause the Hart might have to love this place,
And come and make his death-bed near the well.

'Here on the grass perhaps asleep he sank,
Lulled by the fountain in the summer-tide;
This water was perhaps the first he drank
When he had wandered from his mother's side.

'In April here beneath the flowering thorn
He heard the birds their morning carols sing;
And he, perhaps, for aught we know, was born
Not half a furlong from that self-same spring.   *60*

'Now, here is neither grass nor pleasant shade;
The sun on drearier hollow never shone;
So will it be, as I have often said,
Till trees, and stones, and fountain, all are gone.'

'Grey-headed Shepherd, thou hast spoken well;
Small difference lies, between thy creed and mine:
This Beast not unobserved by Nature fell;
His death was mourned by sympathy divine.

'The Being, that is in the clouds and air,
That is in the green leaves among the groves,   *70*
Maintains a deep and reverential care
For the unoffending creatures whom he loves.

'The pleasure-house is dust:—behind, before,
This is no common waste, no common gloom;
But Nature, in due course of time, once more
Shall here put on her beauty and her bloom.

'She leaves these objects to a slow decay,
That what we are, and have been, may be known;
But at the coming of the milder day,
These monuments shall all be overgrown.   *80*

'One lesson, Shepherd, let us two divide,
Taught both by what she shows, and what conceals;
Never to blend our pleasures or our pride
With sorrow of the meanest thing that feels.'

MICHAEL

A PASTORAL POEM

IF from the public way you turn your steps
Up the tumultuous brook of Greenhead Ghyll,
You will suppose that with an upright path
Your feet must struggle; in such bold ascent
The pastoral mountains front you, face to face.
But, courage! for around that boisterous brook
The mountains have all opened out themselves,
And made a hidden valley of their own.
No habitation can be seen; but they
Who journey thither find themselves alone   *10*
With a few sheep, with rocks and stones, and kites
That overhead are sailing in the sky.
It is in truth an utter solitude;
Nor should I have made mention of this Dell
But for one object which you might pass by,
Might see and notice not.   Beside the brook
Appears a straggling heap of unhewn stones!
And to that simple object appertains
A story—unenriched with strange events,
Yet not unfit, I deem, for the fireside,   *20*
Or for the summer shade.   It was the first
Of those domestic tales that spake to me
Of shepherds, dwellers in the valleys, men
Whom I already loved; not verily
For their own sakes, but for the fields and hills
Where was their occupation and abode.
And hence this Tale, while I was yet a Boy
Careless of books, yet having felt the power
Of Nature, by the gentle agency
Of natural objects, led me on to feel   *30*
For passions that were not my own, and think
(At random and imperfectly indeed)
On man, the heart of man, and human life.
She was a woman of a stirring life,
Whose heart was in her house: two wheels she had
Of antique form; this large, for spinning wool;
That small, for flax; and if one wheel had rest
It was because the other was at work.
The Pair had but one inmate in their house,

Upon the forest-side in Grasmere Vale   *40*
There dwelt a Shepherd, Michael was his name;
An old man, stout of heart, and strong of limb.
His bodily frame had been from youth to age
Of an unusual strength: his mind was keen,
Intense, and frugal, apt for all affairs,
And in his shepherd's calling he was prompt
And watchful more than ordinary men.
Hence had he learned the meaning of all winds,
Of blasts of every tone; and, oftentimes,
When others heeded not, He heard the South   *50*
Make subterraneous music, like the noise
Of bagpipers on distant Highland hills.
The Shepherd, at such warning, of his flock
Bethought him, and he to himself would say,
'The winds are now devising work for me!'
And, truly, at all times, the storm, that drives
The traveller to a shelter, summoned him
Up to the mountains: he had been alone
Amid the heart of many thousand mists,
That came to him, and left him, on the heights.   *60*
So lived he till his eightieth year was past.
And grossly that man errs, who should suppose
That the green valleys, and the streams and rocks,
Were things indifferent to the Shepherd's thoughts.
Fields, where with cheerful spirits he had breathed
The common air; hills, which with vigorous step
He had so often climbed; which had impressed
So many incidents upon his mind
Of hardship, skill or courage, joy or fear;
Which, like a book, preserved the memory   *70*
Of the dumb animals, whom he had saved,
Had fed or sheltered, linking to such acts
The certainty of honourable gain;
Those fields, those hills—what could they less? had laid
Strong hold on his affections, were to him
A pleasurable feeling of blind love,
The pleasure which there is in life itself.
His days had not been passed in singleness.
His Helpmate was a comely matron, old—
Though younger than himself full twenty years.   *80*
She was a woman of a stirring life,
Whose heart was in her house: two wheels she had
Of antique form; this large, for spinning wool;
That small, for flax; and if one wheel had rest
It was because the other was at work.
The Pair had but one inmate in their house,

An only Child, who had been born to them
When Michael, telling o'er his years, began
To deem that he was old,—in shepherd's phrase,
With one foot in the grave. This only Son,   *90*
With two brave sheep-dogs tried in many a storm,
The one of an inestimable worth,
Made all their household.   I may truly say,
That they were as a proverb in the vale
For endless industry.   When day was gone,
And from their occupations out of doors
The Son and Father were come home, even then,
Their labour did not cease; unless when all
Turned to the cleanly supper-board, and there,
Each with a mess of pottage and skimmed milk,   *100*
Sat round the basket piled with oaten cakes,
And their plain home-made cheese.   Yet when the meal
Was ended, Luke (for so the Son was named)
And his old Father both betook themselves
To such convenient work as might employ
Their hands by the fireside; perhaps to card
Wool for the Housewife's spindle, or repair
Some injury done to sickle, flail, or scythe,
Or other implement of house or field.
   Down from the ceiling, by the chimney's edge,   *110*
That in our ancient uncouth country style
With huge and black projection overbrowed
Large space beneath, as duly as the light
Of day grew dim the Housewife hung a lamp;
An aged utensil, which had performed
Service beyond all others of its kind.
Early at evening did it burn—and late,
Surviving comrade of uncounted hours,
Which, going by from year to year, had found,
And left, the couple neither gay perhaps   *120*
Nor cheerful, yet with objects and with hopes,
Living a life of eager industry.
And now, when Luke had reached his eighteenth year,
There by the light of this old lamp they sate,
Father and Son, while far into the night
The Housewife plied her own peculiar work,
Making the cottage through the silent hours
Murmur as with the sound of summer flies.
This light was famous in its neighbourhood,
And was a public symbol of the life   *130*
That thrifty Pair had lived.   For, as it chanced,
Their cottage on a plot of rising ground
Stood single, with large prospect, north and south,
High into Easedale, up to Dunmail-Raise,

And westward to the village near the lake;
And from this constant light, so regular
And so far seen, the House itself, by all
Who dwelt within the limits of the vale,
Both old and young, was named THE EVENING STAR.
   Thus living on through such a length of years,   *140*
The Shepherd, if he loved himself, must needs
Have loved his Helpmate; but to Michael's heart
This son of his old age was yet more dear—
Less from instinctive tenderness, the same
Fond spirit that blindly works in the blood of all—
Than that a child, more than all other gifts
That earth can offer to declining man,
Brings hope with it, and forward-looking thoughts,
And stirrings of inquietude, when they
By tendency of nature needs must fail.   *150*
Exceeding was the love he bare to him,
His heart and his heart's joy! For oftentimes
Old Michael, while he was a babe in arms,
Had done him female service, not alone
For pastime and delight, as is the use
Of fathers, but with patient mind enforced
To acts of tenderness; and he had rocked
His cradle, as with a woman's gentle hand.
   And, in a later time, ere yet the Boy
Had put on boy's attire, did Michael love,   *160*
Albeit of a stern unbending mind,
To have the Young-one in his sight, when he
Wrought in the field, or on his shepherd's stool
Sate with a fettered sheep before him stretched
Under the large old oak, that near his door
Stood single, and, from matchless depth of shade,
Chosen for the Shearer's covert from the sun,
Thence in our rustic dialect was called
The CLIPPING TREE, a name which yet it bears.
There, while they two were sitting in the shade,   *170*
With others round them, earnest all and blithe,
Would Michael exercise his heart with looks
Of fond correction and reproof bestowed
Upon the Child, if he disturbed the sheep
By catching at their legs, or with his shouts
Scared them, while they lay still beneath the shears.
   And when by Heaven's good grace the boy grew up
A healthy Lad, and carried in his cheek
Two steady roses that were five years old;
Then Michael from a winter coppice cut   *180*
With his own hand a sapling, which he hooped
With iron, making it throughout in all

Due requisites a perfect shepherd's staff,
And gave it to the Boy; wherewith equipt
He as a watchman oftentimes was placed
At gate or gap, to stem or turn the flock;
And, to his office prematurely called,
There stood the urchin, as you will divine,
Something between a hindrance and a help;
And for this cause not always, I believe,　　　　　　*190*
Receiving from his Father hire of praise;
Though nought was left undone which staff, or voice,
Or looks, or threatening gestures, could perform.
　But soon as Luke, full ten years old, could stand
Against the mountain blasts; and to the heights,
Not fearing toil, nor length of weary ways,
He with his Father daily went, and they
Were as companions, why should I relate
That objects which the Shepherd loved before
Were dearer now? that from the Boy there came　　　*200*
Feelings and emanations—things which were
Light to the sun and music to the wind;
And that the old Man's heart seemed born again?
　Thus in his Father's sight the Boy grew up:
And now, when he had reached his eighteenth year,
He was his comfort and his daily hope.
　While in this sort the simple household lived
From day to day, to Michael's ear there came
Distressful tidings.　Long before the time
Of which I speak, the Shepherd had been bound　　　*210*
In surety for his brother's son, a man
Of an industrious life, and ample means;
But unforeseen misfortunes suddenly
Had prest upon him; and old Michael now
Was summoned to discharge the forfeiture,
A grievous penalty, but little less
Than half his substance.　This unlooked-for claim,
At the first hearing, for a moment took
More hope out of his life than he supposed
That any old man ever could have lost.　　　　　　*220*
As soon as he had armed himself with strength
To look his trouble in the face, it seemed
The Shepherd's sole resource to sell at once
A portion of his patrimonial fields.
Such was his first resolve; he thought again,
And his heart failed him. 'Isabel,' said he,
Two evenings after he had heard the news,
'I have been toiling more than seventy years,
And in the open sunshine of God's love

Have we all lived: yet if these fields of ours   *230*
Should pass into a stranger's hand, I think
That I could not lie quiet in my grave.
Our lot is a hard lot; the sun himself
Has scarcely been more diligent than I;
And I have lived to be a fool at last
To my own family. An evil man
That was, and made an evil choice, if he
Were false to us; and if he were not false,
There are ten thousand to whom loss like this
Had been no sorrow. I forgive him;—but   *240*
'Twere better to be dumb than to talk thus.
  'When I began, my purpose was to speak
Of remedies and of a cheerful hope.
Our Luke shall leave us, Isabel; the land
Shall not go from us, and it shall be free;
He shall possess it, free as is the wind
That passes over it. We have, thou know'st,
Another kinsman—he will be our friend
In this distress. He is a prosperous man,
Thriving in trade—and Luke to him shall go,   *250*
And with his kinsman's help and his own thrift
He quickly will repair this loss, and then
He may return to us. If here he stay,
What can be done? Where every one is poor,
What can be gained?'
             At this the old Man paused,
And Isabel sat silent, for her mind
Was busy, looking back into past times.
There's Richard Bateman, thought she to herself,
He was a parish-boy—at the church-door
They made a gathering for him, shillings, pence   *260*
And halfpennies, wherewith the neighbours bought
A basket, which they filled with pedlar's wares;
And, with this basket on his arm, the lad
Went up to London, found a master there,
Who, out of many, chose the trusty boy
To go and overlook his merchandise
Beyond the seas; where he grew wondrous rich,
And left estates and monies to the poor,
And, at his birth-place, built a chapel, floored
With marble which he sent from foreign lands.   *270*
These thoughts, and many others of like sort,
Passed quickly through the mind of Isabel,
And her face brightened. The old Man was glad,
And thus resumed:—'Well, Isabel! this scheme
These two days, has been meat and drink to me.

Far more than we have lost is left us yet.
—We have enough—I wish indeed that I
Were younger;—but this hope is a good hope.
—Make ready Luke's best garments, of the best
Buy for him more, and let us send him forth   280
To-morrow, or the next day, or to-night:
—If he *could* go, the Boy should go to-night.'
  Here Michael ceased, and to the fields went forth
With a light heart.   The Housewife for five days
Was restless morn and night, and all day long
Wrought on with her best fingers to prepare
Things needful for the journey of her son.
But Isabel was glad when Sunday came
To stop her in her work: for, when she lay
By Michael's side, she through the last two nights   290
Heard him, how he was troubled in his sleep:
And when they rose at morning she could see
That all his hopes were gone.   That day at noon
She said to Luke, while they two by themselves
Were sitting at the door, 'Thou must not go:
We have no other Child but thee to lose,
None to remember—do not go away,
For if thou leave thy Father he will die.'
The Youth made answer with a jocund voice;
And Isabel, when she had told her fears,   300
Recovered heart.   That evening her best fare
Did she bring forth, and all together sat
Like happy people round a Christmas fire.
  With daylight Isabel resumed her work;
And all the ensuing week the house appeared
As cheerful as a grove in Spring: at length
The expected letter from their kinsman came,
With kind assurances that he would do
His utmost for the welfare of the Boy;
To which, requests were added, that forthwith   310
He might be sent to him.   Ten times or more
The letter was read over; Isabel
Went forth to show it to the neighbours round,
Nor was there at that time on English land
A prouder heart than Luke's.   When Isabel
Had to her house returned, the old Man said,
'He shall depart to-morrow.'   To this word
The Housewife answered, talking much of things
Which, if at such short notice he should go,
Would surely be forgotten.   But at length   320
She gave consent, and Michael was at ease.
  Near the tumultuous brook of Greenhead Ghyll,

In that deep valley, Michael had designed
To build a Sheepfold; and, before he heard
The tidings of his melancholy loss,
For this same purpose he had gathered up
A heap of stones, which by the streamlet's edge
Lay thrown together, ready for the work.
With Luke that evening thitherward he walked:
And soon as they had reached the place he stopped,   *330*
And thus the old Man spake to him:—'My Son,
To-morrow thou wilt leave me: with full heart
I look upon thee, for thou art the same
That wert a promise to me ere thy birth,
And all thy life hast been my daily joy.
I will relate to thee some little part
Of our two histories; 'twill do thee good
When thou art from me, even if I should touch
On things thou canst not know of.——After thou
First cam'st into the world—as oft befalls   *340*
To new-born infants—thou didst sleep away
Two days, and blessings from thy Father's tongue
Then fell upon thee. Day by day passed on,
And still I loved thee with increasing love.
Never to living ear came sweeter sounds
Than when I heard thee by our own fireside
First uttering, without words, a natural tune;
While thou, a feeding babe, didst in thy joy
Sing at thy Mother's breast. Month followed month,
And in the open fields my life was passed   *350*
And on the mountains; else I think that thou
Hadst been brought up upon thy Father's knees.
But we were playmates, Luke: among these hills,
As well thou knowest, in us the old and young
Have played together, nor with me didst thou
Lack any pleasure which a boy can know.'
Luke had a manly heart; but at these words
He sobbed aloud. The old Man grasped his hand,
And said, 'Nay, do not take it so—I see
That these are things of which I need not speak.   *360*
—Even to the utmost I have been to thee
A kind and a good Father: and herein
I but repay a gift which I myself
Received at others' hands; for, though now old
Beyond the common life of man, I still
Remember them who loved me in my youth.
Both of them sleep together: here they lived,
As all their Forefathers had done; and when
At length their time was come, they were not loth

To give their bodies to the family mould.   *370*
I wished that thou should'st live the life they lived:
But, 'tis a long time to look back, my Son,
And see so little gain from threescore years.
These fields were burthened when they came to me;
Till I was forty years of age, not more
Than half of my inheritance was mine.
I toiled and toiled; God blessed me in my work,
And till these three weeks past the land was free.
—It looks as if it never could endure
Another Master.   Heaven forgive me, Luke,   *380*
If I judge ill for thee, but it seems good
That thou should'st go.'
                 At this the old Man paused;
Then, pointing to the stones near which they stood,
Thus, after a short silence, he resumed:
'This was a work for us; and now, my Son,
It is a work for me.   But, lay one stone—
Here, lay it for me, Luke, with thine own hands.
Nay, Boy, be of good hope;—we both may live
To see a better day.   At eighty-four
I still am strong and hale;—do thou thy part;   *390*
I will do mine.—I will begin again
With many tasks that were resigned to thee:
Up to the heights, and in among the storms,
Will I without thee go again, and do
All works which I was wont to do alone,
Before I knew thy face.—Heaven bless thee, Boy!
Thy heart these two weeks has been beating fast
With many hopes; it should be so—yes—yes—
I knew that thou could'st never have a wish
To leave me, Luke: thou hast been bound to me   *400*
Only by links of love: when thou art gone,
What will be left to us!—But, I forget
My purposes.   Lay now the corner-stone,
As I requested; and hereafter, Luke,
When thou art gone away, should evil men
Be thy companions, think of me, my Son,
And of this moment; hither turn thy thoughts,
And God will strengthen thee: amid all fear
And all temptation, Luke, I pray that thou
May'st bear in mind the life thy Fathers lived   *410*
Who, being innocent, did for that cause
Bestir them in good deeds.   Now, fare thee well—
When thou return'st, thou in this place wilt see
A work which is not here: a covenant
'Twill be between us; but, whatever fate

Befall thee, I shall love thee to the last,
And bear thy memory with me to the grave.'
   The Shepherd ended here; and Luke stooped down,
And, as his Father had requested, laid
The first stone of the Sheepfold.   At the sight   420
The old Man's grief broke from him; to his heart
He pressed his Son, he kissèd him and wept;
And to the house together they returned.
—Hushed was that House in peace, or seeming peace,
Ere the night fell:—with morrow's dawn the Boy
Began his journey, and when he had reached
The public way, he put on a bold face;
And all the neighbours, as he passed their doors,
Came forth with wishes and with farewell prayers,
That followed him till he was out of sight.   430
   A good report did from their Kinsman come,
Of Luke and his well-doing: and the Boy
Wrote loving letters, full of wondrous news,
Which, as the Housewife phrased it, were throughout
'The prettiest letters that were ever seen.'
Both parents read them with rejoicing hearts.
So, many months passed on: and once again
The Shepherd went about his daily work
With confident and cheerful thoughts; and now
Sometimes when he could find a leisure hour   440
He to that valley took his way, and there
Wrought at the Sheepfold.   Meantime Luke began
To slacken in his duty; and, at length,
He in the dissolute city gave himself
To evil courses: ignominy and shame
Fell on him, so that he was driven at last
To seek a hiding-place beyond the seas.

   There is a comfort in the strength of love;
'Twill make a thing endurable, which else
Would overset the brain, or break the heart: 450
I have conversed with more than one who well
Remember the old Man, and what he was
Years after he had heard this heavy news.
His bodily frame had been from youth to age
Of an unusual strength.   Among the rocks
He went, and still looked up to sun and cloud,
And listened to the wind; and, as before,
Performed all kinds of labour for his sheep,
And for the land, his small inheritance.
And to that hollow dell from time to time   460
Did he repair, to build the Fold of which

His flock had need.   'Tis not forgotten yet
The pity which was then in every heart
For the old Man—and 'tis believed by all
That many and many a day he thither went,
And never lifted up a single stone.
    There, by the Sheepfold, sometimes was he seen
Sitting alone, or with his faithful Dog,
Then old, beside him, lying at his feet.
The length of full seven years, from time to time,   470
He at the building of this Sheepfold wrought,
And left the work unfinished when he died.
Three years, or little more, did Isabel
Survive her Husband: at her death the estate
Was sold, and went into a stranger's hand.
The Cottage which was named the EVENING STAR
Is gone—the ploughshare has been through the ground
On which it stood; great changes have been wrought
In all the neighbourhood:—yet the oak is left
That grew beside their door; and the remains   480
Of the unfinished Sheepfold may be seen
Beside the boisterous brook of Greenhead Ghyll.

'’TIS SAID, THAT SOME HAVE DIED FOR LOVE'

'TIS said, that some have died for love:
    And here and there a churchyard grave is found
In the cold north's unhallowed ground,
Because the wretched man himself had slain,
His love was such a grievous pain.

And there is one whom I five years have known;
He dwells alone
Upon Helvellyn's side:
He loved—the pretty Barbara died;
And thus he makes his moan: 10
Three years had Barbara in her grave been laid
When thus his moan he made:

'Oh, move, thou Cottage, from behind that oak!
Or let the aged tree uprooted lie,
That in some other way yon smoke
May mount into the sky!
The clouds pass on; they from the heavens depart.
I look—the sky is empty space;
I know not what I trace;
But when I cease to look, my hand is on my heart.   20

'Oh! what a weight is in these shades! Ye leaves,
That murmur once so dear, when will it cease?
Your sound my heart of rest bereaves,
It robs my heart of peace.
Thou Thrush, that singest loud—and loud and free,
Into yon row of willows flit,
Upon that alder sit;
Or sing another song, or choose another tree.

'Roll back, sweet Rill! back to thy mountain-bounds,
And there for ever be thy waters chained!   *30*
For thou dost haunt the air with sounds
That cannot be sustained;
If still beneath that pine-tree's ragged bough
Headlong yon waterfall must come,
Oh let it then be dumb!
Be anything, sweet Rill, but that which thou art now.

'Thou Eglantine, so bright with sunny showers,
Proud as a rainbow spanning half the vale,
Thou one fair shrub, oh! shed thy flowers,
And stir not in the gale.   *40*
For thus to see thee nodding in the air,
To see thy arch thus stretch and bend,
Thus rise and thus descend,—
Disturbs me till the sight is more than I can bear.'

The Man who makes this feverish complaint
Is one of giant stature, who could dance
Equipped from head to foot in iron mail.
Ah gentle Love! if ever thought was thine
To store up kindred hours for me, thy face
Turn from me, gentle Love! nor let me walk   *50*
Within the sound of Emma's voice, nor know
Such happiness as I have known to-day.

PETER BELL

A TALE

What's in a *Name*?

.   .   .   .   .   .

'Brutus' will start a Spirit as soon as 'Caesar'!

PROLOGUE

THERE's something in a flying horse,
  There's something in a huge balloon;
But through the clouds I'll never float
Until I have a little Boat,
Shaped like the crescent-moon.

And now I *have* a little Boat
In shape a very crescent-moon:
Fast through the clouds my boat can sail;
But if perchance your faith should fail,
Look up—and you shall see me soon!   10

The woods, my Friends, are round you roaring,
Rocking and roaring like a sea;
The noise of danger's in your ears,
And ye have all a thousand fears
Both for my little Boat and me!

Meanwhile untroubled I admire
The pointed horns of my canoe;
And, did not pity touch my breast,
To see how ye are all distrest,
Till my ribs ached, I'd laugh at you!   20

Away we go, my Boat and I—
Frail man ne'er sate in such another;
Whether among the winds we strive,
Or deep into the clouds we dive,
Each is contented with the other.

Away we go—and what care we
For treasons, tumults, and for wars?
We are as calm in our delight
As is the crescent-moon so bright
Among the scattered stars.   30

Up goes my Boat among the stars
Through many a breathless field of light,
Through many a long blue field of ether,
Leaving ten thousand stars beneath her:
Up goes my little Boat so bright!

The Crab, the Scorpion, and the Bull—
We pry among them all; have shot
High o'er the red-haired race of Mars,
Covered from top to toe with scars;
Such company I like it not!   40

The towns in Saturn are decayed,
And melancholy Spectres throng them;—
The Pleiads, that appear to kiss
Each other in the vast abyss,
With joy I sail among them.

Swift Mercury resounds with mirth,
Great Jove is full of stately bowers;
But these, and all that they contain,
What are they to that tiny grain,
That little Earth of ours?   50

Then back to Earth, the dear green Earth:—
Whole ages if I here should roam,
The world for my remarks and me
Would not a whit the better be;
I've left my heart at home.

See! there she is, the matchless Earth!
There spreads the famed Pacific Ocean!
Old Andes thrusts yon craggy spear
Through the grey clouds; the Alps are here,
Like waters in commotion!   60

Yon tawny slip is Libya's sands;
That silver thread the river Dnieper!
And look, where clothed in brightest green
Is a sweet Isle, of isles the Queen;
Ye fairies, from all evil keep her!

And see the town where I was born!
Around those happy fields we span
In boyish gambols;—I was lost
Where I have been, but on this coast
I feel I am a man.   70

Never did fifty things at once
Appear so lovely, never, never;—
How tunefully the forests ring!
To hear the earth's soft murmuring
Thus could I hang for ever!

'Shame on you!' cried my little Boat,
'Was ever such a homesick Loon,
Within a living Boat to sit,
And make no better use of it;
A Boat twin-sister of the crescent-moon!   *80*

'Ne'er in the breast of full-grown Poet
Fluttered so faint a heart before;—
Was it the music of the spheres
That overpowered your mortal ears?
—Such din shall trouble them no more.

'These nether precincts do not lack
Charms of their own;—then come with me;
I want a comrade, and for you
There's nothing that I would not do;
Nought is there that you shall not see.   *90*

'Haste! and above Siberian snows
We'll sport amid the boreal morning;
Will mingle with her lustres gliding
Among the stars, the stars now hiding,
And now the stars adorning.

'I know the secrets of a land
Where human foot did never stray;
Fair is that land as evening skies,
And cool, though in the depth it lies
Of burning Africa.   *100*

'Or we'll into the realm of Faery,
Among the lovely shades of things;
The shadowy forms of mountains bare,
And streams, and bowers, and ladies fair,
The shades of palaces and kings!

'Or, if you thirst with hardy zeal
Less quiet regions to explore,
Prompt voyage shall to you reveal
How earth and heaven are taught to feel
The might of magic lore!'   *110*

'My little vagrant Form of light,
My gay and beautiful Canoe,
Well have you played your friendly part;
As kindly take what from my heart
Experience forces—then adieu!

'Temptation lurks among your words;
But, while these pleasures you're pursuing
Without impediment or let,
No wonder if you quite forget
What on the earth is doing.   *120*

'There was a time when all mankind
Did listen with a faith sincere
To tuneful tongues in mystery versed;
Then Poets fearlessly rehearsed
The wonders of a wild career.

'Go—(but the world's a sleepy world,
And 'tis, I fear, an age too late)
Take with you some ambitious Youth!
For, restless Wanderer! I, in truth,
Am all unfit to be your mate.   *130*

'Long have I loved what I behold,
The night that calms, the day that cheers;
The common growth of mother-earth
Suffices me—her tears, her mirth,
Her humblest mirth and tears.

'The dragon's wing, the magic ring,
I shall not covet for my dower,
If I along that lowly way
With sympathetic heart may stray,
And with a soul of power.   *140*

'These given, what more need I desire
To stir, to soothe, or elevate?
What nobler marvels than the mind
May in life's daily prospect find,
May find or there create?

'A potent wand doth Sorrow wield;
What spell so strong as guilty Fear!
Repentance is a tender Sprite;
If aught on earth have heavenly might,
'Tis lodged within her silent tear.   *150*

'But grant my wishes,—let us now
Descend from this ethereal height;
Then take thy way, adventurous Skiff,
More daring far than Hippogriff,
And be thy own delight!

'To the stone-table in my garden,
Loved haunt of many a summer hour,
The Squire is come: his daughter Bess
Beside him in the cool recess
Sits blooming like a flower.   160

'With these are many more convened;
They know not I have been so far;—
I see them there, in number nine,
Beneath the spreading Weymouth-pine!
I see them—there they are!

'There sits the Vicar and his Dame;
And there my good friend, Stephen Otter;
And, ere the light of evening fail,
To them I must relate the Tale
Of Peter Bell the Potter.'   170

Off flew the Boat—away she flees,
Spurning her freight with indignation!
And I, as well as I was able,
On two poor legs, toward my stone-table
Limped on with sore vexation.

'O, here he is!' cried little Bess—
She saw me at the garden-door;
'We've waited anxiously and long,'
They cried, and all around me throng,
Full nine of them or more!   180

'Reproach me not—your fears be still—
Be thankful we again have met;—
Resume, my Friends! within the shade
Your seats, and quickly shall be paid
The well-remembered debt.'

I spake with faltering voice, like one
Not wholly rescued from the pale
Of a wild dream, or worse illusion;
But, straight, to cover my confusion,
Began the promised Tale.   190

PART FIRST

ALL by the moonlight river-side
Groaned the poor Beast—alas! in vain;
The staff was raised to loftier height,
And the blows fell with heavier weight
As Peter struck—and struck again.

'Hold!' cried the Squire, 'against the rules
Of common sense you're surely sinning;
This leap is for us all too bold;
Who Peter was, let that be told,
And start from the beginning.'   *10*

——'A Potter, Sir, he was by trade,'
Said I, becoming quite collected;
'And wheresoever he appeared,
Full twenty times was Peter feared
For once that Peter was respected.

'He, two-and-thirty years or more,
Had been a wild and woodland rover;
Had heard the Atlantic surges roar
On farthest Cornwall's rocky shore,
And trod the cliffs of Dover.   *20*

'And he had seen Caernarvon's towers,
And well he knew the spire of Sarum;
And he had been where Lincoln bell
Flings o'er the fen that ponderous knell—
A far-renowned alarum!

'At Doncaster, at York, and Leeds,
And merry Carlisle had he been;
And all along the Lowlands fair,
All through the bonny shire of Ayr
And far as Aberdeen.   *30*

'And he had been at Inverness;
And Peter, by the mountain-rills,
Had danced his round with Highland lasses;
And he had lain beside his asses
On lofty Cheviot Hills:

'And he had trudged through Yorkshire dales,
Among the rocks and winding *scars*;
Where deep and low the hamlets lie
Beneath their little patch of sky
And little lot of stars: *40*

'And all along the indented coast,
Bespattered with the salt-sea foam;
Where'er a knot of houses lay
On headland, or in hollow bay;—
Sure never man like him did roam!

'As well might Peter in the Fleet
Have been fast bound, a begging debtor;—
He travelled here, he travelled there;—
But not the value of a hair
Was heart or head the better.   *50*

'He roved among the vales and streams,
In the green wood and hollow dell;
They were his dwellings night and day,—
But nature ne'er could find the way
Into the heart of Peter Bell.

'In vain, through every changeful year,
Did Nature lead him as before;
A primrose by a river's brim
A yellow primrose was to him,
And it was nothing more.   *60*

'Small change it made on Peter's heart
To see his gentle panniered train
With more than vernal pleasure feeding,
Where'er the tender grass was leading
Its earliest green along the lane.

'In vain, through water, earth, and air,
The soul of happy sound was spread,
When Peter on some April morn,
Beneath the broom or budding thorn,
Made the warm earth his lazy bed.   *70*

'At noon, when, by the forest's edge
He lay beneath the branches high,
The soft blue sky did never melt
Into his heart; he never felt
The witchery of the soft blue sky!

'On a fair prospect some have looked
And felt, as I have heard them say,
As if the moving time had been
A thing as steadfast as the scene
On which they gazed themselves away.   *80*

'Within the breast of Peter Bell
These silent raptures found no place;
He was a Carl as wild and rude
As ever hue-and-cry pursued,
As ever ran a felon's race.

'Of all that lead a lawless life,
Of all that love their lawless lives,
In city or in village small,
He was the wildest far of all;—
He had a dozen wedded wives.   90

'Nay, start not!—wedded wives—and twelve!
But how one wife could e'er come near him,
In simple truth I cannot tell;
For, be it said of Peter Bell,
To see him was to fear him.

'Though Nature could not touch his heart
By lovely forms, and silent weather,
And tender sounds, yet you might see
At once, that Peter Bell and she
Had often been together.   100

'A savage wildness round him hung
As of a dweller out of doors;
In his whole figure and his mien
A savage character was seen
Of mountains and of dreary moors.

'To all the unshaped half-human thoughts
Which solitary Nature feeds
'Mid summer storms or winter's ice,
Had Peter joined whatever vice
The cruel city breeds.   110

'His face was keen as is the wind
That cuts along the hawthorn-fence;
Of courage you saw little there,
But, in its stead, a medley air
Of cunning and of impudence.

'He had a dark and sidelong walk,
And long and slouching was his gait;
Beneath his looks so bare and bold,
You might perceive, his spirit cold
Was playing with some inward bait.   120

'His forehead wrinkled was and furred;
A work, one half of which was done
By thinking of his "*whens*" and "*hows*;"
And half, by knitting of his brows
Beneath the glaring sun.

'There was a hardness in his cheek,
There was a hardness in his eye,
As if the man had fixed his face,
In many a solitary place,
Against the wind and open sky!'   *130*

———

ONE NIGHT, (and now, my little Bess!
We've reached at last the promised Tale;)
One beautiful November night,
When the full moon was shining bright
Upon the rapid river Swale,

Along the river's winding banks
Peter was travelling all alone;—
Whether to buy or sell, or led
By pleasure running in his head,
To me was never known.   *140*

He trudged along through copse and brake,
He trudged along o'er hill and dale;
Nor for the moon cared he a tittle,
And for the stars he cared as little,
And for the murmuring river Swale.

But, chancing to espy a path
That promised to cut short the way,
As many a wiser man hath done,
He left a trusty guide for one
That might his steps betray.   *150*

To a thick wood he soon is brought
Where cheerily his course he weaves,
And whistling loud may yet be heard,
Though often buried, like a bird
Darkling, among the boughs and leaves.

But quickly Peter's mood is changed,
And on he drives with cheeks that burn
In downright fury and in wrath;—
There's little sign the treacherous path
Will to the road return!

The path grows dim, and dimmer still;
Now up, now down, the Rover wends,
With all the sail that he can carry,
Till brought to a deserted quarry—
And there the pathway ends.   *160*

He paused—for shadows of strange shape,
Massy and black, before him lay;
But through the dark, and through the cold,
And through the yawning fissures old,
Did Peter boldly press his way.

Right through the quarry;—and behold
A scene of soft and lovely hue!
Where blue and grey, and tender green
Together make as sweet a scene
As ever human eye did view.   *170*

Beneath the clear blue sky he saw
A little field of meadow ground;
But field or meadow name it not;
Call it of earth a small green plot,
With rocks encompassed round.

The Swale flowed under the grey rocks,
But he flowed quiet and unseen;—
You need a strong and stormy gale
To bring the noises of the Swale
To that green spot, so calm and green!   *180*

And is there no one dwelling here,
No hermit with his beads and glass?
And does no little cottage look
Upon this soft and fertile nook?
Does no one live near this green grass?

Across the deep and quiet spot
Is Peter driving through the grass—
And now has reached the skirting trees;
When, turning round his head, he sees
A solitary Ass.   *190*

'A Prize!' cries Peter—but he first
Must spy about him far and near:
There's not a single house in sight,
No woodman's hut, no cottage light—
Peter, you need not fear!

There's nothing to be seen but woods,
And rocks that spread a hoary gleam,
And this one Beast, that from the bed
Of the green meadow hangs his head
Over the silent stream.   *200*

His head is with a halter bound;
The halter seizing, Peter leapt
Upon the Creature's back, and plied
With ready heels his shaggy side;
But still the Ass his station kept.

Then Peter gave a sudden jerk,
A jerk that from a dungeon-floor
Would have pulled up an iron ring;
But still the heavy-headed Thing
Stood just as he had stood before!   *210*

Quoth Peter, leaping from his seat,
'There is some plot against me laid;'
Once more the little meadow-ground
And all the hoary cliffs around
He cautiously surveyed.

All, all is silent—rocks and woods,
All still and silent—far and near!
Only the Ass, with motion dull,
Upon the pivot of his skull
Turns round his long left ear.   *220*

Thought Peter, What can mean all this?
Some ugly witchcraft must be here!
—Once more the Ass, with motion dull,
Upon the pivot of his skull
Turned round his long left ear.

Suspicion ripened into dread;
Yet with deliberate action slow,
His staff high-raising, in the pride
Of skill, upon the sounding hide,
He dealt a sturdy blow.   *230*

The poor Ass staggered with the shock;
And then, as if to take his ease,
In quiet uncomplaining mood,
Upon the spot where he had stood,
Dropped gently down upon his knees;

As gently on his side he fell;
And by the river's brink did lie;
And, while he lay like one that mourned,
The patient Beast on Peter turned
His shining hazel eye.   240

'Twas but one mild, reproachful look,
A look more tender than severe;
And straight in sorrow, not in dread,
He turned the eye-ball in his head
Towards the smooth river deep and clear.

Upon the Beast the sapling rings;
His lank sides heaved, his limbs they stirred;
He gave a groan, and then another,
Of that which went before the brother,
And then he gave a third.   250

All by the moonlight river side
He gave three miserable groans;
And not till now hath Peter seen
How gaunt the Creature is,—how lean
And sharp his staring bones!

With legs stretched out and stiff he lay:—
No word of kind commiseration
Fell at the sight from Peter's tongue;
With hard contempt his heart was wrung,
With hatred and vexation.   260

The meagre beast lay still as death;
And Peter's lips with fury quiver;
Quoth he, 'You little mulish dog,
I'll fling your carcase like a log
Head-foremost down the river!'

An impious oath confirmed the threat—
Whereat from the earth on which he lay
To all the echoes, south and north,
And east and west, the Ass sent forth
A long and clamorous bray!   270

This outcry, on the heart of Peter,
Seems like a note of joy to strike,—
Joy at the heart of Peter knocks;
But in the echo of the rocks
Was something Peter did not like.

Whether to cheer his coward breast,
Or that he could not break the chain,
In this serene and solemn hour,
Twined round him by demoniac power,
To the blind work he turned again.   *280*

Among the rocks and winding crags;
Among the mountains far away;
Once more the Ass did lengthen out
More ruefully a deep-drawn shout,
The hard dry see-saw of his horrible bray!

What is there now in Peter's heart!
Or whence the might of this strange sound?
The moon uneasy looked and dimmer,
The broad blue heavens appeared to glimmer.
And the rocks staggered all around—   *290*

From Peter's hand the sapling dropped!
Threat has he none to execute;
'If any one should come and see
That I am here, they'll think,' quoth he,
'I'm helping this poor dying brute.'

He scans the Ass from limb to limb,
And ventures now to uplift his eyes;
More steady looks the moon, and clear,
More like themselves the rocks appear
And touch more quiet skies.   *300*

His scorn returns—his hate revives,
He stoops the Ass's neck to seize
With malice—that again takes flight;
For in the pool a startling sight
Meets him, among the inverted trees.

Is it the moon's distorted face?
The ghost-like image of a cloud?
Is it a gallows there portrayed?
Is Peter of himself afraid?
Is it a coffin,—or a shroud?   *310*

A grisly idol hewn in stone?
Or imp from witch's lap let fall?
Perhaps a ring of shining fairies?
Such as pursue their feared vagaries
In sylvan bower, or haunted hall?

Is it a fiend that to a stake
Of fire his desperate self is tethering?
Or stubborn spirit doomed to yell
In solitary ward or cell,
Ten thousand miles from all his brethren?   *320*

Never did pulse so quickly throb,
And never heart so loudly panted;
He looks, he cannot choose but look;
Like some one reading in a book—
A book that is enchanted.

Ah, well-a-day for Peter Bell!
He will be turned to iron soon,
Meet Statue for the court of Fear!
His hat is up—and every hair
Bristles, and whitens in the moon!   *330*

He looks, he ponders, looks again;
He sees a motion—hears a groan;
His eyes will burst—his heart will break—
He gives a loud and frightful shriek,
And back he falls, as if his life were flown!

PART SECOND

WE left our Hero in a trance,
Beneath the alders, near the river;
The Ass is by the river-side,
And, where the feeble breezes glide,
Upon the stream the moonbeams quiver.

A happy respite! but at length
He feels the glimmering of the moon;
Wakes with glazed eye, and feebly sighing—
To sink, perhaps, where he is lying,
Into a second swoon!   *10*

He lifts his head, he sees his staff;
He touches—'tis to him a treasure!
Faint recollection seems to tell
That he is yet where mortals dwell—
A thought received with languid pleasure!

His head upon his elbow propped,
Becoming less and less perplexed,
Sky-ward he looks—to rock and wood—
And then—upon the glassy flood
His wandering eye is fixed.   20

Thought he, that is the face of one
In his last sleep securely bound!
So toward the stream his head he bent,
And downward thrust his staff, intent
The river's depth to sound.

Now—like a tempest-shattered bark,
That overwhelmed and prostrate lies,
And in a moment to the verge
Is lifted of a foaming surge—
Full suddenly the Ass doth rise!   30

His staring bones all shake with joy,
And close by Peter's side he stands:
While Peter o'er the river bends,
The little Ass his neck extends,
And fondly licks his hands.

Such life is in the Ass's eyes,
Such life is in his limbs and ears;
That Peter Bell, if he had been
The veriest coward ever seen,
Must now have thrown aside his fears.   40

The Ass looks on—and to his work
Is Peter quietly resigned;
He touches here—he touches there—
And now among the dead man's hair
His sapling Peter has entwined.

He pulls—and looks—and pulls again;
And he whom the poor Ass had lost,
The man who had been four days dead,
Head-foremost from the river's bed
Uprises like a ghost!   50

And Peter draws him to dry land;
And through the brain of Peter pass
Some poignant twitches, fast and faster;
'No doubt,' quoth he, 'he is the Master
Of this poor miserable Ass!'

The meagre Shadow that looks on—
What would he now? what is he doing?
His sudden fit of joy is flown,—
He on his knees hath laid him down,
As if he were his grief renewing;   *60*

But no—that Peter on his back
Must mount, he shows well as he can:
Thought Peter then, come weal or woe,
I'll do what he would have me do,
In pity to this poor drowned man.

With that resolve he boldly mounts
Upon the pleased and thankful Ass;
And then, without a moment's stay,
That earnest Creature turned away,
Leaving the body on the grass.   *70*

Intent upon his faithful watch,
The Beast four days and nights had past;
A sweeter meadow ne'er was seen,
And there the Ass four days had been,
Nor ever once did break his fast:

Yet firm his step, and stout his heart;
The mead is crossed—the quarry's mouth
Is reached; but there the trusty guide
Into a thicket turns aside,
And deftly ambles towards the south.   *80*

When hark a burst of doleful sound!
And Peter honestly might say,
The like came never to his ears,
Though he has been, full thirty years,
A rover—night and day!

'Tis not a plover of the moors,
'Tis not a bittern of the fen;
Nor can it be a barking fox,
Nor night-bird chambered in the rocks,
Nor wild-cat in a woody glen!   *90*

The Ass is startled—and stops short
Right in the middle of the thicket;
And Peter, wont to whistle loud
Whether alone or in a crowd,
Is silent as a silent cricket.

What ails you now, my little Bess?
Well may you tremble and look grave!
This cry—that rings along the wood,
This cry—that floats adown the flood,
Comes from the entrance of a cave: *100*

I see a blooming Wood-boy there,
And if I had the power to say
How sorrowful the wanderer is,
Your heart would be as sad as his
Till you had kissed his tears away!

Grasping a hawthorn branch in hand,
All bright with berries ripe and red,
Into the cavern's mouth he peeps;
Thence back into the moonlight creeps;
Whom seeks he—whom?—the silent dead: *110*

His father!—Him doth he require—
Him hath he sought with fruitless pains,
Among the rocks, behind the trees;
Now creeping on his hands and knees,
Now running o'er the open plains.

And hither is he come at last,
When he through such a day has gone,
By this dark cave to be distrest
Like a poor bird—her plundered nest
Hovering around with dolorous moan!   *120*

Of that intense and piercing cry
The listening Ass conjectures well;
Wild as it is, he there can read
Some intermingled notes that plead
With touches irresistible.

But Peter—when he saw the Ass
Not only stop but turn, and change
The cherished tenor of his pace
That lamentable cry to chase—
It wrought in him conviction strange;   *130*

A faith that, for the dead man's sake
And this poor slave who loved him well,
Vengeance upon his head will fall,
Some visitation worse than all
Which ever till this night befell.

Meanwhile the Ass to reach his home,
Is striving stoutly as he may;
But, while he climbs the woody hill,
The cry grows weak—and weaker still;
And now at last it dies away.   *140*

So with his freight the Creature turns
Into a gloomy grove of beech,
Along the shade with footsteps true
Descending slowly, till the two
The open moonlight reach.

And there, along the narrow dell,
A fair smooth pathway you discern,
A length of green and open road—
As if it from a fountain flowed—
Winding away between the fern.   *150*

The rocks that tower on either side
Build up a wild fantastic scene;
Temples like those among the Hindoos,
And mosques, and spires, and abbey windows,
And castles all with ivy green!

And, while the Ass pursues his way
Along this solitary dell,
As pensively his steps advance,
The mosques and spires change countenance,
And look at Peter Bell!   *160*

That unintelligible cry
Hath left him high in preparation,—
Convinced that he, or soon or late,
This very night will meet his fate—
And so he sits in expectation!

The strenuous Animal hath clomb
With the green path; and now he wends
Where, shining like the smoothest sea,
In undisturbed immensity
A level plain extends.   *170*

But whence this faintly-rustling sound
By which the journeying pair are chased?
—A withered leaf is close behind,
Light plaything for the sportive wind
Upon that solitary waste.

When Peter spied the moving thing,
It only doubled his distress;
'Where there is not a bush or tree,
The very leaves they follow me—
So huge hath been my wickedness!'   *180*

To a close lane they now are come,
Where, as before, the enduring Ass
Moves on without a moment's stop,
Nor once turns round his head to crop
A bramble-leaf or blade of grass.

Between the hedges as they go,
The white dust sleeps upon the lane;
And Peter, ever and anon
Back-looking, sees, upon a stone,
Or in the dust, a crimson stain.   *190*

A stain—as of a drop of blood
By moonlight made more faint and wan;
Ha! why these sinkings of despair?
He knows not how the blood comes there—
And Peter is a wicked man.

At length he spies a bleeding wound,
Where he had struck the Ass's head;
He sees the blood, knows what it is,—
A glimpse of sudden joy was his,
But then it quickly fled;   *200*

Of him whom sudden death had seized
He thought,—of thee, O faithful Ass!
And once again those ghastly pains
Shoot to and fro through heart and reins,
And through his brain like lightning pass.

PART THIRD

I'VE heard of one, a gentle Soul,
Though given to sadness and to gloom,
And for the fact will vouch,—one night
It chanced that by a taper's light
This man was reading in his room;

Bending, as you or I might bend
At night o'er any pious book,
When sudden blackness overspread
The snow-white page on which he read,
And made the good man round him look.   *10*

The chamber walls were dark all round,—
And to his book he turned again;
—The light had left the lonely taper,
And formed itself upon the paper
Into large letters—bright and plain!

The godly book was in his hand—
And, on the page, more black than coal,
Appeared set forth in strange array,
A *word*—which to his dying day
Perplexed the good man's gentle soul.   *20*

The ghostly word, thus plainly seen,
Did never from his lips depart;
But he hath said, poor gentle wight!
It brought full many a sin to light
Out of the bottom of his heart.

Dread Spirits! to confound the meek
Why wander from your course so far,
Disordering colour, form, and stature!
—Let good men feel the soul of nature,
And see things as they are.   *30*

Yet, potent Spirits! well I know,
How ye, that play with soul and sense,
Are not unused to trouble friends
Of goodness, for most gracious ends—
And this I speak in reverence!

But might I give advice to you,
Whom in my fear I love so well;
From men of pensive virtue go,
Dread Beings! and your empire show
On hearts like that of Peter Bell.   *40*

Your presence often have I felt
In darkness and the stormy night;
And with like force, if need there be,
Ye can put forth your agency
When earth is calm, and heaven is bright.

Then, coming from the wayward world,
That powerful world in which ye dwell,
Come, spirits of the Mind! and try
To-night, beneath the moonlight sky,
What may be done with Peter Bell!   50

—O, would that some more skilful voice
My further labour might prevent!
Kind Listeners, that around me sit,
I feel that I am all unfit
For such high argument.

—I've played, I've danced, with my narration;
I loitered long ere I began:
Ye waited then on my good pleasure;
Pour our indulgence still, in measure
As liberal as ye can!   60

Our Travellers, ye remember well,
Are thridding a sequestered lane;
And Peter many tricks is trying,
And many anodynes applying,
To ease his conscience of its pain.

By this his heart is lighter far;
And, finding that he can account
So snugly for that crimson stain,
His evil spirit up again
Does like an empty bucket mount.   70

And Peter is a deep logician
Who hath no lack of wit mercurial;
'Blood drops—leaves rustle—yet,' quoth he,
'This poor man never, but for me,
Could have had Christian burial.

'And, say the best you can, 'tis plain,
That here has been some wicked dealing;
No doubt the devil in me wrought;
I'm not the man who could have thought
An Ass like this was worth the stealing!' 80

So from his pocket Peter takes
His shining horn tobacco-box;
And, in a light and careless way,
As men who with their purpose play,
Upon the lid he knocks.

Let them whose voice can stop the clouds,
Whose cunning eye can see the wind,
Tell to a curious world the cause
Why, making here a sudden pause,
The Ass turned round his head, and *grinned*.   90

Appalling process!   I have marked
The like on heath, in lonely wood;
And, verily, have seldom met
A spectacle more hideous—yet
It suited Peter's present mood.

And, grinning in his turn, his teeth
He in jocose defiance showed—
When, to upset his spiteful mirth,
A murmur, pent within the earth,
In the dead earth beneath the road   100

Rolled audibly! it swept along,
A muffled noise—a rumbling sound!—
'Twas by a troop of miners made,
Plying with gunpowder their trade,
Some twenty fathoms under ground.

Small cause of dire effect! for, surely,
If ever mortal, King or Cotter,
Believed that earth was charged to quake
And yawn for his unworthy sake,
'Twas Peter Bell the Potter.   110

But, as an oak in breathless air
Will stand though to the centre hewn;
Or as the weakest things, if frost
Have stiffened them, maintain their post;
So he, beneath the gazing moon!—

The Beast bestriding thus, he reached
A spot where, in a sheltering cove,
A little chapel stands alone,
With greenest ivy overgrown,
And tufted with an ivy grove;   120

Dying insensibly away
From human thoughts and purposes,
It seemed—wall, window, roof and tower—
To bow to some transforming power,
And blend with the surrounding trees.

As ruinous a place it was,
Thought Peter, in the shire of Fife
That served my turn, when following still
From land to land a reckless will
I married my sixth wife!   *130*

The unheeding Ass moved slowly on,
And now is passing by an inn
Brim-full of a carousing crew,
That make, with curses not a few,
An uproar and a drunken din.

I cannot well express the thoughts
Which Peter in those noises found;—
A stifling power compressed his frame,
While-as a swimming darkness came
Over that dull and dreary sound.   *140*

For well did Peter know the sound;
The language of those drunken joys
To him, a jovial soul, I ween,
But a few hours ago, had been
A gladsome and a welcome noise.

Now, turned adrift into the past,
He finds no solace in his course;
Like planet-stricken men of yore,
He trembles, smitten to the core
By strong compunction and remorse.   *150*

But, more than all, his heart is stung
To think of one, almost a child;
A sweet and playful Highland girl,
As light and beauteous as a squirrel,
As beauteous and as wild!

Her dwelling was a lonely house,
A cottage in a heathy dell;
And she put on her gown of green,
And left her mother at sixteen,
And followed Peter Bell.   *160*

But many good and pious thoughts
Had she; and, in the kirk to pray,
Two long Scotch miles, through rain or snow,
To kirk she had been used to go,
Twice every Sabbath-day.

And, when she followed Peter Bell,
It was to lead an honest life;
For he, with tongue not used to falter,
Had pledged his troth before the altar
To love her as his wedded wife.   *170*

A mother's hope is hers;—but soon
She drooped and pined like one forlorn;
From Scripture she a name did borrow;
Benoni, or the child of sorrow,
She called her babe unborn.

For she had learned how Peter lived,
And took it in most grievous part;
She to the very bone was worn,
And, ere that little child was born,
Died of a broken heart.   *180*

And now the Spirits of the Mind
Are busy with poor Peter Bell;
Upon the rights of visual sense
Usurping, with a prevalence
More terrible than magic spell.

Close by a brake of flowering furze
(Above it shivering aspens play)
He sees an unsubstantial creature,
His very self in form and feature,
Not four yards from the broad highway: *190*

And stretched beneath the furze he sees
The Highland girl—it is no other;
And hears her crying as she cried,
The very moment that she died,
'My mother! oh my mother!'

The sweat pours down from Peter's face,
So grievous is his heart's contrition;
With agony his eye-balls ache
While he beholds by the furze-brake
This miserable vision!   *200*

Calm is the well-deserving brute,
His peace hath no offence betrayed;
But now, while down that slope he wends
A voice to Peter's ear ascends,
Resounding from the woody glade:

The voice, though clamorous as a horn
Re-echoed by a naked rock,
Comes from that tabernacle—List!
Within, a fervent Methodist
Is preaching to no heedless flock!   *210*

'Repent! repent!' he cries aloud,
'While yet ye may find mercy;—strive
To love the Lord with all your might;
Turn to him, seek him day and night,
And save your souls alive!

'Repent! repent! though ye have gone,
Through paths of wickedness and woe,
After the Babylonian harlot;
And, though your sins be red as scarlet,
They shall be white as snow!'   *220*

Even as he passed the door, these words
Did plainly come to Peter's ears;
And they such joyful tidings were,
The joy was more than he could bear!—
He melted into tears.

Sweet tears of hope and tenderness!
And fast they fell, a plenteous shower!
His nerves, his sinews seemed to melt,
Through all his iron frame was felt
A gentle, a relaxing power!   *230*

Each fibre of his frame was weak;
Weak all the animal within;
But, in its helplessness, grew mild
And gentle as an infant child,
An infant that has known no sin.

'Tis said, meek Beast! that, through Heaven's grace,
He not unmoved did notice now
The cross upon thy shoulder scored,
For lasting impress, by the Lord
To whom all human-kind shall bow;   *240*

Memorial of his touch—that day
When Jesus humbly deigned to ride,
Entering the proud Jerusalem,
By an immeasurable stream
Of shouting people deified!

Meanwhile the persevering Ass
Turned towards a gate that hung in view
Across a shady lane; his chest
Against the yielding gate he pressed
And quietly passed through.   *250*

And up the stony lane he goes;
No ghost more softly ever trod;
Among the stones and pebbles, he
Sets down his hoofs inaudibly.
As if with felt his hoofs were shod.

Along the lane the trusty Ass
Went twice two hundred yards or more,
And no one could have guessed his aim,—
Till to a lonely house he came,
And stopped beside the door.   *260*

Thought Peter, 'tis the poor man's home!
He listens—not a sound is heard,
Save from the trickling household rill;
But, stepping o'er the cottage-sill,
Forthwith a little Girl appeared.

She to the Meeting-house was bound
In hopes some tidings there to gather:
No glimpse it is, no doubtful gleam;
She saw—and uttered with a scream,
'My father! here's my father!'   *270*

The very word was plainly heard,
Heard plainly by the wretched Mother—
Her joy was like a deep affright:
And forth she rushed into the light,
And saw it was another!

And, instantly, upon the earth,
Beneath the full moon shining bright,
Close to the Ass's feet she fell;
At the same moment Peter Bell
Dismounts in most unhappy plight.   *280*

As he beheld the Woman lie
Breathless and motionless, the mind
Of Peter sadly was confused;
But, though to such demands unused,
And helpless almost as the blind,

He raised her up; and, while he held
Her body propped against his knee,
The Woman waked—and when she spied
The poor Ass standing by her side,
She moaned most bitterly.   *290*

'Oh! God be praised—my heart's at ease—
For he is dead—I know it well!'
—At this she wept a bitter flood;
And, in the best way that he could,
His tale did Peter tell.

He trembles—he is pale as death;
His voice is weak with perturbation;
He turns aside his head, he pauses;
Poor Peter, from a thousand causes,
Is crippled sore in his narration.   *300*

At length she learned how he espied
The Ass in that small meadow-ground;
And that her Husband now lay dead,
Beside that luckless river's bed
In which he had been drowned.

A piercing look the Widow cast
Upon the Beast that near her stands;
She sees 'tis he, that 'tis the same;
She calls the poor Ass by his name,
And wrings, and wrings her hands.   *310*

'O wretched loss—untimely stroke!
If he had died upon his bed!
He knew not one forewarning pain;
He never will come home again—
Is dead, for ever dead!'

Beside the Woman Peter stands;
His heart is opening more and more;
A holy sense pervades his mind;
He feels what he for human kind
Had never felt before.   *320*

At length, by Peter's arm sustained,
The Woman rises from the ground—
'Oh, mercy! something must be done,
My little Rachel, you must run,—
Some willing neighbour must be found.

'Make haste—my little Rachel—do,
The first you meet with—bid him come,
Ask him to lend his horse to-night,
And this good Man, whom Heaven requite,
Will help to bring the body home.'   *330*

Away goes Rachel weeping loud;—
An Infant, waked by her distress,
Makes in the house a piteous cry;
And Peter hears the Mother sigh,
'Seven are they, and all fatherless!'

And now is Peter taught to feel
That man's heart is a holy thing;
And Nature, through a world of death,
Breathes into him a second breath,
More searching than the breath of spring.   *340*

Upon a stone the Woman sits
In agony of silent grief—
From his own thoughts did Peter start;
He longs to press her to his heart,
From love that cannot find relief.

But roused, as if through every limb
Had past a sudden shock of dread,
The Mother o'er the threshold flies,
And up the cottage stairs she hies,
And on the pillow lays her burning head.   *350*

And Peter turns his steps aside
Into a shade of darksome trees,
Where he sits down, he knows not how,
With his hands pressed against his brow,
His elbows on his tremulous knees.

There, self-involved, does Peter sit
Until no sign of life he makes,
As if his mind were sinking deep
Through years that have been long asleep!
The trance is passed away—he wakes;   *360*

He lifts his head—and sees the Ass
Yet standing in the clear moonshine;
'When shall I be as good as thou?
Oh! would, poor beast, that I had now
A heart but half as good as thine!'

But *He*—who deviously hath sought
His Father through the lonesome woods,
Hath sought, proclaiming to the ear
Of night his grief and sorrowful fear—
He comes, escaped from fields and floods;—   *370*

With weary pace is drawing nigh;
He sees the Ass—and nothing living
Had ever such a fit of joy
As hath this little orphan Boy,
For he has no misgiving!

Forth to the gentle Ass he springs,
And up about his neck he climbs;
In loving words he talks to him,
He kisses, kisses face and limb,—
He kisses him a thousand times!   *380*

This Peter sees, while in the shade
He stood beside the cottage-door;
And Peter Bell, the ruffian wild,
Sobs loud, he sobs even like a child,
'O God! I can endure no more!'

—Here ends my Tale: for in a trice
Arrived a neighbour with his horse;
Peter went forth with him straightway;
And, with due care, ere break of day
Together they brought back the Corse.   *390*

And many years did this poor Ass,
Whom once it was my luck to see
Cropping the shrubs of Leming-Lane,
Help by his labour to maintain
The Widow and her family.

And Peter Bell, who, till that night,
Had been the wildest of his clan,
Forsook his crimes, renounced his folly,
And, after ten months' melancholy,
Became a good and honest man.   *400*

TO A BUTTERFLY

I

STAY near me—do not take thy flight!
  A little longer stay in sight!
Much converse do I find in thee,
Historian of my infancy!
Float near me; do not yet depart!
Dead times revive in thee:
Thou bring'st, gay creature as thou art!
A solemn image to my heart,
My father's family!   *10*

Oh! pleasant, pleasant were the days,
The time, when, in our childish plays,
My sister Emmeline and I
Together chased the butterfly!
A very hunter did I rush
Upon the prey:—with leaps and springs
I followed on from brake to bush;
But she, God love her, feared to brush
The dust from off its wings.   *20*

II

I'VE watched you now a full half-hour,
  Self-poised upon that yellow flower;
And, little Butterfly! indeed
I know not if you sleep or feed.
How motionless!—not frozen seas
More motionless! and then
What joy awaits you, when the breeze
Hath found you out among the trees,
And calls you forth again!   *10*

This plot of orchard-ground is ours;
My trees they are, my Sister's flowers;
Here rest your wings when they are weary;
Here lodge as in a sanctuary!
Come often to us, fear no wrong;
Sit near us on the bough!
We'll talk of sunshine and of song,
And summer days, when we were young:
Sweet childish days, that were as long
As twenty days are now.   *20*

TO THE CUCKOO

O BLITHE New-comer! I have heard,
  I hear thee and rejoice.
O Cuckoo! shall I call thee Bird,
Or but a wandering Voice?

While I am lying on the grass
Thy twofold shout I hear;
From hill to hill it seems to pass,
At once far off, and near.

Though babbling only to the Vale,
Of sunshine and of flowers,   *10*
Thou bringest unto me a tale
Of visionary hours.

Thrice welcome, darling of the Spring!
Even yet thou art to me
No bird, but an invisible thing,
A voice, a mystery;

The same whom in my school-boy days
I listened to; that Cry
Which made me look a thousand ways
In bush, and tree, and sky.   *20*

To seek thee did I often rove
Through woods and on the green;
And thou wert still a hope, a love;
Still longed for, never seen.

And I can listen to thee yet;
Can lie upon the plain
And listen, till I do beget
That golden time again.

O blessèd Bird! the earth we pace
Again appears to be   *30*
An unsubstantial, faery place;
That is fit home for Thee!

'MY HEART LEAPS UP'

My heart leaps up when I behold
        A rainbow in the sky:
So was it when my life began;
So is it now I am a man;
So be it when I shall grow old,
        Or let me die!
The Child is father of the Man;
And I could wish my days to be
Bound each to each by natural piety.

ODE:

INTIMATIONS OF IMMORTALITY FROM RECOLLECTIONS
OF EARLY CHILDHOOD

The Child is father of the Man;
And I could wish my days to be
Bound each to each by natural piety.

I

THERE was a time when meadow, grove, and stream,
    The earth, and every common sight,
        To me did seem
        Apparelled in celestial light,
The glory and the freshness of a dream.
It is not now as it hath been of yore;—
        Turn wheresoe'er I may,
        By night or day,
The things which I have seen I now can see no more.

II

The Rainbow comes and goes,   *10*
    And lovely is the Rose,
    The Moon doth with delight
Look round her when the heavens are bare,
    Waters on a starry night
    Are beautiful and fair;
    The sunshine is a glorious birth;
    But yet I know, where'er I go,
That there hath past away a glory from the earth.

III

Now, while the birds thus sing a joyous song,
    And while the young lambs bound   *20*
        As to the tabor's sound,
To me alone there came a thought of grief:
A timely utterance gave that thought relief,
        And I again am strong:
The cataracts blow their trumpets from the steep;
No more shall grief of mine the season wrong;
I hear the Echoes through the mountains throng,
The Winds come to me from the fields of sleep,
        And all the earth is gay;
        Land and sea   *30*
    Give themselves up to jollity,
        And with the heart of May
    Doth every Beast keep holiday;—
        Thou Child of Joy,
Shout round me, let me hear thy shouts, thou happy
        Shepherd-boy!

IV

Ye blessèd Creatures, I have heard the call
    Ye to each other make; I see
The heavens laugh with you in your jubilee;
    My heart is at your festival,   *40*
    My head hath its coronal,
The fulness of your bliss, I feel—I feel it all.
    Oh evil day! if I were sullen
    While Earth herself is adorning,
        This sweet May-morning,
    And the Children are culling
        On every side,
    In a thousand valleys far and wide,
    Fresh flowers; while the sun shines warm,
And the Babe leaps up on his Mother's arm:—   *50*
    I hear, I hear, with joy I hear!
    —But there's a Tree [1] of many, one,
A single Field which I have looked upon,

Both of them speak of something that is gone:
    The Pansy at my feet
    Doth the same tale repeat:
Whither is fled the visionary gleam?
Where is it now, the glory and the dream?

          V

Our birth is but a sleep and a forgetting:
The Soul that rises with us, our life's Star,   *60*
    Hath had elsewhere its setting,
      And cometh from afar:
    Not in entire forgetfulness,
    And not in utter nakedness,
But trailing clouds of glory do we come
    From God, who is our home:
Heaven lies about us in our infancy!
Shades of the prison-house begin to close
    Upon the growing Boy,
             But He
Beholds the light, and whence it flows,   *70*
    He sees it in his joy;
The Youth, who daily farther from the east
    Must travel, still is Nature's Priest,
    And by the vision splendid
    Is on his way attended;
At length the Man perceives it die away,
And fade into the light of common day.

          VI

Earth fills her lap with pleasures of her own;
Yearnings she hath in her own natural kind,
And, even with something of a Mother's mind,   *80*
    And no unworthy aim
    The homely Nurse doth all she can
To make her Foster-child, her Inmate Man,
    Forget the glories he hath known,
And that imperial palace whence he came.

          VII

Behold the Child among his new-born blisses,
A six years' Darling of a pigmy size! [1]
See, where 'mid work of his own hand he lies.

Fretted by sallies of his mother's kisses,
With light upon him from his father's eyes!   *90*
See, at his feet, some little plan or chart,
Some fragment from his dream of human life,
Shaped by himself with newly-learned art;
  A wedding or a festival,
  A mourning or a funeral;
   And this hath now his heart,
  And unto this he frames his song:
   Then will he fit his tongue
To dialogues of business, love, or strife;
   But it will not be long   *100*
   Ere this be thrown aside,
   And with new joy and pride
The little Actor cons another part;
Filling from time to time his 'humorous stage'
With all the Persons, down to palsied Age,
That Life brings with her in her equipage;
  As if his whole vocation
  Were endless imitation.

VIII

Thou, whose exterior semblance doth belie
  Thy Soul's immensity;   *110*
Thou best Philosopher, who yet dost keep
Thy heritage, thou Eye among the blind,
That, deaf and silent, read'st the eternal deep,
Haunted for ever by the eternal mind,—
  Mighty Prophet! Seer blest!
  On whom those truths do rest,
Which we are toiling all our lives to find,
In darkness lost, the darkness of the grave;
Thou, over whom thy Immortality
Broods like the Day, a Master o'er a Slave,   *120*
A Presence which is not to be put by;
Thou little Child, yet glorious in the might
Of heaven-born freedom on thy being's height,
Why with such earnest pains dost thou provoke
The years to bring the inevitable yoke,
Thus blindly with thy blessedness at strife?
Full soon thy Soul shall have her earthly freight,
And custom lie upon thee with a weight,
Heavy as frost, and deep almost as life!

IX

O joy! that in our embers   *130*
Is something that doth live,
That nature yet remembers
What was so fugitive!
The thought of our past years in me doth breed
Perpetual benediction: not indeed
For that which is most worthy to be blest—
Delight and liberty, the simple creed
Of Childhood, whether busy or at rest,
With new-fledged hope still fluttering in his breast:—
    Not for these I raise   *140*
    The song of thanks and praise;
But for those obstinate questionings
Of sense and outward things,
Fallings from us, vanishings;
Blank misgivings of a Creature
Moving about in worlds not realized,
High instincts before which our mortal Nature
Did tremble like a guilty Thing surprised:
    But for those first affections,
    Those shadowy recollections,   *150*
Which, be they what they may,
Are yet the fountain light of all our day,
Are yet a master light of all our seeing;
    Uphold us, cherish, and have power to make
Our noisy years seem moments in the being
Of the eternal Silence: truths that wake,
    To perish never;
Which neither listlessness, nor mad endeavour,
    Nor Man nor Boy,
Nor all that is at enmity with joy,   *160*
Can utterly abolish or destroy!
    Hence in a season of calm weather
    Though inland far we be,
Our Souls have sight of that immortal sea
    Which brought us hither,
    Can in a moment travel thither,
And see the Children sport upon the shore,
And hear the mighty waters rolling evermore.

X

Then sing, ye Birds, sing, sing a joyous song!
    And let the young Lambs bound   *170*
    As to the tabor's sound!
We in thought will join your throng,
    Ye that pipe and ye that play,
    Ye that through your hearts to-day

Feel the gladness of the May!
What though the radiance which was once so bright
Be now for ever taken from my sight,
   Though nothing can bring back the hour
Of splendour in the grass, of glory in the flower;
      We will grieve not, rather find   *180*
      Strength in what remains behind;
      In the primal sympathy [1]
      Which having been must ever be;
      In the soothing thoughts that spring
      Out of human suffering;
      In the faith that looks through death,
In years that bring the philosophic mind.

XI

And O, ye Fountains, Meadows, Hills, and Groves,
Forebode not any severing of our loves!
Yet in my heart of hearts I feel your might   *190*
I only have relinquished one delight
To live beneath your more habitual sway.
I love the Brooks which down their channels fret,
Even more than when I tripped lightly as they;
The innocent brightness of a new-born Day
      Is lovely yet;
The Clouds that gather round the setting sun
Do take a sober colouring from an eye
That hath kept watch o'er man's mortality;
Another race hath been, and other palms are won.   *200*
Thanks to the human heart by which we live,
Thanks to its tenderness, its joys, and fears,
To me the meanest flower that blows can give
Thoughts that do often lie too deep for tears.

RESOLUTION AND INDEPENDENCE

I

THERE was a roaring in the wind all night;
   The rain came heavily and fell in floods;
But now the sun is rising calm and bright;
The birds are singing in the distant woods;
Over his own sweet voice the Stock-dove broods;
The Jay makes answer as the Magpie chatters;
And all the air is filled with pleasant noise of waters.

II

All things that love the sun are out of doors;
The sky rejoices in the morning's birth;
The grass is bright with rain-drops;—on the moors   *10*
The hare is running races in her mirth;
And with her feet she from the plashy earth
Raises a mist; that, glittering in the sun,
Runs with her all the way, wherever she doth run.

III

I was a Traveller then upon the moor,
I saw the hare that raced about with joy;
I heard the woods and distant waters roar;
Or heard them not, as happy as a boy:
The pleasant season did my heart employ:
My old remembrances went from me wholly;   *20*
And all the ways of men, so vain and melancholy.

IV

But, as it sometimes chanceth, from the might
Of joy in minds that can no further go,
As high as we have mounted in delight
In our dejection do we sink as low;
To me that morning did it happen so;
And fears and fancies thick upon me came;
Dim sadness—and blind thoughts, I knew not, nor could
        name.

V

I heard the sky-lark warbling in the sky;
And I bethought me of the playful hare: *30*
Even such a happy Child of earth am I;
Even as these blissful creatures do I fare;
Far from the world I walk, and from all care;
But there may come another day to me—
Solitude, pain of heart, distress, and poverty.

VI

My whole life I have lived in pleasant thought,
As if life's business were a summer mood;
As if all needful things would come unsought
To genial faith, still rich in genial good;
But how can He expect that others should   *40*
Build for him, sow for him, and at his call
Love him, who for himself will take no heed at all?

VII

I thought of Chatterton, the marvellous Boy,
The sleepless Soul that perished in his pride;
Of Him who walked in glory and in joy
Following his plough, along the mountain-side:
By our own spirits are we deified:
We Poets in our youth begin in gladness;
But thereof come in the end despondency and madness.

VIII

Now, whether it were by peculiar grace,   50
A leading from above, a something given,
Yet it befell, that, in this lonely place,
When I with these untoward thoughts had striven,
Beside a pool bare to the eye of heaven
I saw a Man before me unawares:
The oldest man he seemed that ever wore grey hairs.

IX

As a huge stone is sometimes seen to lie
Couched on the bald top of an eminence;
Wonder to all who do the same espy,
By what means it could thither come, and whence;   60
So that it seems a thing endued with sense:
Like a sea-beast crawled forth, that on a shelf
Of rock or sand reposeth, there to sun itself;

X

Such seemed this Man, not all alive nor dead,
Nor all asleep—in his extreme old age:
His body was bent double, feet and head
Coming together in life's pilgrimage;
As if some dire constraint of pain, or rage
Of sickness felt by him in times long past,
A more than human weight upon his frame had cast.   70

XI

Himself he propped, limbs, body, and pale face,
Upon a long grey staff of shaven wood:
And, still as I drew near with gentle pace,
Upon the margin of that moorish flood
Motionless as a cloud the old Man stood,
That heareth not the loud winds when they call
And moveth all together, if it move at all.

XII

At length, himself unsettling, he the pond
Stirred with his staff, and fixedly did look
Upon the muddy water, which he conned,   *80*
As if he had been reading in a book:
And now a stranger's privilege I took;
And, drawing to his side, to him did say,
'This morning gives us promise of a glorious day.'

XIII

A gentle answer did the old Man make,
In courteous speech which forth he slowly drew:
And him with further words I thus bespake,
'What occupation do you there pursue?
This is a lonesome place for one like you.'
Ere he replied, a flash of mild surprise   *90*
Broke from the sable orbs of his yet-vivid eyes.

XIV

His words came feebly, from a feeble chest,
But each in solemn order followed each,
With something of a lofty utterance drest—
Choice word and measured phrase, above the reach
Of ordinary men; a stately speech;
Such as grave Livers do in Scotland use,
Religious men, who give to God and man their dues.

XV

He told, that to these waters he had come
To gather leeches, being old and poor: *100*
Employment hazardous and wearisome!
And he had many hardships to endure:
From pond to pond he roamed, from moor to moor;
Housing, with God's good help, by choice or chance,
And in this way he gained an honest maintenance.

XVI

The old Man still stood talking by my side;
But now his voice to me was like a stream
Scarce heard; nor word from word could I divide;
And the whole body of the Man did seem
Like one whom I had met with in a dream;   *110*
Or like a man from some far region sent,
To give me human strength, by apt admonishment.

XVII

My former thoughts returned: the fear that kills;
And hope that is unwilling to be fed;
Cold, pain, and labour, and all fleshly ills;
And mighty Poets in their misery dead.
—Perplexed, and longing to be comforted,
My question eagerly did I renew,
'How is it that you live, and what is it you do?'

XVIII

He with a smile did then his words repeat;   *120*
And said, that, gathering leeches, far and wide
He travelled; stirring thus about his feet
The waters of the pools where they abide.
'Once I could meet with them on every side;
But they have dwindled long by slow decay;
Yet still I persevere, and find them where I may.'

XIX

While he was talking thus, the lonely place,
The old Man's shape, and speech—all troubled me:
In my mind's eye I seemed to see him pace
About the weary moors continually,   *130*
Wandering about alone and silently.
While I these thoughts within myself pursued,
He, having made a pause, the same discourse renewed.

XX

And soon with this he other matter blended,
Cheerfully uttered, with demeanour kind,
But stately in the main; and when he ended,
I could have laughed myself to scorn to find
In that decrepit Man so firm a mind.
'God,' said I, 'be my help and stay secure;
I'll think of the Leech-gatherer on the lonely moor!'   *140*

I GRIEVED for Buonaparté, with a vain
And an unthinking grief! The tenderest mood
Of that Man's mind—what can it be? what food
Fed his first hopes? what knowledge could *he* gain?
'Tis not in battles that from youth we train
The Governor who must be wise and good,

And temper with the sternness of the brain
Thoughts motherly, and meek as womanhood.
Wisdom doth live with children round her knees:
Books, leisure, perfect freedom, and the talk   *10*
Man holds with week-day man in the hourly walk
Of the mind's business: these are the degrees
By which true Sway doth mount; this is the stalk
True Power doth grow on; and her rights are these.

COMPOSED UPON WESTMINSTER BRIDGE,

Sept. 3, 1802

Eₐᵣₜₕ has not anything to show more fair:
Dull would he be of soul who could pass by
A sight so touching in its majesty:
This City now doth, like a garment, wear
The beauty of the morning; silent, bare,
Ships, towers, domes, theatres, and temples lie
Open unto the fields, and to the sky;
All bright and glittering in the smokeless air.
Never did sun more beautifully steep
In his first splendour, valley, rock, or hill;   *10*
Ne'er saw I, never felt, a calm so deep!
The river glideth at his own sweet will:
Dear God! the very houses seem asleep;
And all that mighty heart is lying still!

'IT IS A BEAUTEOUS EVENING,
CALM AND FREE'

Iₜ is a beauteous evening, calm and free,
The holy time is quiet as a Nun
Breathless with adoration; the broad sun
Is sinking down in its tranquillity;
The gentleness of heaven broods o'er the Sea:
Listen! the mighty Being is awake,
And doth with his eternal motion make
A sound like thunder—everlastingly.
Dear Child! dear Girl! that walkest with me here,
If thou appear untouched by solemn thought,   *10*
Thy nature is not therefore less divine:
Thou liest in Abraham's bosom all the year;
And worship'st at the Temple's inner shrine,
God being with thee when we know it not.

ON THE EXTINCTION OF THE VENETIAN REPUBLIC

ONCE did She hold the gorgeous east in fee;
    And was the safeguard of the west: the worth
Of Venice did not fall below her birth,
Venice, the eldest Child of Liberty.
She was a maiden City, bright and free;
No guile seduced, no force could violate;
And, when she took unto herself a Mate,
She must espouse the everlasting Sea.
And what if she had seen those glories fade,
Those titles vanish, and that strength decay;   *10*
Yet shall some tribute of regret be paid
When her long life hath reached its final day:
Men are we, and must grieve when even the Shade
Of that which once was great, is passed away.

TO TOUSSAINT L'OUVERTURE

TOUSSAINT, the most unhappy man of men!
    Whether the whistling Rustic tend his plough
Within thy hearing, or thy head be now
Pillowed in some deep dungeon's earless den;—
O miserable Chieftain! where and when
Wilt thou find patience!   Yet die not; do thou
Wear rather in thy bonds a cheerful brow:
Though fallen thyself, never to rise again,
Live, and take comfort.   Thou hast left behind
Powers that will work for thee; air, earth, and skies;   *10*
There's not a breathing of the common wind
That will forget thee; thou hast great allies;
Thy friends are exultations, agonies,
And love, and man's unconquerable mind.

NEAR DOVER, SEPTEMBER 1802

INLAND, within a hollow vale, I stood;
    And saw, while sea was calm and air was clear,
The coast of France—the coast of France how near!
Drawn almost into frightful neighbourhood.
I shrunk; for verily the barrier flood
Was like a lake, or river bright and fair,
A span of waters; yet what power is there!
What mightiness for evil and for good!

Even so doth God protect us if we be
Virtuous and wise. Winds blow, and waters roll, *10*
Strength to the brave, and Power, and Deity;
Yet in themselves are nothing! One decree
Spake laws to *them*, and said that by the soul
Only, the Nations shall be great and free.

LONDON, 1802

MILTON! thou should'st be living at this hour:
England hath need of thee: she is a fen
Of stagnant waters: altar, sword, and pen,
Fireside, the heroic wealth of hall and bower,
Have forfeited their ancient English dower
In inward happiness. We are selfish men;
Oh! raise us up, return to us again;
And give us manners, virtue, freedom, power.
Thy soul was like a Star, and dwelt apart:
Thou hadst a voice whose sound was like the sea: *10*
Pure as the naked heavens, majestic, free,
So didst thou travel on life's common way,
In cheerful godliness; and yet thy heart
The lowliest duties on herself did lay.

TO H. C.

SIX YEARS OLD

O THOU! whose fancies from afar are brought;
Who of thy words dost make a mock apparel,
And fittest to unutterable thought
The breeze-like motion and the self-born carol;
Thou faery voyager! that dost float
In such clear water, that thy boat
May rather seem
To brood on air than on an earthly stream;
Suspended in a stream as clear as sky,
Where earth and heaven do make one imagery; *10*
O blessed vision! happy child!
Thou art so exquisitely wild,
I think of thee with many fears
For what may be thy lot in future years.
    I thought of times when Pain might be thy guest,
Lord of thy house and hospitality;
And Grief, uneasy lover! never rest
But when she sate within the touch of thee.

O too industrious folly!
O vain and causeless melancholy!   20
Nature will either end thee quite;
Or, lengthening out thy season of delight,
Preserve for thee, by individual right,
A young lamb's heart among the full-grown flocks.
What hast thou to do with sorrow,
Or the injuries of to-morrow?
Thou art a dew-drop, which the morn brings forth,
Ill fitted to sustain unkindly shocks,
Or to be trailed along the soiling earth;
A gem that glitters while it lives,   30
And no forewarning gives;
But, at the touch of wrong, without a strife
Slips in a moment out of life.

THERE is a bondage worse, far worse, to bear
    Than his who breathes, by roof, and floor, and wall,
Pent in, a Tyrant's solitary Thrall:
'Tis his who walks about in the open air,
One of a Nation who, henceforth, must wear
Their fetters in their souls.   For who could be,
Who, even the best, in such condition, free
From self-reproach, reproach that he must share
With Human-nature?   Never be it ours
To see the sun how brightly it will shine,   10
And know that noble feelings, manly powers,
Instead of gathering strength, must droop and pine;
And earth with all her pleasant fruits and flowers
Fade, and participate in man's decline.

NUNS fret not at their convent's narrow room;
    And hermits are contented with their cells;
And students with their pensive citadels;
Maids at the wheel, the weaver at his loom,
Sit blithe and happy; bees that soar for bloom,
High as the highest Peak of Furness-fells.
Will murmur by the hour in foxglove bells:
In truth the prison, unto which we doom
Ourselves, no prison is: and hence for me,
In sundry moods, 'twas pastime to be bound   10
Within the Sonnet's scanty plot of ground;

Pleased if some Souls (for such there needs must be)
Who have felt the weight of too much liberty,
Should find brief solace there, as I have found.

METHOUGHT I saw the footsteps of a throne
Which mists and vapours from mine eyes did shroud—
Nor view of who might sit thereon allowed;
But all the steps and ground about were strown
With sights the ruefullest that flesh and bone
Ever put on; a miserable crowd,
Sick, hale, old, young, who cried before that cloud,
'Thou art our king, O Death! to thee we groan.'
Those steps I clomb; the mists before me gave
Smooth way; and I beheld the face of one   *10*
Sleeping alone within a mossy cave,
With her face up to heaven; that seemed to have
Pleasing remembrance of a thought foregone;
A lovely Beauty in a summer grave!

THE world is too much with us; late and soon,
Getting and spending, we lay waste our powers:
Little we see in Nature that is ours;
We have given our hearts away, a sordid boon!
The Sea that bares her bosom to the moon;
The winds that will be howling at all hours,
And are up-gathered now like sleeping flowers;
For this, for everything, we are out of tune;
It moves us not.—Great God! I'd rather be
A Pagan suckled in a creed outworn;   *10*
So might I, standing on this pleasant lea,
Have glimpses that would make me less forlorn;
Have sight of Proteus rising from the sea;
Or hear old Triton blow his wreathèd horn.

ODE TO DUTY

'Jam non consilio bonus, sed more eò perductus, ut non tantum rectè facere possim, sed nisi rectè facere non possim.'

STERN Daughter of the Voice of God!
O Duty! if that name thou love
Who art a light to guide, a rod
To check the erring, and reprove;
Thou, who art victory and law
When empty terrors overawe;
From vain temptations dost set free;
And calm'st the weary strife of frail humanity!

There are who ask not if thine eye
Be on them; who, in love and truth,   *10*
Where no misgiving is, rely
Upon the genial sense of youth:
Glad Hearts! without reproach or blot
Who do thy work, and know it not:
Oh! if through confidence misplaced
They fail, thy saving arms, dread Power! around them cast.

Serene will be our days and bright,
And happy will our nature be,
When love is an unerring light,
And joy its own security.   *20*

And they a blissful course may hold
Even now, who, not unwisely bold,
Live in the spirit of this creed;
Yet seek thy firm support, according to their need.

I, loving freedom, and untried;
No sport of every random gust,
Yet being to myself a guide,
Too blindly have reposed my trust:
And oft, when in my heart was heard
Thy timely mandate, I deferred   *30*
The task, in smoother walks to stray;
But thee I now would serve more strictly, if I may.

Through no disturbance of my soul,
Or strong compunction in me wrought,
I supplicate for thy control;
But in the quietness of thought:
Me this uncharted freedom tires;
I feel the weight of chance-desires:
My hopes no more must change their name,
I long for a repose that ever is the same.   *40*

Yet not the less would I throughout
Still act according to the voice
Of my own wish; and feel past doubt
That my submissiveness was choice:
Not seeking in the school of pride
For 'precepts over dignified,'
Denial and restraint I prize
No farther than they breed a second Will more wise.

Stern Lawgiver! yet thou dost wear
The Godhead's most benignant grace;   *50*
Nor know we anything so fair
As is the smile upon thy face:
Flowers laugh before thee on their beds
And fragrance in thy footing treads;
Thou dost preserve the stars from wrong;
And the most ancient heavens, through Thee, are fresh and
     strong.

To humbler functions, awful Power!
I call thee: I myself commend
Unto thy guidance from this hour;
Oh, let my weakness have an end!   *60*
Give unto me, made lowly wise,
The spirit of self-sacrifice;
The confidence of reason give;
And in the light of truth thy Bondman let me live!

I WANDERED lonely as a cloud
   That floats on high o'er vales and hills,
When all at once I saw a crowd,
A host, of golden daffodils;
Beside the lake, beneath the trees,
Fluttering and dancing in the breeze.

Continuous as the stars that shine
And twinkle on the milky way,
They stretched in never-ending line
Along the margin of a bay: *10*
Ten thousand saw I at a glance,
Tossing their heads in sprightly dance.

The waves beside them danced; but they
Out-did the sparkling waves in glee:
A poet could not but be gay,
In such a jocund company:
I gazed—and gazed—but little thought
What wealth the show to me had brought:

For oft, when on my couch I lie
In vacant or in pensive mood,   *20*
They flash upon that inward eye
Which is the bliss of solitude;
And then my heart with pleasure fills,
And dances with the daffodils.

STEPPING WESTWARD

While my Fellow-traveller and I were walking by the side of Loch
Ketterine, one fine evening after sunset, in our road to a Hut where, in
the course of our Tour, we had been hospitably entertained some weeks
before, we met, in one of the loneliest parts of that solitary region, two
well-dressed Women, one of whom said to us, by way of greeting, 'What,
you are stepping westward?'

' 'W'HAT, *you are stepping westward?*'—' *Yea.*'
    —'Twould be a *wildish* destiny,
If we, who thus together roam
In a strange Land, and far from home,
Were in this place the guests of Chance:
Yet who would stop, or fear to advance,
Though home or shelter he had none,
With such a sky to lead him on?

The dewy ground was dark and cold;
Behind, all gloomy to behold;   *10*
And stepping westward seemed to be
A kind of *heavenly* destiny:
I liked the greeting; 'twas a sound
Of something without place or bound;
And seemed to give me spiritual right
To travel through that region bright.

The voice was soft, and she who spake
Was walking by her native lake:
The salutation had to me
The very sound of courtesy: *20*

Its power was felt; and while my eye
Was fixed upon the glowing Sky,
The echo of the voice enwrought
A human sweetness with the thought
Of travelling through the world that lay
Before me in my endless way.

THE SOLITARY REAPER

BEHOLD her, single in the field,
  Yon solitary Highland Lass!
Reaping and singing by herself;
Stop here, or gently pass!
Alone she cuts and binds the grain,
And sings a melancholy strain;
O listen! for the Vale profound
Is overflowing with the sound.

No Nightingale did ever chaunt
More welcome notes to weary bands   *10*
Of travellers in some shady haunt,
Among Arabian sands:
A voice so thrilling ne'er was heard
In spring-time from the Cuckoo-bird,
Breaking the silence of the seas
Among the farthest Hebrides.

Will no one tell me what she sings?—
Perhaps the plaintive numbers flow
For old, unhappy, far-off things,
And battles long ago: *20*
Or is it some more humble lay,
Familiar matter of to-day?
Some natural sorrow, loss, or pain,
That has been, and may be again?

Whate'er the theme, the Maiden sang
As if her song could have no ending:
I saw her singing at her work,
And o'er the sickle bending;—
I listened, motionless and still;
And, as I mounted up the hill,   *30*
The music in my heart I bore,
Long after it was heard no more.

CHARACTER OF THE HAPPY WARRIOR

WHO is the happy Warrior?   Who is he
    That every man in arms should wish to be?
—It is the generous Spirit, who, when brought
Among the tasks of real life, hath wrought
Upon the plan that pleased his boyish thought:
Whose high endeavours are an inward light
That makes the path before him always bright:
Who, with a natural instinct to discern
What knowledge can perform, is diligent to learn;
Abides by this resolve, and stops not there,   *10*
But makes his moral being his prime care;
Who, doomed to go in company with Pain,
And Fear, and Bloodshed, miserable train!
Turns his necessity to glorious gain;
In face of these doth exercise a power
Which is our human nature's highest dower;
Controls them and subdues, transmutes, bereaves
Of their bad influence, and their good receives:
By objects, which might force the soul to abate
Her feeling, rendered more compassionate;   *20*
Is placable—because occasions rise
So often that demand such sacrifice;
More skilful in self-knowledge, even more pure,
As tempted more; more able to endure,
As more exposed to suffering and distress;
Thence, also, more alive to tenderness.
—'Tis he whose law is reason; who depends
Upon that law as on the best of friends;
Whence, in a state where men are tempted still
To evil for a guard against worse ill,   *30*
And what in quality or act is best
Doth seldom on a right foundation rest,
He labours good on good to fix, and owes
To virtue every triumph that he knows:
—Who, if he rise to station of command,
Rises by open means; and there will stand
On honourable terms, or else retire,
And in himself possess his own desire,
Who comprehends his trust, and to the same
Keeps faithful with a singleness of aim;   *40*
And therefore does not stoop, nor lie in wait
For wealth, or honours, or for worldly state;
Whom they must follow; on whose head must fall,
Like showers of manna, if they come at all:
Whose powers shed round him in the common strife,

Or mild concerns of ordinary life,
A constant influence, a peculiar grace;
But who, if he be called upon to face
Some awful moment to which Heaven has joined
Great issues, good or bad for human kind,   *50*
Is happy as a Lover; and attired
With sudden brightness, like a Man inspired;
And, through the heat of conflict, keeps the law
In calmness made, and sees what he foresaw;
Or if an unexpected call succeed,
Come when it will, is equal to the need:
—He who, though thus endued as with a sense
And faculty for storm and turbulence,
Is yet a Soul whose master-bias leans
To homefelt pleasures and to gentle scenes;   *60*
Sweet images! which, wheresoe'er he be,
Are at his heart; and such fidelity
It is his darling passion to approve;
More brave for this, that he hath much to love:—
'Tis, finally, the Man, who, lifted high,
Conspicuous object in a Nation's eye,
Or left unthought-of in obscurity,—
Who, with a toward or untoward lot,
Prosperous or adverse, to his wish or not—
Plays, in the many games of life, that one   *70*
Where what he most doth value must be won:
Whom neither shape of danger can dismay,
Nor thought of tender happiness betray;
Who, not content that former worth stand fast,
Looks forward, persevering to the last,
From well to better, daily self-surpast:
Who, whether praise of him must walk the earth
For ever, and to noble deeds give birth,
Or he must fall, to sleep without his fame,
And leave a dead unprofitable name—   *80*
Finds comfort in himself and in his cause;
And, while the mortal mist is gathering, draws
His breath in confidence of Heaven's applause:
This is the happy Warrior; this is He
That every Man in arms should wish to be.

ELEGIAC STANZAS

SUGGESTED BY A PICTURE OF PEELE CASTLE, IN A
STORM, PAINTED BY SIR GEORGE BEAUMONT

I WAS thy neighbour once, thou rugged Pile!
 Four summer weeks I dwelt in sight of thee:
I saw thee every day; and all the while
Thy Form was sleeping on a glassy sea.

So pure the sky, so quiet was the air!
So like, so very like, was day to day!
Whene'er I looked, thy Image still was there;
It trembled, but it never passed away.

How perfect was the calm! it seemed no sleep;
No mood, which season takes away, or brings: *10*
I could have fancied that the mighty Deep
Was even the gentlest of all gentle Things.

Ah! THEN, if mine had been the Painter's hand,
To express what then I saw; and add the gleam,
The light that never was, on sea or land,
The consecration, and the Poet's dream;

I would have planted thee, thou hoary Pile,
Amid a world how different from this!
Beside a sea that could not cease to smile;
On tranquil land, beneath a sky of bliss.   *20*

Thou shouldst have seemed a treasure-house divine
Of peaceful years; a chronicle of heaven;—
Of all the sunbeams that did ever shine
The very sweetest had to thee been given.

A Picture had it been of lasting ease,
Elysian quiet, without toil or strife;
No motion but the moving tide, a breeze,
Or merely silent Nature's breathing life.

Such, in the fond illusion of my heart,
Such Picture would I at that time have made: *30*
And seen the soul of truth in every part,
A stedfast peace that might not be betrayed.

So once it would have been,—'tis so no more;
I have submitted to a new control:
A power is gone, which nothing can restore;
A deep distress hath humanized my Soul.

Not for a moment could I now behold
A smiling sea, and be what I have been:
The feeling of my loss will ne'er be old;
This, which I know, I speak with mind serene.   *40*

Then, Beaumont, Friend! who would have been the Friend,
If he had lived, of Him whom I deplore,
This work of thine I blame not, but commend;
This sea in anger, and that dismal shore.

O 'tis a passionate Work!—yet wise and well,
Well chosen is the spirit that is here;
That Hulk which labours in the deadly swell,
This rueful sky, this pageantry of fear!

And this huge Castle, standing here sublime,
I love to see the look with which it braves,   *50*
Cased in the unfeeling armour of old time,
The lightning, the fierce wind, and trampling waves.

Farewell, farewell the heart that lives alone,
Housed in a dream, at distance from the Kind!
Such happiness, wherever it be known,
Is to be pitied, for 'tis surely blind.

But welcome fortitude, and patient cheer,
And frequent sights of what is to be borne!
Such sights, or worse, as are before me here.—
Not without hope we suffer and we mourn.   *60*

LINES

Composed at Grasmere, during a walk one Evening, after a stormy day, the Author having just read in a Newspaper that the dissolution of Mr Fox was hourly expected.

L OUD is the Vale! the Voice is up
  With which she speaks when storms are gone,
A mighty unison of streams!
Of all her Voices, One!

Loud is the Vale;—this inland Depth
In peace is roaring like the Sea;
Yon star upon the mountain-top
Is listening quietly.

Sad was I, even to pain deprest,
Importunate and heavy load!   *10*
The Comforter hath found me here,
Upon this lonely road;

And many thousands now are sad—
Wait the fulfilment of their fear;
For he must die who is their stay,
Their glory disappear.

A Power is passing from the earth
To breathless Nature's dark abyss;
But when the great and good depart
What is it more than this—   *20*

That Man, who is from God sent forth,
Doth yet again to God return?—
Such ebb and flow must ever be,
Then wherefore should we mourn?

THOUGHT OF A BRITON ON THE SUBJUGATION OF SWITZERLAND

Two Voices are there; one is of the sea,
  One of the mountains; each a mighty Voice:
In both from age to age thou didst rejoice,
They were thy chosen music, Liberty!
There came a Tyrant, and with holy glee
Thou fought'st against him; but hast vainly striven:
Thou from thy Alpine holds at length art driven,
Where not a torrent murmurs heard by thee.
Of one deep bliss thine ear hath been bereft:
Then cleave, O cleave to that which still is left;   *10*
For, high-souled Maid, what sorrow would it be
That Mountain floods should thunder as before,
And Ocean bellow from his rocky shore,
And neither awful Voice be heard by thee!

From *THE RECLUSE*

On Man, on Nature, and on Human Life,
Musing in solitude, I oft perceive
Fair trains of imagery before me rise,
Accompanied by feelings of delight
Pure, or with no unpleasing sadness mixed;
And I am conscious of affecting thoughts
And dear remembrances, whose presence soothes
Or elevates the Mind, intent to weigh
The good and evil of our mortal state.
—To these emotions, whencesoe'er they come,   10
Whether from breath of outward circumstance,
Or from the Soul—an impulse to herself—
I would give utterance in numerous verse.
Of Truth, of Grandeur, Beauty, Love, and Hope,
And melancholy Fear subdued by Faith;
Of blessèd consolations in distress;
Of moral strength, and intellectual Power;
Of joy in widest commonalty spread;
Of the individual Mind that keeps her own
Inviolate retirement, subject there   20
To Conscience only, and the law supreme
Of that Intelligence which governs all—
I sing:—'fit audience let me find though few!'

So prayéd, more gaining than he asked, the Bard—
In holiest mood.   Urania, I shall need
Thy guidance, or a greater Muse, if such
Descend to earth or dwell in highest heaven!
For I must tread on shadowy ground, must sink

Deep—and, aloft ascending, breathe in worlds
To which the heaven of heavens is but a veil.   *30*
All strength—all terror, single or in bands,
That ever was put forth in personal form—
Jehovah—with his thunder, and the choir
Of shouting Angels, and the empyreal thrones—
I pass them unalarmed.   Not Chaos, not
The darkest pit of lowest Erebus,
Nor aught of blinder vacancy, scooped out
By help of dreams—can breed such fear and awe
As fall upon us often when we look
Into our Minds, into the Mind of Man—   *40*
My haunt, and the main region of my song.
—Beauty—a living Presence of the earth,
Surpassing the most fair ideal Forms
Which craft of delicate Spirits hath composed
From earth's materials—waits upon my steps;
Pitches her tents before me as I move,
An hourly neighbour.   Paradise, and groves
Elysian, Fortunate Fields—like those of old
Sought in the Atlantic Main—why should they be
A history only of departed things,   *50*
Or a mere fiction of what never was?
For the discerning intellect of Man,
When wedded to this goodly universe
In love and holy passion, shall find these
A simple produce of the common day.
—I, long before the blissful hour arrives,
Would chant, in lonely peace, the spousal verse
Of this great consummation:—and, by words
Which speak of nothing more than what we are,
Would I arouse the sensual from their sleep   *60*
Of Death, and win the vacant and the vain
To noble raptures; while my voice proclaims
How exquisitely the individual Mind
(And the progressive powers perhaps no less
Of the whole species) to the external World
Is fitted:—and how exquisitely, too—
Theme this but little heard of among men—
The external World is fitted to the Mind;
And the creation (by no lower name
Can it be called) which they with blended might   *70*
Accomplish:—this is our high argument.
—Such grateful haunts foregoing, if I oft
Must turn elsewhere—to travel near the tribes
And fellowships of men, and see ill sights
Of madding passions mutually inflamed;

Must hear Humanity in fields and groves
Pipe solitary anguish; or must hang
Brooding above the fierce confederate storm
Of sorrow, barricadoed evermore
Within the walls of cities—may these sounds   *80*
Have their authentic comment; that even these
Hearing, I be not downcast or forlorn!—
Descend, prophetic Spirit! that inspir'st
The human Soul of universal earth,
Dreaming on things to come; and dost possess
A metropolitan temple in the hearts
Of mighty Poets: upon me bestow
A gift of genuine insight; that my Song
With star-like virtue in its place may shine,
Shedding benignant influence, and secure,   *90*
Itself, from all malevolent effect
Of those mutations that extend their sway
Throughout the nether sphere!—And if with this
I mix more lowly matter; with the thing
Contemplated, describe the Mind and Man
Contemplating; and who, and what he was—
The transitory Being that beheld
This Vision; when and where, and how he lived;—
Be not this labour useless.   If such theme
May sort with highest objects, then—dread Power!   *100*
Whose gracious favour is the primal source
Of all illumination,—may my Life
Express the image of a better time,
More wise desires, and simpler manners;—nurse
My Heart in genuine freedom:—all pure thoughts
Be with me;—so shall thy unfailing love
Guide, and support, and cheer me to the end!

From *THE PRELUDE*

BOOK FIRST

INTRODUCTION—CHILDHOOD AND SCHOOL-TIME

Fair seed-time had my soul, and I grew up
Fostered alike by beauty and by fear:
Much favoured in my birth-place, and no less
In that belovèd Vale to which erelong
We were transplanted—there were we let loose
For sports of wider range.   Ere I had told
Ten birth-days, when among the mountain slopes
Frost, and the breath of frosty wind, had snapped
The last autumnal crocus, 'twas my joy
With store of springes o'er my shoulder hung   310
To range the open heights where woodcocks run
Along the smooth green turf.   Through half the night,
Scudding away from snare to snare, I plied
That anxious visitation;—moon and stars
Were shining o'er my head.   I was alone,
And seemed to be a trouble to the peace
That dwelt among them.   Sometimes it befell
In these night wanderings, that a strong desire
O'erpowered my better reason, and the bird
Which was the captive of another's toil   320
Became my prey; and when the deed was done
I heard among the solitary hills
Low breathing coming after me, and sounds
Of undistinguishable motion, steps
Almost as silent as the turf they trod.

Nor less, when spring had warmed the cultured Vale,
Roved we as plunderers where the mother-bird
Had in high places built her lodge; though mean
Our object and inglorious, yet the end
Was not ignoble.   Oh! when I have hung   330
Above the raven's nest, by knots of grass
And half-inch fissures in the slippery rock
But ill sustained, and almost (so it seemed)

Suspended by the blast that blew amain,
Shouldering the naked crag, oh, at that time
While on the perilous ridge I hung alone,
With what strange utterance did the loud dry wind
Blow through my ear! the sky seemed not a sky
Of earth—and with what motion moved the clouds!

Dust as we are, the immortal spirit grows   340
Like harmony in music; there is a dark
Inscrutable workmanship that reconciles
Discordant elements, makes them cling together
In one society.   How strange, that all
The terrors, pains, and early miseries,
Regrets, vexations, lassitudes interfused
Within my mind, should e'er have borne a part,
And that a needful part, in making up
The calm existence that is mine when I
Am worthy of myself!   Praise to the end!   350
Thanks to the means which Nature deigned to employ;
Whether her fearless visitings, or those
That came with soft alarm, like hurtless light
Opening the peaceful clouds; or she may use
Severer interventions, ministry
More palpable, as best might suit her aim.

One summer evening (led by her) I found
A little boat tied to a willow tree
Within a rocky cave, its usual home.
Straight I unloosed her chain, and stepping in   360
Pushed from the shore.   It was an act of stealth
And troubled pleasure, nor without the voice
Of mountain-echoes did my boat move on;
Leaving behind her still, on either side,
Small circles glittering idly in the moon,
Until they melted all into one track
Of sparkling light.   But now, like one who rows,
Proud of his skill, to reach a chosen point
With an unswerving line, I fixed my view
Upon the summit of a craggy ridge,   370
The horizon's utmost boundary; for above
Was nothing but the stars and the grey sky.
She was an elfin pinnace; lustily
I dipped my oars into the silent lake,
And, as I rose upon the stroke, my boat
Went heaving through the water like a swan;
When, from behind that craggy steep till then

The horizon's bound, a huge peak, black and huge,
As if with voluntary power instinct,
Upreared its head.   I struck and struck again,   *380*
And growing still in stature the grim shape
Towered up between me and the stars, and still,
For so it seemed, with purpose of its own
And measured motion like a living thing,
Strode after me.   With trembling oars I turned,
And through the silent water stole my way
Back to the covert of the willow tree;
There in her mooring-place I left my bark,—
And through the meadows homeward went, in grave
And serious mood; but after I had seen   *390*
That spectacle, for many days, my brain
Worked with a dim and undetermined sense
Of unknown modes of being; o'er my thoughts
There hung a darkness, call it solitude
Or blank desertion.   No familiar shapes
Remained, no pleasant images of trees,
Of sea or sky, no colours of green fields;
But huge and mighty forms, that do not live
Like living men, moved slowly through the mind
By day, and were a trouble to my dreams.   *400*

    Wisdom and Spirit of the universe!
Thou Soul that art the eternity of thought,
That givest to forms and images a breath
And everlasting motion, not in vain
By day or star-light thus from my first dawn
Of childhood didst thou intertwine for me
The passions that build up our human soul;
Not with the mean and vulgar works of man,
But with high objects, with enduring things—
With life and nature—purifying thus   *410*
The elements of feeling and of thought,
And sanctifying, by such discipline,
Both pain and fear, until we recognize
A grandeur in the beatings of the heart.
Nor was this fellowship vouchsafed to me
With stinted kindness.   In November days,
When vapours rolling down the valley made
A lonely scene more lonesome, among woods,
At noon and 'mid the calm of summer nights,
When, by the margin of the trembling lake,   *420*
Beneath the gloomy hills homeward I went
In solitude, such intercourse was mine;
Mine was it in the fields both day and night,
And by the waters, all the summer long.

And in the frosty season, when the sun
Was set, and visible for many a mile
The cottage windows blazed through twilight gloom,
I heeded not their summons: happy time
It was indeed for all of us—for me
It was a time of rapture!   Clear and loud   *430*
The village clock tolled six,—I wheeled about,
Proud and exulting like an untired horse
That cares not for his home.   All shod with steel,
We hissed along the polished ice in games
Confederate, imitative of the chase
And woodland pleasures,—the resounding horn,
The pack loud chiming, and the hunted hare.
So through the darkness and the cold we flew,
And not a voice was idle; with the din
Smitten, the precipices rang aloud;   *440*
The leafless trees and every icy crag
Tinkled like iron; while far distant hills
Into the tumult sent an alien sound
Of melancholy not unnoticed, while the stars
Eastward were sparkling clear, and in the west
The orange sky of evening died away.
Not seldom from the uproar I retired
Into a silent bay, or sportively
Glanced sideway, leaving the tumultuous throng,
To cut across the reflex of a star   *450*
That fled, and, flying still before me, gleamed
Upon the glassy plain; and oftentimes,
When we had given our bodies to the wind,
And all the shadowy banks on either side
Came sweeping through the darkness, spinning still
The rapid line of motion, then at once
Have I, reclining back upon my heels,
Stopped short; yet still the solitary cliffs
Wheeled by me—even as if the earth had rolled
With visible motion her diurnal round!   *460*
Behind me did they stretch in solemn train,
Feebler and feebler, and I stood and watched
Till all was tranquil as a dreamless sleep.

Ye Presences of Nature in the sky
And on the earth!   Ye Visions of the hills!
And Souls of lonely places! can I think
A vulgar hope was yours when ye employed
Such ministry, when ye, through many a year
Haunting me thus among my boyish sports,

On caves and trees, upon the woods and hills, 470
Impressed upon all forms the characters
Of danger or desire; and thus did make
The surface of the universal earth,
With triumph and delight, with hope and fear,
Work like a sea?

BOOK THIRD

RESIDENCE AT CAMBRIDGE

The Evangelist St John my patron was:
Three Gothic courts are his, and in the first
Was my abiding-place, a nook obscure;
Right underneath, the College kitchens made
A humming sound, less tuneable than bees, 50
But hardly less industrious; with shrill notes
Of sharp command and scolding intermixed.
Near me hung Trinity's loquacious clock,
Who never let the quarters, night or day,
Slip by him unproclaimed, and told the hours
Twice over with a male and female voice.
Her pealing organ was my neighbour too;
And from my pillow, looking forth by light
Of moon or favouring stars, I could behold
The antechapel where the statue stood 60
Of Newton with his prism and silent face,
The marble index of a mind for ever
Voyaging through strange seas of Thought, alone.

Of College labours, of the Lecturer's room,
All studded round, as thick as chairs could stand,
With loyal students, faithful to their books,
Half-and-half idlers, hardy recusants,
And honest dunces—of important days,
Examinations, when the man was weighed 70
As in a balance! of excessive hopes,
Tremblings withal and commendable fears,
Small jealousies, and triumphs good or bad—
Let others that know more speak as they know.
Such glory was but little sought by me,
And little won.   Yet from the first crude days
Of settling time in this untried abode,
I was disturbed at times by prudent thoughts,
Wishing to hope without a hope, some fears
About my future worldly maintenance, 80
And, more than all, a strangeness in the mind,
A feeling that I was not for that hour,
Nor for that place.   But wherefore be cast down?

For (not to speak of Reason and her pure
Reflective acts to fix the moral law
Deep in the conscience, nor of Christian Hope,
Bowing her head before her sister Faith
As one far mightier), hither I had come,
Bear witness Truth, endowed with holy powers
And faculties, whether to work or feel.   *90*
Oft when the dazzling show no longer new
Had ceased to dazzle, ofttimes did I quit
My comrades, leave the crowd, buildings and groves,
And as I paced alone the level fields
Far from those lovely sights and sounds sublime
With which I had been conversant, the mind
Drooped not; but there into herself returning,
With prompt rebound seemed fresh as heretofore.
At least I more distinctly recognized
Her native instincts: let me dare to speak   *100*
A higher language, say that now I felt
What independent solaces were mine,
To mitigate the injurious sway of place
Or circumstance, how far soever changed
In youth, or to be changed in manhood's prime;
Or for the few who shall be called to look
On the long shadows in our evening years,
Ordained precursors to the night of death.
As if awakened, summoned, roused, constrained,
I looked for universal things; perused   *110*
The common countenance of earth and sky:
Earth, nowhere unembellished by some trace
Of that first Paradise whence man was driven;
And sky, whose beauty and bounty are expressed
By the proud name she bears—the name of Heaven.
I called on both to teach me what they might;
Or, turning the mind in upon herself,
Pored, watched, expected, listened, spread my thoughts
And spread them with a wider creeping; felt
Incumbencies more awful, visitings   *120*
Of the Upholder of the tranquil soul,
That tolerates the indignities of Time,
And, from the centre of Eternity
All finite motions overruling, lives
In glory immutable.   But peace! enough
Here to record that I was mounting now
To such community with highest truth—
A track pursuing, not untrod before,

From strict analogies by thought supplied
Or consciousnesses not to be subdued,   *130*
To every natural form, rock, fruit, or flower,
Even the loose stones that cover the highway,
I gave a moral life: I saw them feel,
Or linked them to some feeling: the great mass
Lay bedded in a quickening soul, and all
That I beheld respired with inward meaning.
Add that whate'er of Terror or of Love
Or Beauty, Nature's daily face put on
From transitory passion, unto this
I was as sensitive as waters are   *140*
To the sky's influence; in a kindred mood
Of passion was obedient as a lute
That waits upon the touches of the wind.
Unknown, unthought of, yet I was most rich—
I had a world about me—'twas my own;
I made it, for it only lived to me,
And to the God who sees into the heart.
Such sympathies, though rarely, were betrayed
By outward gestures and by visible looks:
Some called it madness—so indeed it was,   *150*
If child-like fruitfulness in passing joy,
If steady moods of thoughtfulness matured
To inspiration, sort with such a name;
If prophecy be madness; if things viewed
By poets in old time, and higher up
By the first men, earth's first inhabitants,
May in these tutored days no more be seen
With undisordered sight.   But leaving this,
It was no madness, for the bodily eye
Amid my strongest workings evermore   *160*
Was searching out the lines of difference
As they lie hid in all external forms,
Near or remote, minute or vast; an eye
Which, from a tree, a stone, a withered leaf,
To the broad ocean and the azure heavens
Spangled with kindred multitudes of stars,
Could find no surface where its power might sleep;
Which spake perpetual logic to my soul,
And by an unrelenting agency
Did bind my feelings even as in a chain.   *170*

BOOK FOURTH

SUMMER VACATION

    As one who hangs down-bending from the side
Of a slow-moving boat, upon the breast
Of a still water, solacing himself
With such discoveries as his eye can make
Beneath him in the bottom of the deep,   260
Sees many beauteous sights—weeds, fishes, flowers,
Grots, pebbles, roots of trees, and fancies more,
Yet often is perplexed, and cannot part
The shadow from the substance, rocks and sky,
Mountains and clouds, reflected in the depth
Of the clear flood, from things which there abide
In their true dwelling; now is crossed by gleam
Of his own image, by a sunbeam now,
And wavering motions sent he knows not whence,
Impediments that make his task more sweet;   270
Such pleasant office have we long pursued
Incumbent o'er the surface of past time
With like success, nor often have appeared
Shapes fairer or less doubtfully discerned
Than these to which the Tale, indulgent Friend!
Would now direct thy notice.   Yet in spite
Of pleasure won, and knowledge not withheld,
There was an inner falling off—I loved,
Loved deeply all that had been loved before,
More deeply even than ever: but a swarm   280
Of heady schemes jostling each other, gawds,
And feast and dance, and public revelry,
And sports and games (too grateful in themselves,
Yet in themselves less grateful, I believe,
Than as they were a badge glossy and fresh
Of manliness and freedom) all conspired
To lure my mind from firm habitual quest
Of feeding pleasures, to depress the zeal
And damp those yearnings which had once been mine—
A wild, unworldly-minded youth, given up   290
To his own eager thoughts.   It would demand
Some skill, and longer time than may be spared,
To paint these vanities, and how they wrought
In haunts where they, till now, had been unknown.
It seemed the very garments that I wore
Preyed on my strength, and stopped the quiet stream
Of self-forgetfulness.

                          Yes, that heartless chase
Of trivial pleasures was a poor exchange
For books and nature at that early age.
'Tis true, some casual knowledge might be gained   *300*
Of character or life; but at that time,
Of manners put to school I took small note,
And all my deeper passions lay elsewhere.
Far better had it been to exalt the mind
By solitary study, to uphold
Intense desire through meditative peace;
And yet, for chastisement of these regrets,
The memory of one particular hour
Doth here rise up against me.   'Mid a throng
Of maids and youths, old men, and matrons staid,   *310*
A medley of all tempers, I had passed
The night in dancing, gaiety, and mirth,
With din of instruments and shuffling feet,
And glancing forms, and tapers glittering,
And unaimed prattle flying up and down;
Spirits upon the stretch, and here and there
Slight shocks of young love-liking interspersed,
Whose transient pleasure mounted to the head,
And tingled through the veins.   Ere we retired,
The cock had crowed, and now the eastern sky   *320*
Was kindling, not unseen, from humble copse
And open field, through which the pathway wound,
And homeward led my steps.   Magnificent
The morning rose, in memorable pomp,
Glorious as e'er I had beheld—in front,
The sea lay laughing at a distance; near,
The solid mountains shone, bright as the clouds,
Grain-tinctured, drenched in empyrean light;
And in the meadows and the lower grounds
Was all the sweetness of a common dawn—   *330*
Dews, vapours, and the melody of birds,
And labourers going forth to till the fields.
Ah! need I say, dear Friend! that to the brim
My heart was full; I made no vows, but vows
Were then made for me; bond unknown to me
Was given, that I should be, else sinning greatly,
A dedicated Spirit.   On I walked
In thankful blessedness, which yet survives.

    Strange rendezvous my mind was at that time,
A parti-coloured show of grave and gay,   *340*
Solid and light, short-sighted and profound;
Of inconsiderate habits and sedate,

Consorting in one mansion unreproved.
The worth I knew of powers that I possessed,
Though slighted and too oft misused.   Besides,
That summer, swarming as it did with thoughts
Transient and idle, lacked not intervals
When Folly from the frown of fleeting Time
Shrunk, and the mind experienced in herself
Conformity as just as that of old   *350*
To the end and written spirit of God's works,
Whether held forth in Nature or in Man,
Through pregnant vision, separate or conjoined.

   When from our better selves we have too long
Been parted by the hurrying world, and droop,
Sick of its business, of its pleasures tired,
How gracious, how benign, is Solitude;
How potent a mere image of her sway;
Most potent when impressed upon the mind
With an appropriate human centre—hermit,   *360*
Deep in the bosom of the wilderness;
Votary (in vast cathedral, where no foot
Is treading, where no other face is seen)
Kneeling at prayers; or watchman on the top
Of lighthouse, beaten by Atlantic waves;
Or as the soul of that great Power is met
Sometimes embodied on a public road,
When, for the night deserted, it assumes
A character of quiet more profound
Than pathless wastes.
                                 Once, when those summer months   *370*
Were flown, and autumn brought its annual show
Of oars with oars contending, sails with sails,
Upon Winander's spacious breast, it chanced
That—after I had left a flower-decked room
(Whose in-door pastime, lighted up, survived
To a late hour), and spirits overwrought
Were making night do penance for a day
Spent in a round of strenuous idleness—
My homeward course led up a long ascent,
Where the road's watery surface, to the top   *380*
Of that sharp rising, glittered to the moon
And bore the semblance of another stream
Stealing with silent lapse to join the brook
That murmured in the vale.   All else was still;
No living thing appeared in earth or air,
And, save the flowing water's peaceful voice,
Sound there was none—but, lo! an uncouth shape,

Shown by a sudden turning of the road,
So near that, slipping back into the shade
Of a thick hawthorn, I could mark him well,   *390*
Myself unseen.   He was of stature tall,
A span above man's common measure, tall,
Stiff, lank, and upright; a more meagre man
Was never seen before by night or day.
Long were his arms, pallid his hands; his mouth
Looked ghastly in the moonlight: from behind,
A mile-stone propped him; I could also ken
That he was clothed in military garb,
Though faded, yet entire.   Companionless,
No dog attending, by no staff sustained,   *400*
He stood, and in his very dress appeared
A desolation, a simplicity,
To which the trappings of a gaudy world
Make a strange back-ground.   From his lips, ere long,
Issued low muttered sounds, as if of pain
Or some uneasy thought; yet still his fórm
Kept the same awful steadiness—at his feet
His shadow lay, and moved not.   From self-blame
Not wholly free, I watched him thus; at length
Subduing my heart's specious cowardice,   *410*
I left the shady nook where I had stood
And hailed him.   Slowly from his resting-place
He rose, and with a lean and wasted arm
In measured gesture lifted to his head
Returned my salutation; then resumed
His station as before; and when I asked
His history, the veteran, in reply,
Was neither slow nor eager; but, unmoved,
And with a quiet uncomplaining voice,
A stately air of mild indifference,   *420*
He told in few plain words a soldier's tale—
That in the Tropic Islands he had served,
Whence he had landed scarcely three weeks past;
That on his landing he had been dismissed,
And now was travelling towards his native home.
This heard, I said, in pity, 'Come with me.'
He stooped, and straightway from the ground took up
An oaken staff by me yet unobserved—
A staff which must have dropt from his slack hand
And lay till now neglected in the grass.   *430*
Though weak his step and cautious, he appeared
To travel without pain, and I beheld,
With an astonishment but ill suppressed,
His ghostly figure moving at my side;

Nor could I, while we journeyed thus, forbear
To turn from present hardships to the past,
And speak of war, battle, and pestilence,
Sprinkling this talk with questions, better spared,
On what he might himself have seen or felt.
He all the while was in demeanour calm,   440
Concise in answer; solemn and sublime
He might have seemed, but that in all he said
There was a strange half-absence, as of one
Knowing too well the importance of his theme,
But feeling it no longer.   Our discourse
Soon ended, and together on we passed
In silence through a wood gloomy and still.
Up-turning, then, along an open field,
We reached a cottage.   At the door I knocked,
And earnestly to charitable care   450
Commended him as a poor friendless man,
Belated and by sickness overcome.
Assured that now the traveller would repose
In comfort, I entreated that henceforth
He would not linger in the public ways,
But ask for timely furtherance and help
Such as his state required.   At this reproof,
With the same ghastly mildness in his look,
He said, 'My trust is in the God of Heaven,
And in the eye of him who passes me!'   460

BOOK SIXTH

CAMBRIDGE AND THE ALPS

Whate'er in this wide circuit we beheld,
Or heard, was fitted to our unripe state
Of intellect and heart.   With such a book
Before our eyes, we could not choose but read
Lessons of genuine brotherhood, the plain
And universal reason of mankind,
The truths of young and old.   Nor, side by side
Pacing, two social pilgrims, or alone
Each with his humour, could we fail to abound
In dreams and fictions, pensively composed: 550
Dejection taken up for pleasure's sake,
And gilded sympathies, the willow wreath,
And sober posies of funereal flowers,
Gathered among those solitudes sublime
From formal gardens of the lady Sorrow,
Did sweeten many a meditative hour.

Yet still in me with those soft luxuries
Mixed something of stern mood, an underthirst
Of vigour seldom utterly allayed:
And from that source how different a sadness   *560*
Would issue, let one incident make known.
When from the Vallais we had turned, and clomb
Along the Simplon's steep and rugged road,
Following a band of muleteers, we reached
A halting-place, where all together took
Their noon-tide meal.   Hastily rose our guide,
Leaving us at the board; awhile we lingered,
Then paced the beaten downward way that led
Right to a rough stream's edge, and there broke off;
The only track now visible was one   *570*
That from the torrent's further brink held forth
Conspicuous invitation to ascend
A lofty mountain.   After brief delay
Crossing the unbridged stream, that road we took,
And clomb with eagerness, till anxious fears
Intruded, for we failed to overtake
Our comrades gone before.   By fortunate chance,
While every moment added doubt to doubt,
A peasant met us, from whose mouth we learned
That to the spot which had perplexed us first   *580*
We must descend, and there should find the road,
Which in the stony channel of the stream
Lay a few steps, and then along its banks;
And, that our future course, all plain to sight,
Was downwards, with the current of that stream.
Loth to believe what we so grieved to hear,
For still we had hopes that pointed to the clouds,
We questioned him again, and yet again;
But every word that from the peasant's lips
Came in reply, translated by our feelings,   *590*
Ended in this,—*that we had crossed the Alps.*

Imagination—here the Power so called
Through sad incompetence of human speech,
That awful Power rose from the mind's abyss
Like an unfathered vapour that enwraps,
At once, some lonely traveller.   I was lost;
Halted without an effort to break through;
But to my conscious soul I now can say—
'I recognize thy glory:' in such strength
Of usurpation, when the light of sense   *600*
Goes out, but with a flash that has revealed
The invisible world, doth greatness make abode,

There harbours whether we be young or old.
Our destiny, our being's heart and home,
Is with infinitude, and only there;
With hope it is, hope that can never die,
Effort, and expectation, and desire,
And something evermore about to be.
Under such banners militant, the soul
Seeks for no trophies, struggles for no spoils   *610*
That may attest her prowess, blest in thoughts
That are their own perfection and reward,
Strong in herself and in beatitude
That hides her, like the mighty flood of Nile
Poured from his fount of Abyssinian clouds
To fertilize the whole Egyptian plain.

    The melancholy slackening that ensued
Upon those tidings by the peasant given
Was soon dislodged.   Downwards we hurried fast
And, with the half-shaped road which we had missed,   *620*
Entered a narrow chasm.   The brook and road
Were fellow-travellers in this gloomy strait,
And with them did we journey several hours
At a slow pace.   The immeasurable height
Of woods decaying, never to be decayed,
The stationary blasts of waterfalls,
And in the narrow rent at every turn
Winds thwarting winds, bewildered and forlorn,
The torrents shooting from the clear blue sky,
The rocks that muttered close upon our ears,   *630*
Black drizzling crags that spake by the way-side
As if a voice were in them, the sick sight
And giddy prospect of the raving stream,
The unfettered clouds and region of the Heavens,
Tumult and peace, the darkness and the light—
Were all like workings of one mind, the features
Of the same face, blossoms upon one tree;
Characters of the great Apocalypse,
The types and symbols of Eternity,
Of first, and last, and midst, and without end.   *640*

BOOK TWELFTH

IMAGINATION AND TASTE, HOW IMPAIRED AND RESTORED

    There are in our existence spots of time,
That with distinct pre-eminence retain
A renovating virtue, whence—depressed   *210*
By false opinion and contentious thought,

Or aught of heavier or more deadly weight,
In trivial occupations, and the round
Of ordinary intercourse—our minds
Are nourished and invisibly repaired;
A virtue, by which pleasure is enhanced,
That penetrates, enables us to mount,
When high, more high, and lifts us up when fallen.
This efficacious spirit chiefly lurks
Among those passages of life that give   220
Profoundest knowledge to what point, and how,
The mind is lord and master—outward sense
The obedient servant of her will.   Such moments
Are scattered everywhere, taking their date
From our first childhood.   I remember well,
That once, while yet my inexperienced hand
Could scarcely hold a bridle, with proud hopes
I mounted, and we journeyed towards the hills:
An ancient servant of my father's house
Was with me, my encourager and guide: 230
We had not travelled long, ere some mischance
Disjoined me from my comrade; and, through fear
Dismounting, down the rough and stony moor
I led my horse, and, stumbling on, at length
Came to a bottom, where in former times
A murderer had been hung in iron chains.
The gibbet-mast had mouldered down, the bones
And iron case were gone; but on the turf,
Hard by, soon after that fell deed was wrought,
Some unknown hand had carved the murderer's name.   240
The monumental letters were inscribed
In times long past; but still, from year to year,
By superstition of the neighbourhood,
The grass is cleared away, and to this hour
The characters are fresh and visible:
A casual glance had shown them, and I fled,
Faltering and faint, and ignorant of the road:
Then, reascending the bare common, saw
A naked pool that lay beneath the hills,
The beacon on the summit, and, more near,   250
A girl, who bore a pitcher on her head,
And seemed with difficult steps to force her way
Against the blowing wind.   It was, in truth,
An ordinary sight; but I should need
Colours and words that are unknown to man,
To paint the visionary dreariness
Which, while I looked all round for my lost guide,
Invested moorland waste and naked pool,

The beacon crowning the lone eminence,
The female and her garments vexed and tossed   *260*
By the strong wind.   When, in the blessèd hours
Of early love, the loved one at my side,
I roamed, in daily presence of this scene,
Upon the naked pool and dreary crags,
And on the melancholy beacon, fell
A spirit of pleasure and youth's golden gleam;
And think ye not with radiance more sublime
For these remembrances, and for the power
They had left behind?   So feeling comes in aid
Of feeling, and diversity of strength   *270*
Attends us, if but once we have been strong.
Oh! mystery of man, from what a depth
Proceed thy honours.   I am lost, but see
In simple childhood something of the base
On which thy greatness stands; but this I feel,
That from thyself it comes, that thou must give,
Else never canst receive.   The days gone by
Return upon me almost from the dawn
Of life: the hiding-places of man's power
Open; I would approach them, but they close.   *280*
I see by glimpses now; when age comes on,
May scarcely see at all; and I would give,
While yet we may, as far as words can give,
Substance and life to what I feel, enshrining,
Such is my hope, the spirit of the Past
For future restoration.

BOOK FOURTEENTH

CONCLUSION

IN one of those excursions (may they ne'er
Fade from remembrance!) through the Northern tracts
Of Cambria ranging with a youthful friend,
I left Bethgelert's huts at couching-time,
And westward took my way, to see the sun
Rise, from the top of Snowdon.   To the door
Of a rude cottage at the mountain's base
We came, and roused the shepherd who attends
The adventurous stranger's steps, a trusty guide;
Then, cheered by short refreshment, sallied forth.   *10*

It was a close, warm, breezeless summer night,
Wan, dull, and glaring, with a dripping fog
Low-hung and thick that covered all the sky;

But, undiscouraged, we began to climb
The mountain-side.   The mist soon girt us round,
And, after ordinary travellers' talk
With our conductor, pensively we sank
Each into commerce with his private thoughts:
Thus did we breast the ascent, and by myself
Was nothing either seen or heard that checked   20
Those musings or diverted, save that once
The shepherd's lurcher, who, among the crags,
Had to his joy unearthed a hedgehog, teased
His coiled-up prey with barkings turbulent.
This small adventure, for even such it seemed
In that wild place and at the dead of night,
Being over and forgotten, on we wound
In silence as before.   With forehead bent
Earthward, as if in opposition set
Against an enemy, I panted up   30
With eager pace, and no less eager thoughts.
Thus might we wear a midnight hour away,
Ascending at loose distance each from each,
And I, as chanced, the foremost of the band;
When at my feet the ground appeared to brighten,
And with a step or two seemed brighter still;
Nor was time given to ask or learn the cause,
For instantly a light upon the turf
Fell like a flash, and lo! as I looked up,
The Moon hung naked in a firmament   40
Of azure without cloud, and at my feet
Rested a silent sea of hoary mist.
A hundred hills their dusky backs upheaved
All over this still ocean; and beyond,
Far, far beyond, the solid vapours stretched,
In headlands, tongues, and promontory shapes,
Into the main Atlantic, that appeared
To dwindle, and give up his majesty,
Usurped upon far as the sight could reach.
Not so the ethereal vault; encroachment none   50
Was there, nor loss; only the inferior stars
Had disappeared, or shed a fainter light
In the clear presence of the full-orbed Moon,
Who, from her sovereign elevation, gazed
Upon the billowy ocean, as it lay
All meek and silent, save that through a rift—
Not distant from the shore wheron we stood,
A fixed, abysmal, gloomy, breathing-place—
Mounted the roar of waters, torrents, streams
Innumerable, roaring with one voice!   60

Heard over earth and sea, and, in that hour,
For so it seemed, felt by the starry heavens.

   When into air had partially dissolved
That vision, given to spirits of the night
And three chance human wanderers, in calm thought
Reflected, it appeared to me the type
Of a majestic intellect, its acts
And its possessions, what it has and craves,
What in itself it is, and would become.
There I beheld the emblem of a mind   70
That feeds upon infinity, that broods
Over the dark abyss, intent to hear
Its voices issuing forth to silent light
In one continuous stream; a mind sustained
By recognitions of transcendent power,
In sense conducting to ideal form,
In soul of more than mortal privilege.
One function, above all, of such a mind
Had Nature shadowed there, by putting forth,
'Mid circumstances awful and sublime,   80
That mutual domination which she loves
To exert upon the face of outward things,
So moulded, joined, abstracted, so endowed
With interchangeable supremacy,
That men, least sensitive, see, hear, perceive,
And cannot choose but feel.   The power, which all
Acknowledge when thus moved, which Nature thus
To bodily sense exhibits, is the express
Resemblance of that glorious faculty
That higher minds bear with them as their own.   90
This is the very spirit in which they deal
With the whole compass of the universe:
They from their native selves can send abroad
Kindred mutations; for themselves create
A like existence; and, whene'er it dawns
Created for them, catch it, or are caught
By its inevitable mastery,
Like angels stopped upon the wing by sound
Of harmony from Heaven's remotest spheres.
Them the enduring and the transient both   100
Serve to exalt; they build up greatest things
From least suggestions; ever on the watch,
Willing to work and to be wrought upon,
They need not extraordinary calls
To rouse them; in a world of life they live,
By sensible impressions not enthralled,

But by their quickening impulse made more prompt
To hold fit converse with the spiritual world,
And with the generations of mankind
Spread over time, past, present, and to come,   *110*
Age after age, till Time shall be no more.

From THE EXCURSION

                      Supine the Wanderer lay,
His eyes as if in drowsiness half shut,
The shadows of the breezy elms above   *440*
Dappling his face.   He had not heard the sound
Of my approaching steps, and in the shade
Unnoticed did I stand some minutes' space.
At length I hailed him, seeing that his hat
Was moist with water-drops, as if the brim
Had newly scooped a running stream.   He rose,
And ere our lively greeting into peace
Had settled, ''Tis,' said I, 'a burning day:
My lips are parched with thirst, but you, it seems,
Have somewhere found relief.'   He, at the word,   *450*
Pointing towards a sweet-briar, bade me climb
The fence where that aspiring shrub looked out
Upon the public way.   It was a plot

Of garden ground run wild, its matted weeds
Marked with the steps of those, whom, as they passed,
The gooseberry trees that shot in long lank slips,
Or currants, hanging from their leafless stems,
In scanty strings, had tempted to o'erleap
The broken wall.   I looked around, and there,
Where two tall hedge-rows of thick alder boughs   *460*
Joined in a cold damp nook, espied a well
Shrouded with willow-flowers and plumy fern.
My thirst I slaked, and, from the cheerless spot
Withdrawing, straightway to the shade returned
Where sate the old Man on the cottage-bench;
And, while, beside him, with uncovered head,
I yet was standing, freely to respire,
And cool my temples in the fanning air,
Thus did he speak.   'I see around me here
Things which you cannot see: we die, my Friend,   *470*
Nor we alone, but that which each man loved
And prized in his peculiar nook of earth
Dies with him, or is changed; and very soon
Even of the good is no memorial left.
—The Poets, in their elegies and songs
Lamenting the departed, call the groves,
They call upon the hills and streams, to mourn,
And senseless rocks; nor idly; for they speak,
In these their invocations, with a voice
Obedient to the strong creative power   *480*
Of human passion.   Sympathies there are
More tranquil, yet perhaps of kindred birth,
That steal upon the meditative mind,
And grow with thought.   Beside yon spring I stood,
And eyed its waters till we seemed to feel
One sadness, they and I.   For them a bond
Of brotherhood is broken: time has been
When, every day, the touch of human hand
Dislodged the natural sleep that binds them up
In mortal stillness; and they ministered   *490*
To human comfort.   Stooping down to drink,
Upon the slimy foot-stone I espied
The useless fragment of a wooden bowl,
Green with the moss of years, and subject only
To the soft handling of the elements:
There let it lie—how foolish are such thoughts!
Forgive them;—never—never did my steps
Approach this door but she who dwelt within
A daughter's welcome gave me, and I loved her
As my own child.   Oh, Sir! the good die first,   *500*

And they whose hearts are dry as summer dust
Burn to the socket.   Many a passenger
Hath blessed poor Margaret for her gentle looks,
When she upheld the cool refreshment drawn
From that forsaken spring; and no one came
But he was welcome; no one went away
But that it seemed she loved him.   She is dead,
The light extinguished of her lonely hut,
The hut itself abandoned to decay,
And she forgotten in the quiet grave.   510

   'I speak,' continued he, 'of One whose stock
Of virtues bloomed beneath this lonely roof.
She was a Woman of a steady mind,
Tender and deep in her excess of love;
Not speaking much, pleased rather with the joy
Of her own thoughts: by some especial care
Her temper had been framed, as if to make
A Being, who by adding love to peace
Might live on earth a life of happiness.
Her wedded Partner lacked not on his side   520
The humble worth that satisfied her heart:
Frugal, affectionate, sober, and withal
Keenly industrious.   She with pride would tell
That he was often seated at his loom,
In summer, ere the mower was abroad
Among the dewy grass,—in early spring,
Ere the last star had vanished.—They who passed
At evening, from behind the garden fence
Might hear his busy spade, which he would ply,
After his daily work, until the light   530
Had failed, and every leaf and flower were lost
In the dark hedges.   So their days were spent
In peace and comfort; and a pretty boy
Was their best hope, next to the God in heaven.

   'Not twenty years ago, but you I think
Can scarcely bear it now in mind, there came
Two blighting seasons, when the fields were left
With half a harvest.   It pleased Heaven to add
A worse affliction in the plague of war:
This happy Land was stricken to the heart!   540
A Wanderer then among the cottages,
I, with my freight of winter raiment, saw
The hardships of that season: many rich
Sank down, as in a dream, among the poor;
And of the poor did many cease to be,

And their place knew them not.   Meanwhile, abridged
Of daily comforts, gladly reconciled
To numerous self-denials, Margaret
Went struggling on through those calamitous years
With cheerful hope, until the second autumn,   *550*
When her life's Helpmate on a sick-bed lay,
Smitten with perilous fever.   In disease
He lingered long; and, when his strength returned,
He found the little he had stored, to meet
The hour of accident or crippling age,
Was all consumed.   A second infant now
Was added to the troubles of a time
Laden, for them and all of their degree,
With care and sorrow; shoals of artisans
From ill-requited labour turned adrift   *560*
Sought daily bread from public charity,
They, and their wives and children—happier far
Could they have lived as do the little birds
That peck along the hedge-rows, or the kite
That makes her dwelling on the mountain rocks!

   'A sad reverse it was for him who long
Had filled with plenty, and possessed in peace,
This lonely Cottage.   At the door he stood,
And whistled many a snatch of merry tunes
That had no mirth in them; or with his knife   *570*
Carved uncouth figures on the heads of sticks—
Then, not less idly, sought, through every nook
In house or garden, any casual work
Of use or ornament; and with a strange,
Amusing, yet uneasy, novelty,
He mingled, where he might, the various tasks
Of summer, autumn, winter, and of spring.
But this endured not; his good humour soon
Became a weight in which no pleasure was:
And poverty brought on a petted mood   *580*
And a sore temper: day by day he drooped,
And he would leave his work—and to the town
Would turn without an errand his slack steps;
Or wander here and there among the fields.
One while he would speak lightly of his babes,
And with a cruel tongue: at other times
He tossed them with a false unnatural joy:
And 'twas a rueful thing to see the looks
Of the poor innocent children.   "Every smile,"
Said Margaret to me, here beneath these trees,   *590*
"Made my heart bleed."'

                          At this the Wanderer paused;
And, looking up to those enormous elms,
He said, "'Tis now the hour of deepest noon.
At this still season of repose and peace,
This hour when all things which are not at rest
Are cheerful; while this multitude of flies
With tuneful hum is filling all the air;
Why should a tear be on an old Man's cheek?
Why should we thus, with an untoward mind,
And in the weakness of humanity,   *600*
From natural wisdom turn our hearts away;
To natural comfort shut our eyes and ears;
And, feeding on disquiet, thus disturb
The calm of nature with our restless thoughts?'

                    —————

HE spake with somewhat of a solemn tone:
But, when he ended, there was in his face
Such easy cheerfulness, a look so mild,
That for a little time it stole away
All recollection; and that simple tale
Passed from my mind like a forgotten sound.   *610*
A while on trivial things we held discourse,
To me soon tasteless.   In my own despite,
I thought of that poor Woman as of one
Whom I had known and loved.   He had rehearsed
Her homely tale with such familiar power,
With such an active countenance, an eye
So busy, that the things of which he spake
Seemed present; and, attention now relaxed,
A heart-felt chillness crept along my veins.
I rose; and, having left the breezy shade,   *620*
Stood drinking comfort from the warmer sun,
That had not cheered me long—ere, looking round
Upon that tranquil Ruin, I returned,
And begged of the old Man that, for my sake,
He would resume his story.

                          He replied,
'It were a wantonness, and would demand
Severe reproof, if we were men whose hearts
Could hold vain dalliance with the misery
Even of the dead; contented thence to draw
A momentary pleasure, never marked   *630*
By reason, barren of all future good.
But we have known that there is often found
In mournful thoughts, and always might be found,

A power to virtue friendly; were't not so,
I am a dreamer among men, indeed
An idle dreamer! 'Tis a common tale,
An ordinary sorrow of man's life,
A tale of silent suffering, hardly clothed
In bodily form.—But without further bidding
I will proceed.   640
                        While thus it fared with them,
To whom this cottage, till those hapless years,
Had been a blessed home, it was my chance
To travel in a country far remote;
And when these lofty elms once more appeared
What pleasant expectations lured me on
O'er the flat Common!—With quick step I reached
The threshold, lifted with light hand the latch;
But, when I entered, Margaret looked at me
A little while; then turned her head away
Speechless,—and, sitting down upon a chair,   650
Wept bitterly.   I wist not what to do,
Nor how to speak to her.   Poor Wretch! at last
She rose from off her seat, and then,—O Sir!
I cannot *tell* how she pronounced my name:—
With fervent love, and with a face of grief
Unutterably helpless, and a look
That seemed to cling upon me, she inquired
If I had seen her husband.   As she spake
A strange surprise and fear came to my heart,
Nor had I power to answer ere she told   660
That he had disappeared—not two months gone.
He left his house: two wretched days had past,
And on the third, as wistfully she raised
Her head from off her pillow to look forth,
Like one in trouble, for returning light,
Within her chamber-casement she espied
A folded paper, lying as if placed
To meet her waking eyes.   This tremblingly
She opened—found no writing, but beheld
Pieces of money carefully enclosed,   670
Silver and gold.   "I shuddered at the sight,"
Said Margaret, "for I knew it was his hand
That must have placed it there; and ere that day
Was ended, that long anxious day, I learned,
From one who by my husband had been sent
With the sad news, that he had joined a troop
Of soldiers, going to a distant land.
—He left me thus—he could not gather heart
To take farewell of me; for he feared

That I should follow with my babes, and sink   680
Beneath the misery of that wandering life."

'This tale did Margaret tell with many tears:
And, when she ended, I had little power
To give her comfort, and was glad to take
Such words of hope from her own mouth as served
To cheer us both.   But long we had not talked
Ere we built up a pile of better thoughts,
And with a brighter eye she looked around
As if she had been shedding tears of joy.
We parted.—'Twas the time of early spring;   690
I left her busy with her garden tools;
And well remember, o'er that fence she looked,
And, while I paced along the foot-way path,
Called out, and sent a blessing after me,
With tender cheerfulness, and with a voice
That seemed the very sound of happy thoughts.

'I roved o'er many a hill and many a dale,
With my accustomed load; in heat and cold,
Through many a wood and many an open ground,
In sunshine and in shade, in wet and fair,   700
Drooping or blithe of heart, as might befall;
My best companions now the driving winds,
And now the "trotting brooks" and whispering trees,
And now the music of my own sad steps,
With many a short-lived thought that passed between,
And disappeared.   I journeyed back this way,
When, in the warmth of midsummer, the wheat
Was yellow; and the soft and bladed grass,
Springing afresh, had o'er the hay-field spread
Its tender verdure.   At the door arrived,   710
I found that she was absent.   In the shade,
Where now we sit, I waited her return.
Her cottage, then a cheerful object, wore
Its customary look,—only, it seemed,
The honeysuckle, crowding round the porch,
Hung down in heavier tufts; and that bright weed,
The yellow stone-crop, suffered to take root
Along the window's edge, profusely grew,
Blinding the lower panes.   I turned aside,
And strolled into her garden.   It appeared   720
To lag behind the season, and had lost
Its pride of neatness.   Daisy-flowers and thrift

Had broken their trim border-lines, and straggled
O'er paths they used to deck: carnations, once
Prized for surpassing beauty, and no less
For the peculiar pains they had required,
Declined their languid heads, wanting support.
The cumbrous bind-weed, with its wreaths and bells,
Had twined about her two small rows of peas,
And dragged them to the earth.   730
                              Ere this an hour
Was wasted.—Back I turned my restless steps;
A stranger passed; and, guessing whom I sought,
He said that she was used to ramble far.—
The sun was sinking in the west; and now
I sate with sad impatience.   From within
Her solitary infant cried aloud;
Then, like a blast that dies away self-stilled,
The voice was silent.   From the bench I rose;
But neither could divert nor soothe my thoughts.
The spot, though fair, was very desolate—   740
The longer I remained, more desolate:
And, looking round me, now I first observed
The corner stones, on either side the porch,
With dull red stains discoloured, and stuck o'er
With tufts and hairs of wool, as if the sheep,
That fed upon the Common, thither came
Familiarly, and found a couching-place
Even at her threshold.   Deeper shadows fell
From these tall elms; the cottage-clock struck eight;—
I turned, and saw her distant a few steps.   750
Her face was pale and thin—her figure, too,
Was changed.   As she unlocked the door, she said,
"It grieves me you have waited here so long,
But, in good truth, I've wandered much of late;
And sometimes—to my shame I speak—have need
Of my best prayers to bring me back again."
While on the board she spread our evening meal,
She told me—interrupting not the work
Which gave employment to her listless hands—
That she had parted with her elder child;   760
To a kind master on a distant farm
Now happily apprenticed.—"I perceive
You look at me, and you have cause; to-day
I have been travelling far; and many days
About the fields I wander, knowing this
Only, that what I seek I cannot find;
And so I waste my time: for I am changed;
And to myself," said she, "have done much wrong

And to this helpless infant.   I have slept
Weeping, and weeping have I waked; my tears   770
Have flowed as if my body were not such
As others are; and I could never die.
But I am now in mind and in my heart
More easy; and I hope," said she, "that God
Will give me patience to endure the things
Which I behold at home."
                              It would have grieved
Your very soul to see her.   Sir, I feel
The story linger in my heart; I fear
'Tis long and tedious; but my spirit clings
To that poor Woman:—so familiarly   780
Do I perceive her manner, and her look,
And presence; and so deeply do I feel
Her goodness, that, not seldom, in my walks
A momentary trance comes over me;
And to myself I seem to muse on One
By sorrow laid asleep; or borne away,
A human being destined to awake
To human life, or something very near
To human life, when he shall come again
For whom she suffered.   Yes, it would have grieved   790
Your very soul to see her: evermore
Her eyelids drooped, her eyes downward were cast;
And, when she at her table gave me food,
She did not look at me.   Her voice was low,
Her body was subdued.   In every act
Pertaining to her house-affairs, appeared
The careless stillness of a thinking mind
Self-occupied; to which all outward things
Are like an idle matter.   Still she sighed,
But yet no motion of the breast was seen,   800
No heaving of the heart.   While by the fire
We sate together, sighs came on my ear,
I knew not how, and hardly whence they came.

   'Ere my departure, to her care I gave,
For her son's use, some tokens of regard,
Which with a look of welcome she received;
And I exhorted her to place her trust
In God's good love, and seek His help by prayer.
I took my staff, and, when I kissed her babe,
The tears stood in her eyes.   I left her then   810
With the best hope and comfort I could give:
She thanked me for my wish;—but for my hope
It seemed she did not thank me.

                                        I returned,
And took my rounds along this road again
When on its sunny bank the primrose flower
Peeped forth, to give an earnest of the Spring.
I found her sad and drooping: she had learned
No tidings of her husband; if he lived,
She knew not that he lived; if he were dead,
She knew not he was dead.   She seemed the same   *820*
In person and appearance; but her house
Bespake a sleepy hand of negligence;
The floor was neither dry nor neat, the hearth
Was comfortless, and her small lot of books,
Which, in the cottage-window, heretofore
Had been piled up against the corner panes
In seemly order, now, with straggling leaves
Lay scattered here and there, open or shut,
As they had chanced to fall.   Her infant Babe
Had from his Mother caught the trick of grief,   *830*
And sighed among its playthings.   I withdrew,
And once again entering the garden saw,
More plainly still, that poverty and grief
Were now come nearer to her: weeds defaced
The hardened soil, and knots of withered grass:
No ridges there appeared of clear black mould,
No winter greenness; of her herbs and flowers,
It seemed the better part were gnawed away
Or trampled into earth; a chain of straw,
Which had been twined about the slender stem   *840*
Of a young apple-tree, lay at its root;
The bark was nibbled round by truant sheep.
—Margaret stood near, her infant in her arms,
And, noting that my eye was on the tree,
She said, "I fear it will be dead and gone
Ere Robert come again."   When to the House
We had returned together, she inquired
If I had any hope:—but for her babe
And for her little orphan boy, she said,
She had no wish to live, that she must die   *850*
Of sorrow.   Yet I saw the idle loom
Still in its place; his Sunday garments hung
Upon the selfsame nail; his very staff
Stood undisturbed behind the door.
                                        And when,
In bleak December, I retraced this way,
She told me that her little babe was dead,
And she was left alone.   She now, released
From her maternal cares, had taken up

The employment common through these wilds, and gained,
By spinning hemp, a pittance for herself;   860
And for this end had hired a neighbour's boy
To give her needful help.   That very time
Most willingly she put her work aside,
And walked with me along the miry road,
Heedless how far; and, in such piteous sort
That any heart that ached to hear her, begged
That, wheresoe'er I went, I still would ask
For him whom she had lost.   We parted then—
Our final parting; for from that time forth
Did many seasons pass ere I returned   870
Into this tract again.
                              Nine tedious years;
From their first separation, nine long years,
She lingered in unquiet widowhood;
A Wife and Widow.   Needs must it have been
A sore heart-wasting!   I have heard, my Friend,
That in yon arbour oftentimes she sate
Alone, through half the vacant sabbath day;
And, if a dog passed by, she still would quit
The shade and look abroad.   On this old bench
For hours she sate; and evermore her eye   880
Was busy in the distance, shaping things
That made her heart beat quick.   You see that path,
Now faint,—the grass has crept o'er its grey line;
There, to and fro, she paced through many a day
Of the warm summer, from a belt of hemp
That girt her waist, spinning the long-drawn thread
With backward steps.   Yet ever as there passed
A man whose garments showed the soldier's red,
Or crippled mendicant in sailor's garb,
The little child who sate to turn the wheel   890
Ceased from his task; and she with faltering voice
Made many a fond inquiry; and when they,
Whose presence gave no comfort, were gone by,
Her heart was still more sad.   And by yon gate,
That bars the traveller's road, she often stood,
And when a stranger horseman came, the latch
Would lift, and in his face look wistfully;
Most happy, if, from aught discovered there
Of tender feeling, she might dare repeat
The same sad question.   Meanwhile her poor Hut   900
Sank to decay; for he was gone, whose hand,
At the first nipping of October frost,
Closed up each chink, and with fresh bands of straw
Chequered the green-grown thatch.   And so she lived

Through the long winter, reckless and alone;
Until her house by frost, and thaw, and rain,
Was sapped; and while she slept, the nightly damps
Did chill her breast; and in the stormy day
Her tattered clothes were ruffled by the wind,
Even at the side of her own fire.   Yet still   *910*
She loved this wretched spot, nor would for worlds
Have parted hence; and still that length of road,
And this rude bench, one torturing hope endeared,
Fast rooted at her heart: and here, my Friend,—
In sickness she remained; and here she died;
Last human tenant of these ruined walls!'

   The old Man ceased: he saw that I was moved;
From that low bench, rising instinctively
I turned aside in weakness, nor had power
To thank him for the tale which he had told.   *920*
I stood, and leaning o'er the garden wall
Reviewed that Woman's sufferings; and it seemed
To comfort me while with a brother's love
I blessed her in the impotence of grief.
Then towards the cottage I returned; and traced
Fondly, though with an interest more mild,
That secret spirit of humanity
Which, 'mid the calm oblivious tendencies
Of nature, 'mid her plants, and weeds, and flowers,
And silent overgrowings, still survived.   *930*
The old Man, noting this, resumed, and said,
'My Friend! enough to sorrow you have given,
The purposes of wisdom ask no more:
Nor more would she have craved as due to One
Who, in her worst distress, had ofttimes felt
The unbounded might of prayer; and learned, with soul
Fixed on the Cross, that consolation springs,
From sources deeper far than deepest pain,
For the meek Sufferer.   Why then should we read
The forms of things with an unworthy eye?   *940*
She sleeps in the calm earth, and peace is here.
I well remember that those very plumes,
Those weeds, and the high spear-grass on that wall,
By mist and silent rain-drops silvered o'er,
As once I passed, into my heart conveyed
So still an image of tranquillity,
So calm and still, and looked so beautiful
Amid the uneasy thoughts which filled my mind,
That what we feel of sorrow and despair
From ruin and from change, and all the grief   *950*

That passing shows of Being leave behind,
Appeared an idle dream, that could maintain,
Nowhere, dominion o'er the enlightened spirit
Whose meditative sympathies repose
Upon the breast of Faith.   I turned away,
And walked along my road in happiness.'

   He ceased.   Ere long the sun declining shot
A slant and mellow radiance, which began
To fall upon us, while, beneath the trees,
We sate on that low bench: and now we felt,   960
Admonished thus, the sweet hour coming on.
A linnet warbled from those lofty elms,
A thrush sang loud, and other melodies,
At distance heard, peopled the milder air.
The old Man rose, and, with a sprightly mien
Of hopeful preparation, grasped his staff;
Together casting then a farewell look
Upon those silent walls, we left the shade;
And, ere the stars were visible, had reached
A village-inn,—our evening resting-place.   970

THE WHITE DOE OF RYLSTONE;
OR, THE FATE OF THE NORTONS

'Action is transitory—a step, a blow,
The motion of a muscle—this way or that—
'Tis done; and in the after-vacancy
We wonder at ourselves like men betrayed:
Suffering is permanent, obscure and dark,
And has the nature of infinity.
Yet through that darkness (infinite though it seem
And irremoveable) gracious openings lie,
By which the soul—with patient steps of thought
Now toiling, wafted now on wings of prayer—
May pass in hope, and, though from mortal bonds
Yet undelivered, rise with sure ascent
Even to the fountain-head of peace divine.'

'They that deny a God, destroy Man's nobility: for certainly Man is
of kinn to the Beast by his Body; and if he be not of kinn to God by his
Spirit, he is a base, ignoble Creature. It destroys likewise Magnanimity,
and the raising of humane Nature: for take an example of a Dog, and
mark what a generosity and courage he will put on, when he finds himself
maintained by a Man, who to him is instead of a God, or Melior Natura.
Which courage is manifestly such, as that Creature without that con-
fidence of a better Nature than his own could never attain. So Man,
when he resteth and assureth himself upon Divine protection and favour,
gathereth a force and faith which human Nature in itself could not
obtain.'

LORD BACON.

CANTO FIRST

FROM Bolton's old monastic tower
    The bells ring loud with gladsome power;
The sun shines bright; the fields are gay
With people in their best array
Of stole and doublet, hood and scarf,
Along the banks of crystal Wharf,
Through the Vale retired and lowly,
Trooping to that summons holy.
And, up among the moorlands, see
What sprinklings of blithe company!   *10*
Of lasses and of shepherd grooms,
That down the steep hills force their way,
Like cattle through the budded brooms;
Path, or no path, what care they?
And thus in joyous mood they hie
To Bolton's mouldering Priory.
    What would they there?—Full fifty years
That sumptuous Pile, with all its peers,
Too harshly hath been doomed to taste
The bitterness of wrong and waste: *20*

Its courts are ravaged; but the tower
Is standing with a voice of power,
That ancient voice which wont to call
To mass or some high festival;
And in the shattered fabric's heart
Remaineth one protected part;
A Chapel, like a wild-bird's nest,
Closely embowered and trimly drest;
And thither young and old repair,
This Sabbath-day, for praise and prayer.   30
    Fast the churchyard fills;—anon
Look again, and they all are gone;
The cluster round the porch, and the folk
Who sate in the shade of the Prior's Oak!
And scarcely have they disappeared
Ere the prelusive hymn is heard:—
With one consent the people rejoice,
Filling the church with a lofty voice!
They sing a service which they feel:
For 'tis the sunrise now of zeal;   40
Of a pure faith the vernal prime—
In great Eliza's golden time.
    A moment ends the fervent din,
And all is hushed, without and within;
For though the priest, more tranquilly,
Recites the holy liturgy,
The only voice which you can hear
Is the river murmuring near.
—When soft!—the dusky trees between,
And down the path through the open green,   50
Where is no living thing to be seen;
And through yon gateway, where is found,
Beneath the arch with ivy bound,
Free entrance to the churchyard ground—
Comes gliding in with lovely gleam,
Comes gliding in serene and slow,
Soft and silent as a dream,
A solitary Doe!
White she is as lily of June,
And beauteous as the silver moon   60
When out of sight the clouds are driven
And she is left alone in heaven;
Or like a ship some gentle day
In sunshine sailing far away,
A glittering ship, that hath the plain
Of ocean for her own domain.

    Lie silent in your graves, ye dead!
Lie quiet in your churchyard bed!
Ye living, tend your holy cares;
Ye multitude, pursue your prayers;   70
And blame not me if my heart and sight
Are occupied with one delight!
'Tis a work for sabbath hours
If I with this bright Creature go:
Whether she be of forest bowers,
From the bowers of earth below;
Or a Spirit for one day given,
A pledge of grace from purest heaven.
    What harmonious pensive changes
Wait upon her as she ranges   80
Round and through this Pile of state
Overthrown and desolate!
Now a step or two her way
Leads through space of open day,
Where the enamoured sunny light
Brightens her that was so bright;
Now doth a delicate shadow fall,
Falls upon her like a breath,
From some lofty arch or wall,
As she passes underneath: 90
Now some gloomy nook partakes
Of the glory that she makes,—
High-ribbed vault of stone, or cell,
With perfect cunning framed as well
Of stone, and ivy, and the spread
Of the elder's bushy head;
Some jealous and forbidding cell,
That doth the living stars repel,
And where no flower hath leave to dwell.
    The presence of this wandering Doe   100
Fills many a damp obscure recess
With lustre of a saintly show;
And, reappearing, she no less
Sheds on the flowers that round her blow
A more than sunny liveliness.
But say, among these holy places,
Which thus assiduously she paces,
Comes she with a votary's task,
Rite to perform, or boon to ask?
Fair Pilgrim! harbours she a sense   110
Of sorrow, or of reverence?
Can she be grieved for quire or shrine,
Crushed as if by wrath divine?

For what survives of house where God
Was worshipped, or where Man abode;
For old magnificence undone;
Or for the gentler work begun
By Nature, softening and concealing,
And busy with a hand of healing?
Mourns she for lordly chamber's hearth   *120*
That to the sapling ash gives birth;
For dormitory's length laid bare
Where the wild rose blossoms fair;
Or altar, whence the cross was rent,
Now rich with mossy ornament?
—She sees a warrior carved in stone,
Among the thick weeds, stretched alone;
A warrior, with his shield of pride
Cleaving humbly to his side,
And hands in resignation prest,   *130*
Palm to palm, on his tranquil breast;
As little she regards the sight
As a common creature might:
If she be doomed to inward care,
Or service, it must lie elsewhere.
—But hers are eyes serenely bright,
And on she moves—with pace how light!
Nor spares to stoop her head, and taste
The dewy turf with flowers bestrown;
And thus she fares, until at last   *140*
Beside the ridge of a grassy grave
In quietness she lays her down;
Gentle as a weary wave
Sinks, when the summer breeze hath died
Against an anchored vessel's side;
Even so, without distress, doth she
Lie down in peace, and lovingly.
   The day is placid in its going,
To a lingering motion bound,
Like the crystal stream now flowing   *150*
With its softest summer sound:
So the balmy minutes pass,
While this radiant Creature lies
Couched upon the dewy grass,
Pensively with downcast eyes.
—But now again the people raise
With awful cheer a voice of praise;
It is the last, the parting song;
And from the temple forth they throng,
And quickly spread themselves abroad,   *160*

While each pursues his several road.
But some—a variegated band
Of middle-aged, and old, and young,
And little children by the hand
Upon their leading mothers hung—
With mute obeisance gladly paid
Turn towards the spot, where, full in view,
The white Doe, to her service true,
Her sabbath couch has made.
   It was a solitary mound;   *170*
Which two spears' length of level ground
Did from all other graves divide:
As if in some respect of pride;
Or melancholy's sickly mood,
Still shy of human neighbourhood;
Or guilt, that humbly would express
A penitential loneliness.
   'Look! there she is, my Child! draw near;
She fears not, wherefore should we fear?
She means no harm;'—but still the Boy,   *180*
To whom the words were softly said,
Hung back, and smiled, and blushed for joy,
A shame-faced blush of glowing red!
Again the Mother whispered low,
'Now you have seen the famous Doe;
From Rylstone she hath found her way
Over the hills this sabbath day;
Her work, whate'er it be, is done,
And she will depart when we are gone;
Thus doth she keep, from year to year,   *190*
Her sabbath morning, foul or fair.'
   Bright was the Creature, as in dreams
The Boy had seen her, yea, more bright;
But is she truly what she seems?
He asks with insecure delight,
Asks of himself, and doubts,—and still
The doubt returns against his will:
Though he, and all the standers-by,
Could tell a tragic history
Of facts divulged, wherein appear   *200*
Substantial motive, reason clear,
Why thus the milk-white Doe is found
Couchant beside that lonely mound;
And why she duly loves to pace
The circuit of this hallowed place.
Nor to the Child's inquiring mind
Is such perplexity confined:

For, spite of sober Truth that sees
A world of fixed remembrances
Which to this mystery belong,   *210*
If, undeceived, my skill can trace
The characters of every face,
There lack not strange delusion here,
Conjecture vague, and idle fear,
And superstitious fancies strong,
Which do the gentle Creature wrong.
    That bearded, staff-supported Sire—
Who in his boyhood often fed
Full cheerily on convent-bread
And heard old tales by the convent-fire,   *220*
And to his grave will go with scars,
Relics of long and distant wars—
That Old Man, studious to expound
The spectacle, is mounting high
To days of dim antiquity;
When Lady Aäliza mourned
Her Son, and felt in her despair
The pang of unavailing prayer;
Her Son in Wharf's abysses drowned,
The noble Boy of Egremound.   *230*
From which affliction—when the grace
Of God had in her heart found place—
A pious structure, fair to see,
Rose up, this stately Priory!
The Lady's work;—but now laid low;
To the grief of her soul that doth come and go,
In the beautiful form of this innocent Doe:
Which, though seemingly doomed in its breast to sustain
A softened remembrance of sorrow and pain,
Is spotless, and holy, and gentle, and bright;   *240*
And glides o'er the earth like an angel of light.
    Pass, pass who will, yon chantry door;
And, through the chink in the fractured floor
Look down, and see a griesly sight;
A vault where the bodies are buried upright!
There, face by face, and hand by hand,
The Claphams and Mauleverers stand;
And, in his place, among son and sire,
Is John de Clapham, that fierce Esquire,
A valiant man, and a name of dread   *250*
In the ruthless wars of the White and Red;
Who dragged Earl Pembroke from Banbury church
And smote off his head on the stones of the porch!
Look down among them, if you dare;

Oft does the White Doe loiter there,
Prying into the darksome rent;
Nor can it be with good intent:
So thinks that Dame of haughty air,
Who hath a Page her book to hold,
And wears a frontlet edged with gold.   260
Harsh thoughts with her high mood agree—
Who counts among her ancestry
Earl Pembroke, slain so impiously!
    That slender Youth, a scholar pale,
From Oxford come to his native vale,
He also hath his own conceit:
It is, thinks he, the gracious Fairy,
Who loved the Shepherd-lord to meet
In his wanderings solitary:
Wild notes she in his hearing sang,   270
A song of Nature's hidden powers;
That whistled like the wind, and rang
Among the rocks and holly bowers.
'Twas said that She all shapes could wear;
And oftentimes before him stood,
Amid the trees of some thick wood,
In semblance of a lady fair;
And taught him signs, and showed him sights,
In Craven's dens, on Cumbrian heights;
When under cloud of fear he lay,   280
A shepherd clad in homely grey;
Nor left him at his later day.
And hence, when he, with spear and shield,
Rode full of years to Flodden-field,
His eye could see the hidden spring,
And how the current was to flow;
The fatal end of Scotland's King,
And all that hopeless overthrow.
But not in wars did he delight,
This Clifford wished for worthier might;   290
Nor in broad pomp, or courtly state;
Him his own thoughts did elevate,—
Most happy in the shy recess
Of Barden's lowly quietness.
And choice of studious friends had he
Of Bolton's dear fraternity;
Who, standing on this old church tower,
In many a calm propitious hour,
Perused, with him, the starry sky;
Or, in their cells, with him did pry   300
For other lore,—by keen desire

Urged to close toil with chemic fire;
In quest belike of transmutations
Rich as the mine's most bright creations.
But they and their good works are fled,
And all is now disquieted—
And peace is none, for living or dead!
　　Ah, pensive Scholar, think not so,
But look again at the radiant Doe!
What quiet watch she seems to keep　　　　310
Alone, beside that grassy heap!
Why mention other thoughts unmeet
For vision so composed and sweet?
While stand the people in a ring,
Gazing, doubting, questioning;
Yea, many overcome in spite
Of recollections clear and bright;
Which yet do unto some impart
An undisturbed repose of heart.
And all the assembly own a law　　　　320
Of orderly respect and awe;
But see—they vanish one by one,
And last, the Doe herself is gone.
　　Harp! we have been full long beguiled
By vague thoughts, lured by fancies wild;
To which, with no reluctant strings,
Thou hast attuned thy murmurings;
And now before this Pile we stand
In solitude, and utter peace:
But, Harp! thy murmurs may not cease—　　330
A Spirit, with his angelic wings,
In soft and breeze-like visitings,
Has touched thee—and a Spirit's hand:
A voice is with us—a command
To chant, in strains of heavenly glory,
A tale of tears, a mortal story!

CANTO SECOND

THE Harp in lowliness obeyed;
And first we sang of the greenwood shade
And a solitary Maid;
Beginning, where the song must end,
With her, and with her sylvan Friend;
The Friend who stood before her sight,
Her only unextinguished light;
Her last companion in a dearth
Of love, upon a hopeless earth.

For She it was—this Maid, who wrought   *10*
Meekly, with foreboding thought,
In vermeil colours and in gold
An unblest work; which, standing by,
Her Father did with joy behold,—
Exulting in its imagery;
A Banner, fashioned to fulfil
Too perfectly his headstrong will:
For on his Banner had her hand
Embroidered (such her Sire's command)
The sacred Cross; and figured there   *20*
The five dear wounds our Lord did bear;
Full soon to be uplifted high,
And float in rueful company!
    It was the time when England's Queen
Twelve years had reigned, a Sovereign dread;
Nor yet the restless crown had been
Disturbed upon her virgin head;
But now the inly-working North
Was ripe to send its thousands forth,
A potent vassalage, to fight   *30*
In Percy's and in Neville's right,
Two Earls fast leagued in discontent,
Who gave their wishes open vent;
And boldly urged a general plea,
The rites of ancient piety
To be triumphantly restored,
By the stern justice of the sword!
And that same Banner, on whose breast
The blameless Lady had exprest
Memorials chosen to give life   *40*
And sunshine to a dangerous strife;
That Banner, waiting for the Call,
Stood quietly in Rylstone-hall.
    It came; and Francis Norton said,
'O Father! rise not in this fray—
The hairs are white upon your head;
Dear Father, hear me when I say
It is for you too late a day!
Bethink you of your own good name:
A just and gracious Queen have we,   *50*
A pure religion, and the claim
Of peace on our humanity.—
'Tis meet that I endure your scorn;
I am your son, your eldest born;
But not for lordship or for land,
My Father, do I clasp your knees;

The Banner touch not, stay your hand,
This multitude of men disband,
And live at home in blameless ease;
For these my brethren's sake, for me;   *60*
And, most of all, for Emily!'
  Tumultuous noises filled the hall;
And scarcely could the Father hear
That name—pronounced with a dying fall—
The name of his only Daughter dear,
As on the banner which stood near
He glanced a look of holy pride,
And his moist eyes were glorified;
Then did he seize the staff, and say:
'Thou, Richard, bear'st thy father's name,   *70*
Keep thou this ensign till the day
When I of thee require the same:
Thy place be on my better hand;—
And seven as true as thou, I see,
Will cleave to this good cause and me.'
He spake, and eight brave sons straightway
All followed him, a gallant band!
  Thus, with his sons, when forth he came
The sight was hailed with loud acclaim
And din of arms and minstrelsy,   *80*
From all his warlike tenantry,
All horsed and harnessed with him to ride,—
A voice to which the hills replied!
  But Francis, in the vacant hall,
Stood silent under dreary weight,—
A phantasm, in which roof and wall
Shook, tottered, swam before his sight;
A phantasm like a dream of night!
Thus overwhelmed, and desolate,
He found his way to a postern-gate;   *90*
And, when he waked, his languid eye
Was on the calm and silent sky;
With air about him breathing sweet,
And earth's green grass beneath his feet;
Nor did he fail ere long to hear
A sound of military cheer,
Faint—but it reached that sheltered spot;
He heard, and it disturbed him not.
  There stood he, leaning on a lance
Which he had grasped unknowingly,   *100*
Had blindly grasped in that strong trance,
That dimness of heart-agony;
There stood he, cleansed from the despair

And sorrow of his fruitless prayer.
The past he calmly hath reviewed:
But where will be the fortitude
Of this brave man, when he shall see
That Form beneath the spreading tree,
And know that it is Emily?
  He saw her where in open view   *110*
She sate beneath the spreading yew—
Her head upon her lap, concealing
In solitude her bitter feeling:
'Might ever son *command* a sire,
The act were justified to-day.'
This to himself—and to the Maid,
Whom now he had approached, he said—
'Gone are they,—they have their desire;
And I with thee one hour will stay.
To give thee comfort if I may.'   *120*
  She heard, but looked not up, nor spake;
And sorrow moved him to partake
Her silence; then his thoughts turned round,
And fervent words a passage found.
  'Gone are they, bravely, though misled;
With a dear Father at their head!
The Sons obey a natural lord;
The Father had given solemn word
To noble Percy; and a force
Still stronger, bends him to his course.   *130*
This said, our tears to-day may fall
As at an innocent funeral.
In deep and awful channel runs
This sympathy of Sire and Sons;
Untried our Brothers have been loved
With heart by simple nature moved;
And now their faithfulness is proved:
For faithful we must call them, bearing
That soul of conscientious daring.
—There were they all in circle—there   *140*
Stood Richard, Ambrose, Christopher,
John with a sword that will not fail,
And Marmaduke in fearless mail,
And those bright Twins were side by side;
And there, by fresh hopes beautified,
Stood He, whose arm yet lacks the power
Of man, our youngest, fairest flower!
I, by the right of eldest born,
And in a second father's place,
Presumed to grapple with their scorn,   *150*

And meet their pity face to face;
Yea, trusting in God's holy aid,
I to my Father knelt and prayed;
And one, the pensive Marmaduke,
Methought, was yielding inwardly,
And would have laid his purpose by,
But for a glance of his Father's eye,
Which I myself could scarcely brook.
   'Then be we, each and all, forgiven!
Thou, chiefly thou, my Sister dear,   *160*
Whose pangs are registered in heaven—
The stifled sigh, the hidden tear,
And smiles, that dared to take their place,
Meek filial smiles, upon thy face,
As that unhallowed Banner grew

Beneath a loving old Man's view.
Thy part is done—thy painful part;
Be thou then satisfied in heart!
A further, though far easier, task
Than thine hath been, my duties ask;   *170*
With theirs my efforts cannot blend,
I cannot for such cause contend;
Their aims I utterly forswear;
But I in body will be there.
Unarmed and naked will I go,
Be at their side, come weal or woe:
On kind occasions I may wait,
See, hear, obstruct, or mitigate.
Bare breast I take and an empty hand.'
Therewith he threw away the lance,   *180*
Which he had grasped in that strong trance;
Spurned it, like something that would stand
Between him and the pure intent
Of love on which his soul was bent.
   'For thee, for thee, is left the sense
Of trial past without offence
To God or man; such innocence,
Such consolation, and the excess
Of an unmerited distress;
In that thy very strength must lie.   *190*
—O Sister, I could prophesy!
The time is come that rings the knell
Of all we loved, and loved so well:
Hope nothing, if I thus may speak
To thee, a woman, and thence weak:
Hope nothing, I repeat; for we
Are doomed to perish utterly:

'Tis meet that thou with me divide
The thought while I am by thy side,
Acknowledging a grace in this,   *200*
A comfort in the dark abyss.
But look not for me when I am gone,
And be no farther wrought upon:
Farewell all wishes, all debate,
All prayers for this cause, or for that!
Weep, if that aid thee; but depend
Upon no help of outward friend;
Espouse thy doom at once, and cleave
To fortitude without reprieve.
For we must fall, both we and ours—   *210*
This Mansion and these pleasant bowers,
Walks, pools, and arbours, homestead, hall—
Our fate is theirs, will reach them all;
The young horse must forsake his manger,
And learn to glory in a Stranger;
The hawk forget his perch; the hound
Be parted from his ancient ground:
The blast will sweep us all away—
One desolation, one decay!
And even this Creature!' which words saying,   *220*
He pointed to a lovely Doe,
A few steps distant, feeding, straying;
Fair creature, and more white than snow!
'Even she will to her peaceful woods
Return, and to her murmuring floods,
And be in heart and soul the same
She was before she hither came;
Ere she had learned to love us all,
Herself beloved in Rylstone-hall.
—But thou, my Sister, doomed to be   *230*
The last leaf on a blasted tree;
If not in vain we breathed the breath
Together of a purer faith;
If hand in hand we have been led,
And thou, (O happy thought this day!)
Not seldom foremost in the way;
If on one thought our minds have fed,
And we have in one meaning read;
If, when at home our private weal
Hath suffered from the shock of zeal,   *240*
Together we have learned to prize
Forbearance and self-sacrifice;
If we like combatants have fared,
And for this issue been prepared;

If thou art beautiful, and youth
And thought endue thee with all truth—
Be strong;—be worthy of the grace
Of God, and fill thy destined place:
A Soul, by force of sorrows high,
Uplifted to the purest sky   *250*
Of undisturbed humanity!'
   He ended,—or she heard no more;
He led her from the yew-tree shade,
And at the mansion's silent door,
He kissed the consecrated Maid;
And down the valley then pursued,
Alone, the armèd Multitude.

CANTO THIRD

Now joy for you who from the towers
Of Brancepeth look in doubt and fear,
Telling melancholy hours!
Proclaim it, let your Masters hear
That Norton with his band is near!
The watchmen from their station high
Pronounced the word,—and the Earls descry,
Well-pleased, the armèd Company
Marching down the banks of Were.
   Said fearless Norton to the pair   *10*
Gone forth to greet him on the plain—
'This meeting, noble Lords! looks fair,
I bring with me a goodly train;
Their hearts are with you: hill and dale
Have helped us: Ure we crossed, and Swale,
And horse and harness followed—see
The best part of their Yeomanry!
—Stand forth, my Sons!—these eight are mine!
Whom to this service I commend;
Which way soe'er our fate incline,   *20*
These will be faithful to the end;
They are my all'—voice failed him here—
'My all save one, a Daughter dear!
Whom I have left, Love's mildest birth;
The meekest Child on this blessed earth.
I had—but these are by my side,
These Eight, and this is a day of pride!
The time is ripe. With festive din
Lo! how the people are flocking in,—

Like hungry fowl to the feeder's hand   30
When snow lies heavy upon the land.'
　　He spake bare truth: for far and near
From every side came noisy swarms
Of Peasants in their homely gear;
And, mixed with these, to Brancepeth came
Grave Gentry of estate and name,
And Captains known for worth in arms;
And prayed the Earls in self-defence
To rise, and prove their innocence.—
'Rise, noble Earls, put forth your might   40
For holy Church, and the People's right!'
　　The Norton fixed, at this demand,
His eye upon Northumberland,
And said; 'The Minds of Men will own
No loyal rest while England's Crown
Remains without an Heir, the bait
Of strife and factions desperate;
Who, paying deadly hate in kind
Through all things else, in this can find
A mutual hope, a common mind;   50
And plot, and pant to overwhelm
All ancient honour in the realm.
—Brave Earls! to whose heroic veins
Our noblest blood is given in trust,
To you a suffering State complains,
And ye must raise her from the dust.
With wishes of still bolder scope
On you we look, with dearest hope;
Even for our Altars—for the prize,
In Heaven, of life that never dies;   60
For the old and holy Church we mourn,
And must in joy to her return.
Behold!'—and from his Son whose stand
Was on his right, from that guardian hand
He took the Banner, and unfurled
The precious folds—'behold,' said he,
'The ransom of a sinful world;
Let this your preservation be;
The wounds of hands and feet and side,
And the sacred Cross on which Jesus died.   70
—This bring I from an ancient hearth,
These Records wrought in pledge of love
By hands of no ignoble birth,
A Maid o'er whom the blessed Dove
Vouchsafed in gentleness to brood
While she the holy work pursued.'

'Uplift the Standard!' was the cry
From all the listeners that stood round,
'Plant it,—by this we live or die.'
The Norton ceased not for that sound,   *80*
But said; 'The prayer which ye have heard,
Much-injured Earls! by these preferred,
Is offered to the Saints, the sigh
Of tens of thousands, secretly.'
'Uplift it!' cried once more the Band,
And then a thoughtful pause ensued:
'Uplift it!' said Northumberland—
Whereat, from all the multitude
Who saw the Banner reared on high
In all its dread emblazonry,   *90*
A voice of uttermost joy brake out:
The transport was rolled down the river of Were,
And Durham, the time-honoured Durham, did hear,
And the towers of Saint Cuthbert were stirred by the shout
    Now was the North in arms:—they shine
In warlike trim from Tweed to Tyne,
At Percy's voice: and Neville sees
His followers gathering in from Tees,
From Were, and all the little rills
Concealed among the forkèd hills—   *100*
Seven hundred Knights, Retainers all
Of Neville, at their Master's call
Had sate together in Raby Hall!
Such strength that Earldom held of yore;
Nor wanted at this time rich store
Of well-appointed chivalry.
—Not loth the sleepy lance to wield,
And greet the old paternal shield,
They heard the summons;—and, furthermore,
Horsemen and Foot of each degree,   *110*
Unbound by pledge of fealty,
Appeared, with free and open hate
Of novelties in Church and State;
Knight, burgher, yeoman, and esquire,
And Romish priest, in priest's attire.
And thus, in arms, a zealous Band
Proceeding under joint command,
To Durham first their course they bear;
And in Saint Cuthbert's ancient seat
Sang mass,—and tore the book of prayer,—   *120*
And trod the bible beneath their feet.
    Thence marching southward smooth and free
'They mustered their host at Wetherby,

Full sixteen thousand fair to see,'
The Choicest Warriors of the North!
But none for beauty and for worth
Like those eight Sons—who, in a ring,
(Ripe men, or blooming in life's spring)
Each with a lance, erect and tall,
A falchion, and a buckler small,   *130*
Stood by their Sire, on Clifford-moor,
To guard the Standard which he bore.
On foot they girt their Father round;
And so will keep the appointed ground
Where'er their march: no steed will he
Henceforth bestride;—triumphantly,
He stands upon the gràssy sod,
Trusting himself to the earth, and God.
Rare sight to embolden and inspire!
Proud was the field of Sons and Sire;   *140*
Of him the mòst; and, sooth to say,
No shape of man in all the array
So graced the sunshine of that day.
The monumental pomp of age
Was with this goodly Personage;
A stature undepressed in size,
Unbent, which rather seemed to rise,
In open victory o'er the weight
Of seventy years, to loftier height;
Magnific limbs of withered state;   *150*
A face to fear and venerate;
Eyes dark and strong; and on his head
Bright locks of silver hair, thick spread,
Which a brown morion half-concealed,
Light as a hunter's of the field;
And thus, with girdle round his waist,
Whereon the Banner-staff might rest
At need, he stood, advancing high
The glittering, floating Pageantry.
   Who sees him?—thousands see, and One   *160*
With unparticipated gaze;
Who, 'mong those thousands, friend hath none,
And treads in solitary ways.
He, following wheresoe'er he might,
Hath watched the Banner from afar,
As shepherds watch a lonely star,
Or mariners the distant light
That guides them through a stormy night.
And now, upon a chosen plot
Of rising ground, yon heathy spot!   *170*

He takes alone his far-off stand,
With breast unmailed, unweaponed hand.
Bold is his aspect; but his eye
Is pregnant with anxiety,
While, like a tutelary Power,
He there stands fixed from hour to hour:
Yet sometimes in more humble guise
Upon the turf-clad height he lies
Stretched, herdsman-like, as if to bask
In sunshine were his only task,   180
Or by his mantle's help to find
A shelter from the nipping wind:
And thus, with short oblivion blest,
His weary spirits gather rest.

Again he lifts his eyes; and lo!
The pageant glancing to and fro;
And hope is wakened by the sight,
He thence may learn, ere fall of night,
Which way the tide is doomed to flow.
    To London were the Chieftains bent;   190
But what avails the bold intent?
A Royal army is gone forth
To quell the RISING OF THE NORTH;
They march with Dudley at their head,
And, in seven days' space, will to York be led!—
Can such a mighty Host be raised
Thus suddenly, and brought so near?
The Earls upon each other gazed,
And Neville's cheek grew pale with fear;
For, with a high and valiant name,   200
He bore a heart of timid frame;
And bold if both had been, yet they
'Against so many may not stay.'
Back therefore will they hie to seize
A strong Hold on the banks of Tees;
There wait a favourable hour,
Until Lord Dacre with his power
From Naworth come; and Howard's aid
Be with them openly displayed.
    While through the Host, from man to man,   210
A rumour of this purpose ran,
The Standard trusting to the care
Of him who heretofore did bear
That charge, impatient Norton sought
The Chieftains to unfold his thought,
And thus abruptly spake;—'We yield
(And can it be?) an unfought field!—

How oft has strength, the strength of heaven,
To few triumphantly been given!
Still do our very children boast 　　　　　　　　*220*
Of mitred Thurston—what a Host
He conquered!—Saw we not the Plain
(And flying shall behold again)
Where faith was proved?—while to battle moved
The Standard, on the Sacred Wain
That bore it, compassed round by a bold
Fraternity of Barons old;
And with those grey-haired champions stood,
Under the saintly ensigns three,
The infant Heir of Mowbray's blood— 　　　　*230*
All confident of victory!—
Shall Percy blush, then, for his name?
Must Westmoreland be asked with shame
Whose were the numbers, where the loss,
In that other day of Neville's Cross?
When the Prior of Durham with holy hand
Raised, as the Vision gave command,
Saint Cuthbert's Relic—far and near
Kenned on the point of a lofty spear;
While the Monks prayed in Maiden's Bower 　*240*
To God descending in his power.
Less would not at our need be due
To us, who war against the Untrue,—
The delegates of Heaven we rise,
Convoked the impious to chastise:
We, we, the sanctities of old
Would re-establish and uphold:
Be warned.'—His zeal the Chiefs confounded,
But word was given, and the trumpet sounded:
Back through the melancholy Host 　　　　　*250*
Went Norton, and resumed his post.
Alas! thought he, and have I borne
This Banner raised with joyful pride,
This hope of all posterity,
By those dread symbols sanctified;
Thus to become at once the scorn
Of babbling winds as they go by,
A spot of shame to the sun's bright eye,
To the light clouds a mockery!
—'Even these poor eight of mine would stem—' 　*260*
Half to himself, and half to them
He spake—'would stem, or quell, a force
Ten times their number, man and horse:
This by their own unaided might,

Without their father in their sight,
Without the Cause for which they fight;
A Cause, which on a needful day
Would breed us thousands brave as they.'
—So speaking, he his reverend head
Raised towards that Imagery once more: *270*
But the familiar prospect shed
Despondency unfelt before:
A shock of intimations vain,
Dismay, and superstitious pain,
Fell on him, with the sudden thought
Of her by whom the work was wrought:—
Oh wherefore was her countenance bright
With love divine and gentle light?
She would not, could not, disobey,
But her Faith leaned another way.   *280*
Ill tears she wept; I saw them fall,
I overheard her as she spake
Sad words to that mute Animal,
The White Doe, in the hawthorn brake;
She steeped, but not for Jesu's sake,
This Cross in tears: by her, and One
Unworthier far we are undone—
Her recreant Brother—he prevailed
Over that tender Spirit—assailed
Too oft, alas! by her whose head   *290*
In the cold grave hath long been laid:
She first, in reason's dawn beguiled
Her docile, unsuspecting Child:
Far back—far back my mind must go
To reach the well-spring of this woe!
    While thus he brooded, music sweet
Of border tunes was played to cheer
The footsteps of a quick retreat;
But Norton lingered in the rear,
Stung with sharp thoughts; and ere the last   *300*
From his distracted brain was cast,
Before his Father, Francis stood,
And spake in firm and earnest mood.
    'Though here I bend a suppliant knee
In reverence, and unarmed, I bear
In your indignant thoughts my share;
Am grieved this backward march to see
So careless and disorderly.
I scorn your Chiefs—men who would lead,
And yet want courage at their need: *310*
Then look at them with open eyes!

Deserve they further sacrifice?—
If—when they shrink, nor dare oppose
In open field their gathering foes,
(And fast, from this decisive day,
Yon multitude must melt away;)
If now I ask a grace not claimed
While ground was left for hope; unblamed
Be an endeavour that can do
No injury to them or you.   320
My Father! I would help to find
A place of shelter, till the rage
Of cruel men do like the wind
Exhaust itself and sink to rest;
Be Brother now to Brother joined!
Admit me in the equipage
Of your misfortune, that at least,
Whatever fate remain behind,
I may bear witness in my breast
To your nobility of mind!'   330
   'Thou Enemy, my bane and blight!
Oh! bold to fight the Coward's fight
Against all good'—but why declare,
At length, the issue of a prayer
Which love had prompted, yielding scope
Too free to one bright moment's hope?
Suffice it that the Son, who strove
With fruitless effort to allay
That passion, prudently gave way;
Nor did he turn aside to prove   340
His Brothers' wisdom or their love—
But calmly from the spot withdrew;
His best endeavours to renew,
Should e'er a kindlier time ensue.

CANTO FOURTH

'TIS night: in silence looking down,
The Moon, from cloudless ether, sees
A Camp, and a beleaguered Town,
And Castle, like a stately crown
On the steep rocks of winding Tees;—
And southward far, with moor between,
Hill-top, and flood, and forest green,

The bright Moon sees that valley small
Where Rylstone's old sequestered Hall
A venerable image yields   *10*
Of quiet to the neighbouring fields;
While from one pillared chimney breathes
The smoke, and mounts in silver wreaths.
—The courts are hushed;—for timely sleep
The greyhounds to their kennel creep;
The peacock in the broad ash tree
Aloft is roosted for the night,
He who in proud prosperity
Of colours manifold and bright
Walked round, affronting the daylight;   *20*
And higher still, above the bower
Where he is perched, from yon lone Tower
The hall-clock in the clear moonshine
With glittering finger points at nine.
    Ah! who could think that sadness here
Hath any sway? or pain, or fear?
A soft and lulling sound is heard
Of streams inaudible by day;
The garden pool's dark surface, stirred
By the night insects in their play,   *30*
Breaks into dimples small and bright;
A thousand, thousand rings of light
That shape themselves and disappear
Almost as soon as seen:—and lo!
Not distant far, the milk-white Doe—
The same who quietly was feeding
On the green herb, and nothing heeding,
When Francis, uttering to the Maid
His last words in the yew-tree shade,
Involved whate'er by love was brought   *40*
Out of his heart, or crossed his thought,
Or chance presented to his eye,
In one sad sweep of destiny—
The same fair Creature who hath found
Her way into forbidden ground;
Where now—within this spacious plot
For pleasure made, a goodly spot,
With lawns and beds of flowers, and shades
Of trellis-work in long arcades,
And cirque and crescent framed by wall   *50*
Of close-clipt foliage green and tall,
Coverging walks, and fountains gay,
And terraces in trim array—
Beneath yon cypress spiring high,

With pine and cedar spreading wide
Their darksome boughs on either side,
In open moonlight doth she lie;
Happy as others of her kind,
That, far from human neighbourhood,
Range unrestricted as the wind,   *60*
Through park, or chase, or savage wood
　But see the consecrated Maid
Emerging from a cedar shade
To open moonshine, where the Doe
Beneath the cypress-spire is laid;
Like a patch of April snow—
Upon a bed of herbage green,
Lingering in a woody glade
Or behind a rocky screen—
Lonely relic! which, if seen   *70*
By the shepherd, is passed by
With an inattentive eye.
No more regard doth She bestow
Upon the uncomplaining Doe
Now couched at ease, though oft this day
Not unperplexed nor free from pain,
When she had tried, and tried in vain,
Approaching in her gentle way,
To win some look of love, or gain
Encouragement to sport or play;   *80*
Attempts which still the heart-sick Maid
Rejected, or with slight repaid.
　　Yet Emily is soothed;—the breeze
Came fraught with kindly sympathies.
As she approached yon rustic Shed
Hung with late-flowering woodbine, spread
Along the walls and overhead,
The fragrance of the breathing flowers
Revived a memory of those hours
When here, in this remote alcove,   *90*
(While from the pendent woodbine came
Like odours, sweet as if the same)
A fondly-anxious Mother strove
To teach her salutary fears
And mysteries above her years.
Yes, she is soothed: an Image faint,
And yet not faint—a presence bright
Returns to her—that blessèd Saint
Who with mild looks and language mild
Instructed here her darling Child,   *100*
While yet a prattler on the knee,

To worship in simplicity
The invisible God, and take for guide
The faith reformed and purified.
   'Tis flown—the Vision, and the sense
Of that beguiling influence;
'But oh! thou Angel from above,
Mute Spirit of maternal love,
That stood'st before my eyes, more clear
Than ghosts are fabled to appear   *110*
Sent upon embassies of fear;
As thou thy presence hast to me
Vouchsafed, in radiant ministry
Descend on Francis; nor forbear
To greet him with a voice, and say;—
"If hope be a rejected stay,
Do thou, my christian Son, beware
Of that most lamentable snare,
The self-reliance of despair!"'
   Then from within the embowered retreat   *120*
Where she had found a grateful seat
Perturbed she issues.   She will go!
Herself will follow to the war,
And clasp her Father's knees;—ah, no!
She meets the insuperable bar,
The injunction by her Brother laid;
His parting charge—but ill obeyed—
That interdicted all debate,
All prayer for this cause or for that;
All efforts that would turn aside   *130*
The headstrong current of their fate:
Her duty is to stand and wait; [1]
In resignation to abide
The shock, AND FINALLY SECURE
O'ER PAIN AND GRIEF A TRIUMPH PURE.
—She feels it, and her pangs are checked.
But now, as silently she paced
The turf, and thought by thought was chased,
Came One who, with sedate respect,
Approached, and, greeting her, thus spake; *140*
'An old man's privilege I take:
Dark is the time—a woeful day!
Dear daughter of affliction, say
How can I serve you? point the way.'
   'Rights have you, and may well be bold;
You with my Father have grown old
In friendship—strive—for his sake go—
Turn from us all the coming woe:

This would I beg; but on my mind
A passive stillness is enjoined.   *150*
On you, if room for mortal aid
Be left, is no restriction laid;
You not forbidden to recline
With hope upon the Will divine.'
  'Hope,' said the old Man, 'must abide
With all of us, whate'er betide.
In Craven's Wilds is many a den,
To shelter persecuted men:
Far under ground is many a cave,
Where they might lie as in the grave,   *160*
Until this storm hath ceased to rave:
Or let them cross the River Tweed,
And be at once from peril freed!'
  'Ah tempt me not!' she faintly sighed;
'I will not counsel nor exhort,
With my condition satisfied;
But you, at least, may make report
Of what befalls;—be this your task—
This may be done;—'tis all I ask!'   *170*
  She spake—and from the Lady's sight
The Sire, unconscious of his age,
Departed promptly as a Page
Bound on some errand of delight.
—The noble Francis—wise as brave,
Thought he, may want not skill to save.
With hopes in tenderness concealed,
Unarmed he followed to the field;
Him will I seek: the insurgent Powers
Are now besieging Barnard's Towers,—
'Grant that the Moon which shines this night   *180*
May guide them in a prudent flight!'
  But quick the turns of chance and change,
And knowledge has a narrow range;
Whence idle fears, and needless pain,
And wishes blind, and efforts vain.—
The Moon may shine, but cannot be
Their guide in flight—already she
Hath witnessed their captivity.
She saw the desperate assault
Upon that hostile castle made;—   *190*
But dark and dismal is the vault
Where Norton and his sons are laid!
Disastrous issue!—he had said
'This night yon faithless Towers must yield,
Or we for ever quit the field.

—Neville is utterly dismayed,
For promise fails of Howard's aid;
And Dacre to our call replies
That *he* is unprepared to rise.
My heart is sick;—this weary pause   *200*
Must needs be fatal to our cause.
The breach is open—on the wall,
This night, the Banner shall be planted!'
—'Twas done: his Sons were with him—all;
They belt him round with hearts undaunted
And others follow;—Sire and Son
Leap down into the court;—' 'Tis won'—
They shout aloud—but Heaven decreed
That with their joyful shout should close
The triumph of a desperate deed   *210*
Which struck with terror friends and foes!
The friend shrinks back—the foe recoils
From Norton and his filial band;
But they, now caught within the toils,
Against a thousand cannot stand;—
The foe from numbers courage drew,
And overpowered that gallant few.
'A rescue for the Standard!' cried
The Father from within the walls;
But, see, the sacred Standard falls!—   *220*
Confusion through the Camp spread wide:
Some fled; and some their fears detained:
But ere the Moon had sunk to rest
In her pale chambers of the west,
Of that rash levy nought remained.

CANTO FIFTH

HIGH on a point of rugged ground
Among the wastes of Rylstone Fell,
Above the loftiest ridge or mound
Where foresters or shepherds dwell,
An edifice of warlike frame
Stands single—Norton Tower its name—
It fronts all quarters, and looks round
O'er path and road, and plain and dell,
Dark moor, and gleam of pool and stream,
Upon a prospect without bound.   *10*
    The summit of this bold ascent—
Though bleak and bare, and seldom free

As Pendle-hill or Pennygent
From wind, or frost, or vapours wet—
Had often heard the sound of glee
When there the youthful Nortons met,
To practise games and archery:
How proud and happy they! the crowd
Of Lookers-on how pleased and proud!
And from the scorching noon-tide sun,   20
From showers, or when the prize was won,
They to the Tower withdrew, and there
Would mirth run round, with generous fare;
And the stern old Lord of Rylstone-hall
Was happiest, proudest, of them all!
　　But now, his Child, with anguish pale,
Upon the height walks to and fro;
'Tis well that she hath heard the tale,
Received the bitterness of woe:
For she *had* hoped, had hoped and feared,   30
Such rights did feeble nature claim;
And oft her steps had hither steered,
Though not unconscious of self-blame;
For she her brother's charge revered,
His farewell words; and by the same,
Yea, by her brother's very name,
Had, in her solitude, been cheered.
　　Beside the lonely watch-tower stood
That grey-haired Man of gentle blood,
Who with her Father had grown old   40
In friendship; rival hunters they,
And fellow warriors in their day;
To Rylstone he the tidings brought;
Then on this height the Maid had sought,
And, gently as he could, had told
The end of that dire Tragedy,
Which it had been his lot to see.
　　To him the Lady turned; 'You said
That Francis lives, *he* is not dead?'
'Your noble brother hath been spared;   50
To take his life they have not dared;
On him and on his high endeavour
The light of praise shall shine for ever!
Nor did he (such Heaven's will) in vain
His solitary course maintain;
Not vainly struggled in the might
Of duty, seeing with clear sight;
He was their comfort to the last,
Their joy till every pang was past.

'I witnessed when to York they came—   60
What, Lady, if their feet were tied;
They might deserve a good Man's blame;
But marks of infamy and shame—
These were their triumph, these their pride.
Nor wanted 'mid the pressing crowd
Deep feeling, that found utterance loud,
"Lo, Francis comes," there were who cried,
"A prisoner once, but now set free!
'Tis well, for he the worst defied
Through force of natural piety;   70
He rose not in this quarrel; he
For concord's sake and England's good,
Suit to his Brothers often made
With tears, and of his Father prayed—
And when he had in vain withstood
Their purpose—then did he divide,
He parted from them; but at their side
Now walks in unanimity.
Then peace to cruelty and scorn,
While to the prison they are borne,   80
Peace, peace to all indignity!"
   'And so in Prison were they laid—
Oh hear me, hear me, gentle Maid,
For I am come with power to bless,
By scattering gleams, through your distress,
Of a redeeming happiness.
Me did a reverent pity move
And privilege of ancient love;
And, in your service, making bold,
Entrance I gained to that stronghold.   90
   'Your Father gave me cordial greeting;
But to his purposes, that burned
Within him, instantly returned:
He was commanding and entreating,
And said—"We need not stop, my Son!
Thoughts press, and time is hurrying on"—
And so to Francis he renewed
His words, more calmly thus pursued.
   '"Might this our enterprise have sped,
Change wide and deep the Land had seen,   100
A renovation from the dead,
A spring-time of immortal green:
The darksome altars would have blazed
Like stars when clouds are rolled away;
Salvation to all eyes that gazed,
Once more the Rood had been upraised

To spread its arms, and stand for aye.
Then, then—had I survived to see
New life in Bolton Priory;
The voice restored, the eye of Truth   *110*
Re-opened that inspired my youth;
To see her in her pomp arrayed—
This Banner (for such vow I made)
Should on the consecrated breast
Of that same Temple have found rest:
I would myself have hung it high,
Fit offering of glad victory!
   '"A shadow of such thought remains
To cheer this sad and pensive time;
A solemn fancy yet sustains   *120*
One feeble Being—bids me climb
Even to the last—one effort more
To attest my Faith, if not restore.
   '"Hear then," said he, "while I impart,
My Son, the last wish of my heart.
The Banner strive thou to regain;
And, if the endeavour prove not vain,
Bear it—to whom if not to thee
Shall I this lonely thought consign?—
Bear it to Bolton Priory,   *130*
And lay it on Saint Mary's shrine;
To wither in the sun and breeze
'Mid those decaying sanctities.
There let at least the gift be laid,
The testimony there displayed;
Bold proof that with no selfish aim,
But for lost Faith and Christ's dear name,
I helmeted a brow though white,
And took a place in all men's sight;
Yea offered up this noble Brood,   *140*
This fair unrivalled Brotherhood,
And turned away from thee, my Son!
And left—but be the rest unsaid,
The name untouched, the tear unshed;—
My wish is known, and I have done:
Now promise, grant this one request,
This dying prayer, and be thou blest!"
   'Then Francis answered—"Trust thy Son,
For, with God's will, it shall be done!"—
   'The pledge obtained, the solemn word   *150*
Thus scarcely given, a noise was heard,
And Officers appeared in state
To lead the prisoners to their fate.

They rose, oh! wherefore should I fear
To tell, or, Lady, you to hear?
They rose—embraces none were given—
They stood like trees when earth and heaven
Are calm; they knew each other's worth,
And reverently the Band went forth.
They met, when they had reached the door,   *160*
One with profane and harsh intent
Placed there—that he might go before,
And, with that rueful Banner borne
Aloft in sign of taunting scorn,
Conduct them to their punishment:
So cruel Sussex, unrestrained
By human feeling, had ordained.
The unhappy Banner Francis saw,
And, with a look of calm command
Inspiring universal awe,   *170*
He took it from the soldier's hand;
And all the people that stood round
Confirmed the deed in peace profound.
—High transport did the Father shed
Upon his Son—and they were led,
Led on, and yielded up their breath;
Together died, a happy death!—
But Francis, soon as he had braved
That insult, and the Banner saved,
Athwart the unresisting tide   *180*
Of the spectators occupied
In admiration or dismay,
Bore instantly his Charge away.'
    These things, which thus had in the sight
And hearing passed of him who stood
With Emily, on the Watch-tower height,
In Rylstone's woeful neighbourhood,
He told; and oftentimes with voice
Of power to comfort or rejoice;
For deepest sorrows that aspire   *190*
Go high, no transport ever higher.
'Yes—God is rich in mercy,' said
The old Man to the silent Maid,
'Yet, Lady! shines, through this black night,
One star of aspect heavenly bright;
Your Brother lives—he lives—is come
Perhaps already to his home;
Then let us leave this dreary place.'
She yielded, and with gentle pace,
Though without one uplifted look,   *200*
To Rylstone-hall her way she took.

CANTO SIXTH

WHY comes not Francis?—From the doleful City
He fled,—and, in his flight, could hear
The death-sounds of the Minster-bell:
That sullen stroke pronounced farewell
To Marmaduke, cut off from pity!
To Ambrose that! and then a knell
For him, the sweet half-opened Flower!
For all—all dying in one hour!
—Why comes not Francis?   Thoughts of love
Should bear him to his Sister dear   *10*
With the fleet motion of a dove;
Yea, like a heavenly messenger
Of speediest wing, should he appear.
Why comes he not?—for westward fast
Along the plain of York he passed;
Reckless of what impels or leads,
Unchecked he hurries on;—nor heeds
The sorrow, through the Villages,
Spread by triumphant cruelties
Of vengeful military force,   *20*
And punishment without remorse.
He marked not, heard not, as he fled;
All but the suffering heart was dead
For him, abandoned to blank awe,
To vacancy, and horror strong:
And the first object which he saw,
With conscious sight, as he swept along—
It was the Banner in his hand!
He felt—and made a sudden stand.

   He looked about like one betrayed: *30*
What hath he done? what promise made?
Oh weak, weak moment! to what end
Can such a vain oblation tend,
And he the Bearer?—Can he go
Carrying this instrument of woe,
And find, find any where, a right
To excuse him in his Country's sight?
No; will not all men deem the change
A downward course, perverse and strange?
Here is it;—but how? when? must she,   *40*
The unoffending Emily,
Again this piteous object see?
   Such conflict long did he maintain,

Nor liberty nor rest could gain:
His own life into danger brought
By this sad burden—even that thought,
Exciting self-suspicion strong,
Swayed the brave man to his wrong.
And how—unless it were the sense
Of all-disposing Providence,   *50*
Its will unquestionably shown—
How has the Banner clung so fast
To a palsied, and unconscious hand;
Clung to the hand to which it passed
Without impediment?   And why,
But that Heaven's purpose might be known,
Doth now no hindrance meet his eye,
No intervention, to withstand
Fulfilment of a Father's prayer
Breathed to a Son forgiven, and blest   *60*
When all resentments were at rest,
And life in death laid the heart bare?—
Then, like a spectre sweeping by,
Rushed through his mind the prophecy
Of utter desolation made
To Emily in the yew-tree shade:
He sighed, submitting will and power
To the stern embrace of that grasping hour.
'No choice is left, the deed is mine—
Dead are they, dead!—and I will go,   *70*
And, for their sakes, come weal or woe,
Will lay the Relic on the shrine.'
   So forward with a steady will
He went, and traversed plain and hill;
And up the vale of Wharf his way
Pursued;—and, at the dawn of day,
Attained a summit whence his eyes
Could see the Tower of Bolton rise.
There Francis for a moment's space
Made halt—but hark! a noise behind   *80*
Of horsemen at an eager pace!
He heard, and with misgiving mind.
—'Tis Sir George Bowes who leads the Band:
They come, by cruel Sussex sent;
Who, when the Nortons from the hand
Of death had drunk their punishment,
Bethought him, angry and ashamed,
How Francis, with the Banner claimed
As his own charge, had disappeared,
By all the standers-by revered.   *90*

His whole bold carriage (which had quelled
Thus far the Opposer, and repelled
All censure, enterprise so bright
That even bad men had vainly striven
Against that overcoming light)
Was then reviewed, and prompt word given
That to what place soever fled
He should be seized, alive or dead.
    The troop of horse have gained the height
Where Francis stood in open sight.   *100*
They hem him round—'Behold the proof,'
They cried, 'the Ensign in his hand!
He did not arm, he walked aloof!
For why?—to save his Father's land;
Worst Traitor of them all is he,
A Traitor dark and cowardly!'
   'I am no Traitor,' Francis said,
'Though this unhappy freight I bear;
And must not part with.   But beware;—
Err not by hasty zeal misled,   *110*
Nor do a suffering Spirit wrong,
Whose self-reproaches are too strong!'
At this he from the beaten road
Retreated towards a brake of thorn,
That like a place of vantage showed;
And there stood bravely, though forlorn.
In self-defence with warlike brow
He stood,—nor weaponless was now;
He from a Soldier's hand had snatched
A spear,—and, so protected, watched   *120*
The Assailants, turning round and round;
But from behind with treacherous wound
A Spearman brought him to the ground.
The guardian lance, as Francis fell,
Dropped from him; but his other hand
The Banner clenched; till, from out the Band,
One, the most eager for the prize,
Rushed in; and—while, O grief to tell!
A glimmering sense still left, with eyes
Unclosed the noble Francis lay—   *130*
Seized it, as hunters seize their prey;
But not before the warm life-blood
Had tinged more deeply, as it flowed,
The wounds the broidered Banner showed,
Thy fatal work, O Maiden, innocent as good!
    Proudly the Horsemen bore away
The Standard; and where Francis lay

There was he left alone, unwept,
And for two days unnoticed slept.
For at that time bewildering fear   *140*
Possessed the country, far and near;
But, on the third day, passing by
One of the Norton Tenantry
Espied the uncovered Corse; the Man
Shrunk as he recognized the face,
And to the nearest homesteads ran
And called the people to the place.
—How desolate is Rylstone-hall!
This was the instant thought of all;
And if the lonely Lady there   *150*
Should be; to her they cannot bear
This weight of anguish and despair.
So, when upon sad thoughts had prest
Thoughts sadder still, they deemed it best
That, if the Priest should yield assent
And no one hinder their intent,
Then, they, for Christian pity's sake,
In holy ground a grave would make;
And straightway buried he should be
In the Churchyard of the Priory.   *160*
    Apart, some little space, was made
The grave where Francis must be laid.
In no confusion or neglect
This did they,—but in pure respect
That he was born of gentle blood;
And that there was no neighbourhood
Of kindred for him in that ground:
So to the Churchyard they are bound,
Bearing the body on a bier;
And psalms they sing—a holy sound   *170*
That hill and vale with sadness hear.
    But Emily hath raised her head,
And is again disquieted;
She must behold!—so many gone,
Where is the solitary One?
And forth from Rylstone-hall stepped she,—
To seek her Brother forth she went,
And tremblingly her course she bent
Toward Bolton's ruined Priory.
She comes, and in the vale hath heard   *180*
The funeral dirge;—she sees the knot
Of people, sees them in one spot—
And darting like a wounded bird
She reached the grave, and with her breast

Upon the ground received the rest,—
The consummation, the whole ruth
And sorrow of this final truth!

CANTO SEVENTH

'Powers there are
That touch each other to the quick—in modes
Which the gross world no sense hath to perceive,
No soul to dream of.'

THOU Spirit, whose angelic hand
Was to the harp a strong command,
Called the submissive strings to wake
In glory for this Maiden's sake,
Say, Spirit! whither hath she fled
To hide her poor afflicted head?
What mighty forest in its gloom
Enfolds her?—is a rifted tomb
Within the wilderness her seat?
Some island which the wild waves beat—   *10*
Is that the Sufferer's last retreat?
Or some aspiring rock, that shrouds
Its perilous front in mists and clouds?
High-climbing rock, low sunless dale,
Sea, desert, what do these avail?
Oh take her anguish and her fears
Into a deep recess of years!
   'Tis done;—despoil and desolation
O'er Rylstone's fair domain have blown;
Pools, terraces, and walks are sown   *20*
With weeds; the bowers are overthrown,
Or have given way to slow mutation,
While, in their ancient habitation
The Norton name hath been unknown.
The lordly Mansion of its pride
Is stripped; the ravage hath spread wide
Through park and field, a perishing
That mocks the gladness of the Spring!
And, with this silent gloom agreeing,
Appears a joyless human Being,   *30*
Of aspect such as if the waste
Were under her dominion placed.
Upon a primrose bank, her throne
Of quietness, she sits alone;

Among the ruins of a wood,
Erewhile a covert bright and green,
And where full many a brave tree stood,
That used to spread its boughs, and ring
With the sweet bird's carolling.
Behold her, like a virgin Queen,   *40*
Neglecting in imperial state
These outward images of fate,
And carrying inward a serene
And perfect sway, through many a thought
Of chance and change, that hath been brought
To the subjection of a holy,
Though stern and rigorous, melancholy!
The like authority, with grace
Of awfulness, is in her face,—
There hath she fixed it; yet it seems   *50*
To o'ershadow by no native right
That face, which cannot lose the gleams,
Lose utterly the tender gleams,
Of gentleness and meek delight,
And loving-kindness ever bright:
Such is her sovereign mien:—her dress
(A vest with woollen cincture tied,
A hood of mountain-wool undyed)
Is homely,—fashioned to express
A wandering Pilgrim's humbleness.   *60*
    And she *hath* wandered, long and far,
Beneath the light of sun and star;
Hath roamed in trouble and in grief,
Driven forward like a withered leaf,
Yea like a ship at random blown
To distant places and unknown.
But now she dares to seek a haven
Among her native wilds of Craven;
Hath seen again her Father's roof,
And put her fortitude to proof;   *70*
The mighty sorrow hath been borne,
And she is thoroughly forlorn:
Her soul doth in itself stand fast,
Sustained by memory of the past
And strength of Reason; held above
The infirmities of mortal love;
Undaunted, lofty, calm, and stable,
And awfully impenetrable.
    And so—beneath a mouldered tree,
A self-surviving leafless oak   *80*
By unregarded age from stroke

Of ravage saved—sate Emily.
There did she rest, with head reclined,
Herself most like a stately flower,
(Such have I seen) whom chance of birth
Hath separated from its kind,
To live and die in a shady bower,
Single on the gladsome earth.
    When, with a noise like distant thunder,
A troop of deer came sweeping by;   *90*
And, suddenly, behold a wonder!
For One, among those rushing deer,
A single One, in mid career
Hath stopped, and fixed her large full eye
Upon the Lady Emily;
A Doe most beautiful, clear-white,
A radiant creature, silver-bright!
    Thus checked, a little while it stayed;
A little thoughtful pause it made;
And then advanced with stealth-like pace,   *100*
Drew softly near her, and more near—
Looked round—but saw no cause for fear;
So to her feet the Creature came,
And laid its head upon her knee,
And looked into the Lady's face,
A look of pure benignity,
And fond unclouded memory.
It is, thought Emily, the same,
The very Doe of other years!—
The pleading look the Lady viewed,   *110*
And, by her gushing thoughts subdued,
She melted into tears—
A flood of tears, that flowed apace,
Upon the happy Creature's face.
    Oh, moment ever blest!   O Pair
Beloved of Heaven, Heaven's chosen care,
This was for you a precious greeting;
And may it prove a fruitful meeting!
Joìned are they, and the sylvan Doe
Can she depart? can she forego   *120*
The Lady, once her playful peer,
And now her sainted Mistress dear?
And will not Emily receive
This lovely chronicler of things
Long past, delights and sorrowings?
Lone Sufferer! will not she believe
The promise in that speaking face;
And welcome, as a gift of grace,
The saddest thought the Creature brings?

That day, the first of a re-union   *130*
Which was to teem with high communion,
That day of balmy April weather,
They tarried in the wood together.
And when, ere fall of evening dew,
She from her sylvan haunt withdrew,
The White Doe tracked with faithful pace
The Lady to her dwelling-place;
That nook where, on paternal ground,
A habitation she had found,
The Master of whose humble board   *140*
Once owned her Father for his Lord;
A hut, by tufted trees defended,
Where Rylstone brook with Wharf is blended.
 When Emily by morning light
Went forth, the Doe stood there in sight.
She shrunk:—with one frail shock of pain
Received and followed by a prayer,
She saw the Creature once again;
Shun will she not, she feels, will bear;—
But, wheresoever she looked round,   *150*
All now was trouble-haunted ground;
And therefore now she deems it good
Once more this restless neighbourhood
To leave.—Unwooed, yet unforbidden,
The White Doe followed up the vale,
Up to another cottage, hidden
In the deep fork of Amerdale;
And there may Emily restore
Herself, in spots unseen before.
—Why tell of mossy rock, or tree,   *160*
By lurking Dernbrook's pathless side,
Haunts of a strengthening amity
That calmed her, cheered, and fortified?
For she hath ventured now to read
Of time, and place, and thought, and deed—
Endless history that lies
In her silent Follower's eyes;
Who with a power like human reason
Discerns the favourable season,
Skilled to approach or to retire,—   *170*
From looks conceiving her desire;
From look, deportment, voice, or mien,
That vary to the heart within.
If she too passionately wreathed
Her arms, or over-deeply breathed,
Walked quick or slowly, every mood
In its degree was understood;

Then well may their accord be true,
And kindliest intercourse ensue.
—Oh! surely 'twas a gentle rousing   *180*
When she by sudden glimpse espied
The White Doe on the mountain browsing,
Or in the meadow wandered wide!
How pleased, when down the Straggler sank
Beside her, on some sunny bank!
How soothed, when in thick bower enclosed,
They, like a nested pair, reposed!
Fair Vision! when it crossed the Maid
Within some rocky cavern laid,
The dark cave's portal gliding by,   *190*
White as whitest cloud on high
Floating through the azure sky.
—What now is left for pain or fear?
That Presence, dearer and more dear,
While they, side by side, were straying,
And the shepherd's pipe was playing,
Did now a very gladness yield
At morning to the dewy field,
And with a deeper peace endued
The hour of moonlight solitude.   *200*
    With her Companion, in such frame
Of mind, to Rylstone back she came;
And, ranging through the wasted groves,
Received the memory of old loves,
Undisturbed and undistrest,
Into a soul which now was blest
With a soft spring-day of holy,
Mild, and grateful, melancholy:
Not sunless gloom or unenlightened,
But by tender fancies brightened.   *210*
    When the bells of Rylstone played
Their sabbath music—'GOD US AYDE!'
That was the sound they seemed to speak;
Inscriptive legend which I ween
May on those holy bells be seen,
That legend and her Grandsire's name;
And oftentimes the Lady meek
Had in her childhood read the same;
Words which she slighted at that day;
But now, when such sad change was wrought,   *220*
And of that lonely name she thought,
The bells of Rylstone seemed to say,
While she sate listening in the shade,
With vocal music, 'GOD US AYDE;'

And all the hills were glad to bear
Their part in this effectual prayer.
   Nor lacked she Reason's firmest power;
But with the White Doe at her side
Up would she climb to Norton Tower,
And thence look round her far and wide,   *230*
Her fate there measuring;—all is stilled,—
The weak One hath subdued her heart;
Behold the prophecy fulfilled,
Fulfilled, and she sustains her part!
But here her Brother's words have failed;
Here hath a milder doom prevailed;
That she, of him and all bereft,
Hath yet this faithful Partner left;
This one Associate, that disproves
His words, remains for her, and loves.   *240*
If tears are shed, they do not fall
For loss of him—for one, or all;
Yet, sometimes, sometimes doth she weep,
Moved gently in her soul's soft sleep;
A few tears down her cheek descend
For this her last and living Friend.
   Bless, tender Hearts, their mutual lot,
And bless for both this savage spot;
Which Emily doth sacred hold
For reasons dear and manifold—   *250*
Here hath she, here before her sight,
Close to the summit of this height,
The grassy rock-encircled Pound
In which the Creature first was found.
So beautiful the timid Thrall
(A spotless Youngling white as foam)
Her youngest Brother brought it home;
The youngest, then a lusty boy,
Bore it, or led, to Rylstone-hall
With heart brimful of pride and joy!   *260*
   But most to Bolton's sacred Pile,
On favouring nights, she loved to go;
There ranged through cloister, court, and aisle,
Attended by the soft-paced Doe;
Nor feared she in the still moonshine
To look upon Saint Mary's shrine;
Nor on the lonely turf that showed
Where Francis slept in his last abode.
For that she came; there oft she sate
Forlorn, but not disconsolate: *270*
And when she from the abyss returned

Of thought, she neither shrunk nor mourned;
Was happy that she lived to greet
Her mute Companion as it lay
In love and pity at her feet;
How happy in its turn to meet
The recognition! the mild glance
Beamed from that gracious countenance;
Communication, like the ray
Of a new morning, to the nature   *280*
And prospects of the inferior Creature!
   A mortal Song we sing, by dower
Encouraged of celestial power;
Power which the viewless Spirit shed
By whom we were first visited;
Whose voice we heard, whose hand and wings
Swept like a breeze the conscious strings,
When, left in solitude, erewhile
We stood before this ruined Pile,
And, quitting unsubstantial dreams,   *290*
Sang in this Presence kindred themes;
Distress and desolation spread
Through human hearts, and pleasure dead,—
Dead—but to live again on earth,
A second and yet nobler birth;
Dire overthrow, and yet how high
The re-ascent in sanctity!
From fair to fairer; day by day
A more divine and loftier way!
Even such this blessèd Pilgrim trod,   *300*
By sorrow lifted towards her God;
Uplifted to the purest sky
Of undisturbed mortality.
Her own thoughts loved she; and could bend
A dear look to her lowly Friend;
There stopped; her thirst was satisfied
With what this innocent spring supplied:
Her sanction inwardly she bore,
And stood apart from human cares:
But to the world returned no more,   *310*
Although with no unwilling mind
Help did she give at need, and joined
The Wharfdale peasants in their prayers.
At length, thus faintly, faintly tied
To earth, she was set free, and died.
Thy soul, exalted Emily,
Maid of the blasted family,
Rose to the God from whom it came!

—In Rylstone Church her mortal frame
Was buried by her Mother's side.   *320*
  Most glorious sunset! and a ray
Survives—the twilight of this day—
In that fair Creature whom the fields
Support, and whom the forest shields;
Who, having filled a holy place,
Partakes, in her degree, Heaven's grace;
And bears a memory and a mind
Raised far above the law of kind;
Haunting the spots with lonely cheer
Which her dear Mistress once held dear: *330*
Loves most what Emily loved most—
The enclosure of this churchyard ground;
Here wanders like a gliding ghost,
And every sabbath here is found;
Comes with the people when the bells
Are heard among the moorland dells,
Finds entrance through yon arch, where way
Lies open on the sabbath day;
Here walks amid the mournful waste
Of prostrate altars, shrines defaced,   *340*
And floors encumbered with rich show
Of fret-work imagery laid low;
Paces softly, or makes halt,
By fractured cell, or tomb, or vault;
By plate of monumental brass
Dim-gleaming among weeds and grass,
And sculptured Forms of Warriors brave:
But chiefly by that single grave,
That one sequestered hillock green,
The pensive visitant is seen   *350*
There doth the gentle Creature lie
With those adversities unmoved;
Calm spectacle, by earth and sky
In their benignity approved!
And aye, methinks, this hoary Pile
Subdued by outrage and decay,
Looks down upon her with a smile,
A gracious smile, that seems to say—
'Thou, thou art not a Child of Time,
But Daughter of the Eternal Prime!'   *360*

LATER POEMS

CHARACTERISTICS OF A CHILD THREE YEARS OLD

L OVING she is, and tractable, though wild;
  And Innocence hath privilege in her
To dignify arch looks and laughing eyes
And feats of cunning; and the pretty round
Of trespasses, affected to provoke
Mock-chastisement and partnership in play.
And, as a faggot sparkles on the hearth,
Not less if unattended and alone
Than when both young and old sit gathered round
And take delight in its activity;   *10*
Even so this happy Creature of herself
Is all-sufficient; solitude to her
Is blithe society, who fills the air
With gladness and involuntary songs.
Light are her sallies as the tripping fawn's
Forth-startled from the fern where she lay couched;
Unthought-of, unexpected, as the stir
Of the soft breeze ruffling the meadow-flowers,
Or from before it chasing wantonly
The many-coloured images imprest   *20*
Upon the bosom of a placid lake.

'SURPRISED BY JOY—IMPATIENT AS THE WIND'

Surprised by joy—impatient as the Wind
I turned to share the transport—Oh! with whom
But Thee, deep buried in the silent tomb,
That spot which no vicissitude can find?.
Love, faithful love, recalled thee to my mind—
But how could I forget thee?   Through what power,
Even for the least division of an hour,
Have I been so beguiled as to be blind
To my most grievous loss?—That thought's return
Was the worst pang that sorrow ever bore,   *10*
Save one, one only, when I stood forlorn,
Knowing my heart's best treasure was no more;
That neither present time, nor years unborn
Could to my sight that heavenly face restore.

LAODAMIA

'With sacrifice before the rising morn
Vows have I made by fruitless hope inspired;
And from the infernal Gods, 'mid shades forlorn
Of night, my slaughtered Lord have I required;
Celestial pity I again implore;—
Restore him to my sight—great Jove, restore!'

So speaking, and by fervent love endowed
With faith, the Suppliant heavenwards lifts her hands;
While, like the sun emerging from a cloud,
Her countenance brightens—and her eye expands;   *10*
Her bosom heaves and spreads, her stature grows;
And she expects the issue in repose.

O terror! what hath she perceived?—O joy!
What doth she look on?—whom doth she behold?
Her Hero slain upon the beach of Troy?
His vital presence? his corporeal mould?
It is—if sense deceive her not—'tis He!
And a God leads him, wingèd Mercury!

Mild Hermes spake—and touched her with his wand
That calms all fear; 'Such grace hath crowned thy prayer,   20
Laodamia! that at Jove's command
Thy Husband walks the paths of upper air:
He comes to tarry with thee three hours' space;
Accept the gift, behold him face to face!'

Forth sprang the impassioned Queen her Lord to clasp;
Again that consummation she essayed;
But unsubstantial Form eludes her grasp
As often as that eager grasp was made.
The Phantom parts—but parts to re-unite,
And re-assume his place before her sight.   30

'Protesiláus, lo! thy guide is gone!
Confirm, I pray, the vision with thy voice:
This is our palace,—yonder is thy throne;
Speak, and the floor thou tread'st on will rejoice.
Not to appal me have the gods bestowed
This precious boon; and blest a sad abode.'

'Great Jove, Laodamia! doth not leave
His gifts imperfect:—Spectre though I be,
I am not sent to scare thee or deceive;
But in reward of thy fidelity.   40
And something also did my worth obtain;
For fearless virtue bringeth boundless gain.

'Thou knowest, the Delphic oracle foretold
That the first Greek who touched the Trojan strand
Should die; but me the threat could not withhold:
A generous cause a victim did demand;
And forth I leapt upon the sandy plain;
A self-devoted chief—by Hector slain.'

'Supreme of Heroes—bravest, noblest, best!
Thy matchless courage I bewail no more,   50
Which then, when tens of thousands were deprest
By doubt, propelled thee to the fatal shore;
Thou found'st—and I forgive thee—here thou art—
A nobler counsellor than my poor heart.

'But thou, though capable of sternest deed,
Wert kind as resolute, and good as brave;
And he, whose power restores thee, hath decreed
Thou should'st elude the malice of the grave:
Redundant are thy locks, thy lips as fair
As when their breath enriched Thessalian air.   60

'No Spectre greets me,—no vain Shadow this;
Come, blooming Hero, place thee by my side!
Give, on this well-known couch, one nuptial kiss
To me, this day, a second time thy bride!'
Jove frowned in heaven: the conscious Parcæ threw
Upon those roseate lips a Stygian hue.

'This visage tells thee that my doom is past:
Nor should the change be mourned, even if the joys
Of sense were able to return as fast
And surely as they vanish.   Earth destroys   70
Those raptures duly—Erebus disdains:
Calm pleasures there abide—majestic pains.

'Be taught, O faithful Consort, to control
Rebellious passion: for the Gods approve
The depth, and not the tumult, of the soul;
A fervent, not ungovernable, love.
Thy transports moderate; and meekly mourn
When I depart, for brief is my sojourn—'

'Ah, wherefore?—Did not Hercules by force
Wrest from the guardian Monster of the tomb   80
Alcestis, a reanimated corse,
Given back to dwell on earth in vernal bloom?
Medea's spells dispersed the weight of years,
And Æson stood a youth 'mid youthful peers.

'The Gods to us are merciful—and they
Yet further may relent: for mightier far
Than strength of nerve and sinew, or the sway
Of magic potent over sun and star,
Is love, though oft to agony distrest,
And though his favourite seat be feeble woman's breast.   90

'But if thou goest, I follow—' 'Peace!' he said,—
She looked upon him and was calmed and cheered;
The ghastly colour from his lips had fled;
In his deportment, shape, and mien, appeared
Elysian beauty, melancholy grace,
Brought from a pensive though a happy place.

He spake of love, such love as Spirits feel
In worlds whose course is equable and pure;
No fears to beat away—no strife to heal—
The past unsighed for, and the future sure;   100
Spake of heroic arts in graver mood
Revived, with finer harmony pursued;

Of all that is most beauteous—imaged there
In happier beauty; more pellucid streams,
An ampler ether, a diviner air,
And fields invested with purpureal gleams;
Climes which the sun, who sheds the brightest day
Earth knows, is all unworthy to survey.

Yet there the Soul shall enter which hath earned
That privilege by virtue.—'Ill,' said he,   *110*
'The end of man's existence I discerned,
Who from ignoble games and revelry
Could draw, when we had parted, vain delight,
While tears were thy best pastime, day and night;

'And while my youthful peers before my eyes
(Each hero following his peculiar bent)
Prepared themselves for glorious enterprise
By martial sports,—or, seated in the tent,
Chieftains and kings in council were detained,
What time the fleet at Aulis lay enchained.   *120*

'The wished-for wind was given:—I then revolved
The oracle, upon the silent sea;
And, if no worthier led the way, resolved
That, of a thousand vessels, mine should be
The foremost prow in pressing to the strand,—
Mine the first blood that tinged the Trojan sand.

'Yet bitter, oft-times bitter, was the pang
When of thy loss I thought, belovèd Wife!
On thee too fondly did my memory hang,
And on the joys we shared in mortal life,—   *130*
The paths which we had trod—these fountains, flowers;
My new-planned cities, and unfinished towers.

'But should suspense permit the Foe to cry,
"Behold they tremble!—haughty their array,
Yet of their number no one dares to die"?
In soul I swept the indignity away:
Old frailties then recurred:—but lofty thought,
In act embodied, my deliverance wrought.

'And Thou, though strong in love, art all too weak
In reason, in self-government too slow;   *140*
I counsel thee by fortitude to seek
Our blest re-union in the shades below.
The invisible world with thee hath sympathized;
Be thy affections raised and solemnized.

'Learn, by a mortal yearning, to ascend—
Seeking a higher object.   Love was given,
Encouraged, sanctioned, chiefly for that end;
For this the passion to excess was driven—
That self might be annulled: her bondage prove
The fetters of a dream opposed to love.'——   *150*

Aloud she shrieked! for Hermes re-appears!
Round the dear Shade she would have clung—'tis vain:
The hours are past—too brief had they been years;
And him no mortal effort can detain:
Swift toward the realms that know not earthly day,
He through the portal takes his silent way,
And on the palace-floor a lifeless corse She lay.

Thus, all in vain exhorted and reproved,
She perished; and, as for a wilful crime,
By the just Gods whom no weak pity moved,   *160*
Was doomed to wear out her appointed time,
Apart from happy Ghosts, that gather flowers
Of blissful quiet 'mid unfading bowers.

—Yet tears to human suffering are due;
And mortal hopes defeated and o'erthrown
Are mourned by man, and not by man alone,
As fondly he believes.—Upon the side
Of Hellespont (such faith was entertained)
A knot of spiry trees for ages grew
From out the tomb of him for whom she died;   *170*
And ever, when such stature they had gained
That Ilium's walls were subject to their view,
The trees' tall summits withered at the sight;
A constant interchange of growth and blight.

INSIDE OF KING'S COLLEGE CHAPEL, CAMBRIDGE

TAX not the royal Saint with vain expense,
  With ill-matched aims the Architect who planned—
Albeit labouring for a scanty band
Of white-robed Scholars only—this immense
And glorious Work of fine intelligence!
Give all thou canst; high Heaven rejects the lore
Of nicely-calculated less or more;
So deemed the man who fashioned for the sense
These lofty pillars, spread that branching roof
Self-poised, and scooped into ten thousand cells,   *10*
Where light and shade repose, where music dwells
Lingering—and wandering on as loth to die;
Like thoughts whose very sweetness yieldeth proof
That they were born for immortality.

MUTABILITY

FROM low to high doth dissolution climb,
  And sink from high to low, along a scale
Of awful notes, whose concord shall not fail;
A musical but melancholy chime,
Which they can hear who meddle not with crime,
Nor avarice, nor over-anxious care.
Truth fails not; but her outward forms that bear
The longest date do melt like frosty rime,
That in the morning whitened hill and plain
And is no more; drop like the tower sublime   *10*
Of yesterday, which royally did wear
His crown of weeds, but could not even sustain
Some casual shout that broke the silent air,
Or the unimaginable touch of Time.

EXTEMPORE EFFUSION UPON THE DEATH OF JAMES HOGG

WHEN first, descending from the moorlands,
   I saw the Stream of Yarrow glide
Along a bare and open valley,
   The Ettrick Shepherd was my guide.

When last along its banks I wandered,
   Through groves that had begun to shed
Their golden leaves upon the pathways,
   My steps the Border-minstrel led.

The mighty Minstrel breathes no longer,
   'Mid mouldering ruins low he lies;   *10*
And death upon the braes of Yarrow,
   Has closed the Shepherd-poet's eyes:

Nor has the rolling year twice measured,
   From sign to sign, its steadfast course,
Since every mortal power of Coleridge
   Was frozen at its marvellous source;

The rapt One, of the godlike forehead,
   The heaven-eyed creature sleeps in earth:
And Lamb, the frolic and the gentle,
   Has vanished from his lonely hearth.   *20*

Like clouds that rake the mountain-summits,
   Or waves that own no curbing hand,
How fast has brother followed brother
   From sunshine to the sunless land!

Yet I, whose lids from infant slumber
   Were earlier raised, remain to hear
A timid voice, that asks in whispers,
   'Who next will drop and disappear?'

Our haughty life is crowned with darkness,
   Like London with its own black wreath,   *30*
On which with thee, O Crabbe! forth-looking,
   I gazed from Hampstead's breezy heath.

As if but yesterday departed,
Thou too art gone before; but why,
O'er ripe fruit, seasonably gathered,
Should frail survivors heave a sigh?

Mourn rather for that holy Spirit,
Sweet as the spring, as ocean deep;
For Her who, ere her summer faded,
Has sunk into a breathless sleep.   *40*

No more of old romantic sorrows,
For slaughtered Youth or love-lorn Maid!
With sharper grief is Yarrow smitten,
And Ettrick mourns with her their Poet dead.

NOTES

(*I.F.* indicates notes on his poems dictated by Wordsworth to Isabella Fenwick in 1843.)

The Reverie of Poor Susan (p. 1). Written December 1797. 'This arose out of my observation of the affecting music of these birds hanging in this way [ie. in cages] in the London streets during the freshness and stillness of the Spring morning.' [*I.F.*] In 1800, there was a fifth stanza, probably cancelled because Lamb suggested it 'threw a kind of dubiety upon Susan's moral conduct'—

> Poor Outcast! return—to receive thee once more
> The house of thy Father will open its door,
> And thou once again, in thy plain russet gown,
> May'st hear the thrush sing from a tree of its own.

The Old Cumberland Beggar (p. 1). Written 1797–8. 'Observed, and with great benefit to my own heart, when I was a child: written at Racedown and Alfoxden ... The political economists were about that time beginning their war upon mendicity in all its forms, and by implication, if not directly, on Almsgiving also.' [*I.F.*]
l.179 *House of Industry:* workhouse.

Animal Tranquillity and Decay (p. 6). 'If I recollect right these verses were an overflowing from "The Old Cumberland Beggar".' [*I.F.*] The original printing of 1798 ended with six extra lines:

> —I asked him wither he was bound, and what
> The object of his journey; he replied
> 'Sir! I am going many miles to take
> 'A last leave of my son, a mariner,
> 'Who from a sea-fight has been brought to Falmouth,
> 'And there is dying in an hospital.'

Goody Blake and Harry Gill (p. 6). Written April 1798. Wordsworth based the poem on a story in Erasmus Darwin's *Zoönomia, or the Laws of Organic Life* (1794–6). It illustrates what Mary Moorman calls 'Wordsworth's growing interest in the psychology of fear.'
l.32 *canty:* cheerful.

To My Sister (p. 9). Written May 1798. 'Composed in front of Alfoxden House. My little boy-messenger on this occasion was [Edward] the son of Basil Montague. The larch mentioned in the first stanza was standing when I revisited the place in May, 1841, more than forty years after.' [*I.F.*]

Lines Written in Early Spring (p. 10). Written Spring 1798.
  'Actually composed while I was sitting by the side of the brook
  that runs down the Comb, in which stands the village of Alford,
  through the grounds of Alfoxden.' [*I.F.*]

Anecdote For Fathers (p. 11). Written Spring 1798. The boy was
  Edward, son of Basil Montagu. The epigraph from Eusebius
  (the Delphic oracle speaking) translates 'Restrain your vehemence,
  for if you force me I shall tell you lies.' (Godwin held that children
  were not naturally liars). Like 'We are Seven', the poem illustrates
  the adult's rude intrusions into the different mental world of the
  child. 'The name of Kilve is from a village on the Bristol Channel,
  about a mile from Alfoxden; and the name of Liswyn Farm was
  taken from a beautiful spot on the Wye.' [*I.F.*]

Simon Lee (p. 13). Written Spring 1798. The strong contrast be-
  tween Simon's youth and age was the result of extensive textual
  revisions. 'This old man had been huntsman to the Squires of
  Alfoxden [though the poem is set in Cardiganshire] ... The
  expression when the hounds were out, "I dearly love their voices"
  was word for word from his own lips.' [*I.F.*] Godwin argued that
  gratitude should be socially unnecessary.

We Are Seven (p. 15). Written Spring 1798. 'The little girl who is
  the heroine I met within the area of Goodrich Castle in the year
  1793 [ie. on the tour which took him to Tintern].' [*I.F.*] Words-
  worth composed the last stanza—indeed the last line—first, and
  accepted the prefatory first stanza as composed by Coleridge,
  though he later changed its opening line. See also the *I.F.* note
  to 'Ode: Intimations of Immortality' (p. 219).

The Idiot Boy (p. 17). Written Spring 1798. One of Wordsworth's
  own favourites. In reply to a reader's criticisms, sent to Words-
  worth in a letter, the poet rose to a spirited defence: '... few ever
  consider books but with reference to their power of pleasing ...
  persons and men of a higher rank; few descend lower, among
  cottages and fields, and among children. A man must have done
  this habitually before his judgement upon "The Idiot Boy"
  would be in any way decisive with me. I *know* I have done this
  myself habitually ... I have often applied to idiots, in my own
  mind, that sublime expression of Scripture, that *their life is hidden
  with God* ... I have, indeed, often looked upon the conduct of
  fathers and mothers of the lower classes of society towards idiots
  as the great triumph of the human heart.'

The Thorn (p. 29). Written Spring 1798. 'Arose out of my observing,
  on the ridge of Quantock Hill, on a Stormy day, a thorn which I
  had often passed in calm and bright weather without noticing it.
  I said to myself, "Cannot I by some invention do as much to make
  this Thorn permanently an impressive object as the storm has
  made it to my eyes at this moment?"' [*I.F.*] However, the poem
  also has some literary sources. In the 'Advertisement' to *Lyrical*

Ballads, 1798, Wordsworth claimed that the poem 'is not supposed to be spoken in the author's own person: the character of the loquacious narrator will sufficiently shew itself in the course of the story.'

The Complaint of a Forsaken Indian Woman (p. 35). Written Spring 1798. In the Preface to *Lyrical Ballads*, 1800, Wordsworth describes the poem's aim of following 'the fluxes and refluxes of the mind when agitated by the great and simple affections of our nature' and of delineating 'the last struggles of a human being, at the approach of death, cleaving in solitude to life and society.' Samuel Hearne's *Journey*, referred to at the head of the poem, was published in 1795.

Expostulation and Reply (p. 37). Written, with its companion **'The Tables Turned'**, June 1798. Hazlitt was visiting Coleridge and, as he says, 'got into a metaphysical argument with Wordsworth.' The poet may also have been thinking of William Taylor, his schoolmaster at Hawkshead.

Lines Composed a Few Miles Above Tintern Abbey (p. 39). 'July 1798. No poem of mine was composed under circumstances more pleasant for me to remember than this. I began it upon leaving Tintern, after crossing the Wye, and concluded it just as I was entering Bristol in the evening, after a ramble of 4 or 5 days, with my sister. Not a line of it was altered, and not any part of it written down till I reached Bristol.' [*I.F.*] Wordsworth had first visited Tintern in 1793, on a journey from the Isle of Wight to North Wales.
ll.106–7: Wordsworth noted that he was half-remembering a line from Edward Young's *Night-Thoughts* (1744)—'And half-create the wondrous world they see.'

Nutting (p. 43). Written in Germany, Autumn 1798. '. . . intended as part of a poem on my own life [ie. *The Prelude*], but struck out as not being wanted there.' [*I.F.*]
l.11: The 'frugal Dame' was Ann Tyson, at whose house the poet boarded during his schooldays at Hawkshead.

'There Was a Boy' (p. 44). Written in Germany, October–December 1798. The lines were published in *Lyrical Ballads*, 1800, and in *Poems in Two Volumes*, in 1815; but also fitted into *The Prelude*, Book V. In the original manuscript version, the boy was Wordsworth himself.

'Strange Fits of Passion Have I Known' (p. 45) (December 1798); **'She Dwelt Among The Untrodden Ways'** (p. 46) (December 1798); **'A Slumber Did My Spirit Seal'** (p. 46) (early 1799); **'Three Years She Grew in Sun and Shower'** (p. 46) (Spring 1799): these were written in Germany, and published in *Lyrical Ballads*, 1800. **'I Travelled Among Unknown Men'** (p. 47) was written in April 1801 at Grasmere, and published in *Poems*, 1807. It has been placed with the others here because, together, these five poems constitute what are generally known as the 'Lucy' poems. Guesses as to the exact biographical identity of Lucy seem unnecessary.

Lucy Gray (p. 48). Written in Germany, early 1799. 'It was founded on a circumstance told me by my Sister, of a little girl who, not far from Halifax in Yorkshire, was bewildered in a snow-storm . . . The way in which the incident was treated and the spiritualizing of the character might furnish hints for contrasting the imaginative influences which I have endeavoured to throw over common life with Crabbe's matter of fact style of treating subjects of the same kind.' [*I.F.*] From Crabb Robinson's Diary we learn that Wordsworth's aim in the poem 'was to exhibit poetically entire *solitude*, and he represents the child as observing the day-moon, which no town or village girl would ever notice.'

Matthew (p. 50). Written, with **'The Two April Mornings'** and **'The Fountain'**, in Germany, early 1799. 'Matthew' itself refers to a tablet listing the names of those who had been schoolmasters at Hawkshead School. Thus ostensibly Wordsworth would have William Taylor, his own former teacher, in mind. But the *I.F.* note points to a wider identification: 'This and other poems connected with Matthew would not gain by a literal detail of facts. Like the Wanderer in "The Excursion", this Schoolmaster was made up of several both of his class and men of other occupations.' It seems relevant to remember the wandering Packman who befriended the poet at Hawkshead, and who became the 'Pedlar' of 'The Ruined Cottage' and later the 'Wanderer' of *The Excursion*. (See the Introduction, p. xvi).

A Poet's Epitaph (p. 55). Written in Germany, early 1799. T. E. Casson pointed out its resemblance to the 19th *Epigram* of Theocritus.
l.1 *Statist:* political theorist.

Hart-Leap Well (p. 57). Written January or February 1800 at Grasmere. 'My sister and I had past the place [about five miles from Richmond in Yorkshire] a few weeks before in our wild winter journey from Sockburn on the banks of the Tees to Grasmere. A peasant whom we met near the spot told us the story so far as concerned the name of the well, and the hart, and pointed out the stones.' [*I.F.*]

Michael (p. 62). Written October–December 1800. 'The character and circumstances of Luke were taken from a family to whom had belonged, many years before, the house we lived in at Town-End [Grasmere].' [*I.F.*] Michael himself was based on an old local shepherd who had spent 'seven years in building up a sheepfold in a solitary valley.' In a letter, Wordsworth described his aim of giving 'a picture of a man, of strong mind and lively sensibility, agitated by two of the most powerful affections of the human heart; the parental affection, and the love of property, *landed*

property including the feelings of inheritance, home, and personal and family dependence.'
l.258: Richard Bateman rebuilt Ings Chapel, near Kendal, in 1743.

''Tis Said That Some Have Died For Love' (p. 72). Written 1800.
l.51: *Emma* is one of Wordsworth's names for his sister Dorothy. As in 'Tintern Abbey', he here predisposes her realistically to the event of his own death.

Peter Bell (p. 74). Written April–May 1798, but much revised up to its publication in 1819. The story of the ass and its dead master Wordsworth read in a newspaper. 'The countenance, gait, and figure of Peter, were taken from a wild rover with whom I walked from Builth, on the river Wye, downwards nearly as far as the town of Hay [in 1793]. He told me strange stories . . . In the woods of Alfoxden I used to take great delight in noticing the habits, tricks, and physiognomy of asses; and I have no doubt that I was thus put upon writing the poem out of liking for the creature that is so often dreadfully abused. The crescent-moon, which makes such a figure in the prologue, assumed this character one evening while I was watching its beauty in front of Alfoxden House.' [*I.F.*] The poem can be seen as Wordsworth's equivalent to Coleridge's 'The Ancient Mariner' (finished March 1798), in the early planning of which Wordsworth had played a part. The Prologue signifies Wordsworth's acceptance of the difference between his and Coleridge's imagination.
Both epigraphs are from Shakespeare: *Romeo and Juliet* II.ii. and *Julius Caesar* I.ii., respectively.

To a Butterfly (p. 103). The two poems written March and April respectively, 1802. In her *Journal*, Dorothy recorded: 'The thought first came upon him as we were talking about the pleasure we both always feel at the sight of a butterfly. I told him that I used to chase them a little, but that I was afraid of brushing the dust off their wings.'

To The Cuckoo (p. 104). Dorothy's *Journal* describes Wordsworth working on this poem March 1802. As with 'To a Butterfly' above, and 'My Heart Leaps Up' below, the aim was to establish early childhood memories.

'My Heart Leaps Up' (p. 105). Written March 1802. The last three lines were used as epigraph to 'Ode: Intimations of Immortality', and it is likely that 'My Heart Leaps Up' was the 'timely utterance' referred to in the Ode's third stanza.

Ode: Intimations of Immortality (p. 105). Started March 1802 (first four stanzas) and completed March 1804. 'Nothing was more difficult for me in childhood than to admit the notion of

death as a state applicable to my own being. I have said elsewhere
['We are Seven']—

> "A simple child,
> That lightly draws its breath
> And feels its life in every limb,
> What should it know of death!"

... I was often unable to think of external things as having external
existence, and I communed with all that I saw as something not
apart from, but inherent in, my own immaterial nature. Many
times while going to school have I grasped at a wall or tree to
recall myself from this abyss of idealism to the reality. At that
time I was afraid of such processes. In later periods of life I have
deplored, as we have all reason to do, a subjugation of an opposite
character, and have rejoiced over the remembrances, as is ex-
pressed in the lines—

> "Obstinate questionings,
> Of sense and outward things,
> Fallings from us, vanishings;" etc.

... I took hold of the notion of pre-existence as having sufficient
foundation in humanity for authorizing me to make for my pur-
pose the best use of it I could as a Poet [ie. not as a question of
actual belief].' [*I.F.*]

Resolution and Independence (p. 110). Written May–July 1802.
Dorothy's *Journal* entry for 3 October 1800 describes their
meeting with this leech-gatherer. Wordsworth changed many of
the actual details—most notably making the place an isolated one,
removing Dorothy from the encounter, and ignoring the fact that
the original leech-gatherer had retired from that occupation.
Stanza VII refers to Thomas Chatterton (who fabricated poems
by an invented 15th Century poet, Thomas Rowley, and who
committed suicide in 1770, aged 18); and to Robert Burns.

'I Grieved For Buonaparté' (p. 114). Written May 1802. Up to this
point, Wordsworth had written no sonnets as a mature poet, and
had even thought the sonnet-form 'egregiously absurd'. The new
attraction came through Dorothy's reading to him the sonnets of
Milton.

Composed Upon Westminster Bridge (p. 115). Wordsworth and
Dorothy crossed Westminster Bridge on the Dover coach in the
early morning of 31 July 1802, on their way to Calais to see Annette
Vallon. Dorothy's *Journal* records the same impressions: 'It was a
beautiful morning. The city, St Paul's, with the river and a multi-
tude of little boats, made a most beautiful sight ... The houses
were not overhung by their cloud of smoke ... there was even
something like the purity of one of nature's grand spectacles.'

'It is a Beauteous Evening, Calm and Free' (p. 115). Written at
Calais, August 1802. The 'Dear Child' was Caroline, daughter of
Wordsworth and Annette Vallon, at that time nine years old.

On the Extinction of The Venetian Republic (p. 116). Written at Calais, August 1802. The Venetian Republic was taken by Napoleon in 1797, and given to Austria. Venice had in the twelfth century controlled lands in Asia Minor ('the gorgeous east', l.1). She was 'the safeguard of the west' (l.2) against the Turks after Constantinople fell in 1453. The last line of the octave refers to the Doge's ceremony of dropping, on Ascension Day, a ring into the Adriatic.

To Toussaint L'Ouverture (p. 116). Written August 1802 at Calais. Pierre Dominique Toussaint, called L'Ouverture, led the insurgent negroes of the island of St. Domingo. When the French confirmed the abolition of slavery in 1793, he served under the French government as Commander-in-Chief of the island. In 1801 he resisted Napoleon's edict restoring slavery, was captured, and sent to France, where he died in prison in 1803.

Near Dover, September 1802 (p. 116). Wordsworth sensed that the Peace of Amiens (March 1802–May 1803), which had made his visit to Calais possible, was only a temporary break in the hostilities between England and France.

London, 1802 (p. 117). On his return from Calais, Wordsworth was struck by 'the vanity and parade of our own country, especially in great towns and cities, as contrasted with the quiet, and I may say the desolation, that the revolution had produced in France.' He urges the restoration of the English Puritan virtues epitomized in Milton.

To H. C. Six Years Old (p. 117). Written Autumn 1802. Hartley Coleridge was Coleridge's son.

'There is a Bondage Worse, Far Worse, To Bear' (p. 118). Written 1803.

'Nuns Fret Not at Their Convent's Narrow Room' (p. 118); **'Methought I Saw The Footsteps of a Throne'** (p. 119); **'The World is Too Much With Us'** (p. 119): dates uncertain, but all probably written between June 1802 and February 1804.

Ode to Duty (p. 120). Written probably February–March 1804. The stanza is modelled on Gray's 'Hymn to Adversity'. The epigraph is from Seneca (*Moral Epistle*, CXX: 'Not only sound in judgement, but so governed by habit that it is not so much a matter of his being able to act correctly as of his being unable to act wrongly.' Wordsworth omitted the sixth stanza from all editions after 1807. Its restoration here helps the thought. In that sixth stanza, the phrase 'precepts over dignified' is from Milton's *Doctrine and Discipline of Divorce*.

'I Wandered Lonely as a Cloud' (p. 121). Written early Summer 1804, though the second stanza was added in 1815. Wordsworth acknowledged that the lines 'They flash upon that inward eye/ Which is the bliss of solitude', which he called 'the two best lines', were by his wife. The experience itself had occurred some two years earlier, and was recorded in Dorothy's *Journal*.

Stepping Westward (p. 122). Written June 1805. The incident had occurred during the poet's tour in Scotland with Dorothy and Coleridge, August—September 1803.

The Solitary Reaper (p. 123) Written November 1805. In a note, Wordsworth said that the poem was 'suggested by a beautiful sentence' in Thomas Wilkinson's *Tours to the British Mountains:* 'Passed a female, who was reaping alone: she sung in Erse, as she bended over her sickle; the sweetest human voice I ever heard: her strains were tenderly melancholy, and felt delicious long after they were heard no more.'

Character of The Happy Warrior (p. 124). Written late 1805. The ostensible occasion was the death of Nelson (October 1805), but the *I.F.* note more importantly identifies the character of the poet's brother John (see next note).

Elegiac Stanzas . . . (p. 126). Written July 1806. The painting later formed a frontispiece to *Poems*, 1815. The early stanzas recall an earlier, tranquil view of the castle when Wordsworth spent August 1794 at nearby Rampside (North Lancashire). Stanza nine refers to the effect on Wordsworth of his brother John's death in the wreck of his command ship, the *Earl of Abergavenny*, on 6 February 1805.

Lines Composed at Grasmere (p. 128). Written September 1806. Charles James Fox, the Whig leader and opponent of Pitt's ministry, died on 13 September 1806. Wordsworth had early admired him, had sent him a copy of *Lyrical Ballads* in 1801, and finally met him in London in spring 1806.
l.10 *Importunate and heavy load* is a translation of a phrase by Michael Angelo.

Thought of a Briton on The Subjugation of Switzerland (p. 129). Written late 1806 or early 1807. 'The best I have written.' Napoleon had invaded Switzerland in 1798.

'On Man, On Nature, and On Human Life' (p. 130). These lines (written 1800) stand at the end of Book I of *The Recluse*, the only part of that work actually completed, though it was meant to incorporate *The Prelude* and *The Excursion* as his major poem. When Wordsworth published *The Excursion* in 1814, he quoted these 107 lines in his Preface—as 'a kind of *Prospectus* of the design and scope of the whole Poem.' (See, further, the Introduction).

The Prelude (excerpts, pp. 133 ff.) The aim of *The Prelude* was to trace the growth of the poet's mind up to the point where he felt able and called-upon to write a great philosophical poem. *The*

Prelude itself, however, grew in length and gradual independence, from a two-book form (finished by 1800) to one of five books (nearly finished 1804) to its full length in 1805. This 1805 version was finally revised by 1839, and set aside for posthumous publication in 1850, when its title was decided by Wordsworth's widow.

Bk. I. Written Winter 1798–9 in Germany.
1.304 *that belovèd Vale:* the Vale of Esthwaite, location of Hawkshead.
ll.357 ff.: the episode of the stolen boat took place on Ullswater, 'by the shores of Patterdale' (1805 text).

Bk. III. Written 1801. Wordsworth entered St. John's College, Cambridge in October 1787.
ll.93 ff.: Wordsworth was clearly satisfied to find that his response to Nature was not exclusively dependent on a native Cumberland geography.

Bk. IV. Written 1804.
ll.256 ff.: a simile for the workings of memory.
1.257 *indulgent Friend:* Coleridge, to whom the whole poem is addressed.
ll.309–38: This account of an early visionary experience characteristically shows it occurring in the period of relaxation following physical exertion.
ll.370–460: the MS. of the meeting with this discharged soldier dates probably from 1798, making it one of the earliest experiences of *The Prelude* to be written down. Wordsworth was walking back to Hawkshead from Windermere Ferry. Cf. 'Animal Tranquillity and Decay' (p. 6).

Bk. VI. Written 1804. With a Cambridge friend, Robert Jones, Wordsworth went on a walking tour of France, Switzerland and Germany, July–October 1790.
1.592 *here:* ie., at the present moment of writing the preceding lines.
ll.624–40: these lines show the Imagination at work, reconciling discordant elements.

Bk. XII. Written 1805.
ll. 225 ff.: This is the only episode in *The Prelude* whose location is Penrith.
1.261 *When:* years later, revisiting the scene with his future wife, Mary Hutchinson.

Bk. XIV. Written 1804. In the summer of 1791 the poet had stayed at the Denbighshire home of his Cambridge friend Robert Jones and toured North Wales.
1.12 *glaring:* northern dialect meaning of 'clammy'.
1.22 *lurcher:* cross-bred dog between collie and greyhound.

The Ruined Cottage (p. 151). Wordsworth wrote the first drafts of the story of Margaret and the ruined cottage in the spring of 1797. A year later he expanded the poem by adding an opening, a central transitional passage, a conclusion, and a long character-sketch of the narrator. In 1800 he contemplated publishing the poem separately along with Coleridge's 'Christabel'. In 1806, however, Wordsworth decided to make the poem the starting-point for the work which came to be *The Excursion*, and it is as Book I of that work that 'The Ruined Cottage' was published, in 1814. The character of the Wanderer who tells the story of Margaret was based substantially on the Packman who had befriended Wordsworth at Hawkshead during his school years. (see Introduction, p. xvi).

The author has arranged to meet the Wanderer at the site of a ruined cottage, whose story the Wanderer proceeds to tell.

The White Doe of Rylstone (p. 164). Written October 1807–January 1808. In the summer of 1807 Wordsworth had visited Bolton Priory in Yorkshire. The local legend of the Doe he read in Thomas Whitaker's *History and Antiquities of Craven*. As his source for the Rising in the North of 1569, he used the ballad of that name collected in Thomas Percy's *Reliques of Ancient English Poetry* (1765). The character of Emily is, however, Wordsworth's own creation. He thought the poem 'in conception, the highest work' he had accomplished. In a recorded conversation of 1836, he said: 'The mere physical action was all unsuccessful; but the true action of the poem was spiritual—the subduing of the will and all inferior passions, to the perfect purifying and spiritualizing of the intellectual nature; while the Doe, by connection with Emily is raised, as it were, from its mere animal nature into something mysterious and saint-like.'

The first six lines of the first epigraph are from Wordsworth's play 'The Borderers' (written 1796–97); and the second epigraph is from Bacon's essay 'Of Atheism'. The epigraph at the head of Canto VII is from Wordsworth's 'Address to Kilchurn Castle' (started 1803).

Characteristics of A Child Three Years Old (p. 206). Written first half of 1811. The child was his second daughter, Catherine.

'Surprised by Joy' (p. 207). Exact date unknown. Wordsworth said 'This was suggested by my daughter Catherine long after her death.' Catherine died on 4 June 1812 before her fourth birthday.

Laodamia (p. 207). Written October 1814. 'The incident of the trees growing and withering put the subject into my thoughts, and I wrote with the hope of giving it a loftier tone than, so far as I know, has been given to it by any of the Ancients who have treated of it. It cost me more trouble than almost anything of equal length I have ever written.' [*I.F.*] The 'trouble' was taken over changing an originally happy ending (with Laodamia in Elysium) to the present conclusion, establishing Laodamia's error of immoderate passion.

Protesilaus was the first Greek to land on Trojan soil and, as warned by the oracle at Delphi, the first to die. The gods restored his ghost to his wife Laodamia for three hours.

l.19: *Hermes* in Greek mythology was the son of Zeus, and messenger of the gods.

l.71: *Erebus* = primeval Darkness, part of the Underworld.

l.81: *Alcestis* accepted death instead of her husband Admetus, and was brought back from the shades by Hercules.

l.84: *Aeson* was an old man when his son Jason came back from the Argonautic expedition to recover the golden fleece, but was restored to youth by the magic arts of Medea.

Inside of King's College Chapel, Cambridge (p. 212). The sonnets which comprise *Ecclesiastical Sketches* (1822), to which this and the next sonnet belong, were written March 1821–January 1822.
l.1: The 'royal Saint' was Henry VI, founder of King's College.

Mutability (p. 212). The last line had been used by the poet in an early fragment of a Gothic tale in 1791. Its context in both places suggests the influence of ll.38–42 of John Dyer's *The Ruins of Rome* (1740), a favourite poem of Wordsworth's.

Extempore Effusion upon the Death of James Hogg (p. 213). Written November 1835. Wordsworth had met James Hogg, the 'Ettrick Shepherd' peasant poet, during his visit to Yarrow on the Scottish tour in September 1814. He visited Yarrow with Sir Walter Scott (the 'Border-minstrel' of stanza two) in September 1831. The last of the six dead authors mentioned (in the penultimate stanza) is Felicia Hemans, a poetess who had stayed with the Wordsworths at Rydal Mount in 1830.